Longitudinal Research in Alcoholism

Longitudinal Research in the Behavioral, Social, and Medical Sciences
An International Series

Editor:

SARNOFF A. MEDNICK
University of Southern California and
Psykologisk Institut, Copenhagen

Previously published:

Schulsinger, F., Mednick, S. A., Knop, J.;
LONGITUDINAL RESEARCH: METHODS
AND USES IN BEHAVIORAL SCIENCE

Van Dusen, K.T., Mednick, S.A.;
PROSPECTIVE STUDIES OF CRIME
AND DELINQUENCY

Longitudinal Research in Alcoholism

edited by

Donald W. Goodwin

Katherine Teilmann Van Dusen

Sarnoff A. Mednick *(eds.)*

Kluwer-Nijhoff Publishing
a member of the Kluwer Academic Publishers Group
Boston/The Hague/Dordrecht/Lancaster

Distributors for North America:
Kluwer Academic Publishers
190 Old Derby Street
Hingham, MA 02043, U.S.A.

Distributors Outside North America:
Kluwer Academic Publishers Group
Distribution Centre
P. O. Box 322
3300AH Dordrecht, The Netherlands

Six papers in this book (chapters 2, 3, 6, 8, 9, and 12) were presented at the Annual Meeting of the Society for Life History Research at Asilonar Center, Monterey, California, November 22–25, 1981.

We are grateful to the Viking Press, Inc., New York, for permission to publish excerpts from Lewis Thomas' essay, "The Technology of Medicine," which appeared in his 1974 book, The Lives of a Cell. The essay originally appeared in the New England Journal of Medicine.

Library of Congress Cataloging in Publication Data
Main entry under title:

Longitudinal research in alcoholism.

(Longitudinal research in the behavioral, social, and medical sciences)
Bibliography: p.
Includes index.
1. Alcoholism—Longitudinal studies. I. Goodwin, Donald W. II. Van Dusen, Katherine Teilmann. III. Mednick, Sarnoff A. IV. Series. [DNLM: 1. Alcoholism. 2. Longitudinal studies. WM 274 L855]
RC565.L65 1984   616.86'1'00722   83-9896
ISBN 0-89838-133-9

Printed in the United States of America

Contents

v

Contributing Authors

Thomas F. Babor, Department of Psychiatry, University of Connecticut Health Center, Farmington, Connecticut

Peter M. Bentler, Department of Psychology, University of California at Los Angeles, Los Angeles, California

Stephen F. Bingham, VA Medical Center, Perry Point, Maryland

C. Robert Cloninger, Professor, Department of Psychiatry, Washington University School of Medicine, St. Louis, Missouri

Donald W. Goodwin, Professor of Psychiatry, Chairman of the Department, University of Kansas Medical Center, Kansas City, Kansas

Samuel B. Guze, Spencer T. Olin Professor and Head, Department of Psychiatry, Washington University School of Medicine, St. Louis, Missouri

Michie N. Hesselbrock, Department of Psychiatry, University of Connecticut Health Center, Farmington, Connecticut

Victor M. Hesselbrock, Department of Psychiatry, University of Connecticut Health Center, Farmington, Connecticut

George J. Huba, Department of Psychology, University of California at Los Angeles, Los Angeles, California

Joachim Knop, Psykologisk Institut, Department of Psychiatry, Kommunehospitalet; Copenhagen K, Denmark

Bruce S. Liese, Psychology Service, Kansas City VA Medical Center, Kansas City, Missouri

Ronald L. Martin, Associate Professor, Department of Psychiatry, University of Kansas Medical Center, Kansas City, Kansas

Sarnoff Mednick, Social Science Research Institute, University of Southern California, Los Angeles, California

Roger E. Meyer, Department of Psychiatry, University of Connecticut Health Center, Farmington, Connecticut

Eva S. Milofsky, Harvard University Health Services, Cambridge, Massachusetts

Leif Öjesjö, Center for Social and Forensic Psychiatry, Linköping, Sweden

Ekkehard Othmer, Department of Psychiatry, University of Kansas Medical Center, Kansas City, Kansas

Elizabeth C. Pennick, Department of Psychiatry, University of Kansas Medical Center, Kansas City, Kansas; Psychology Service, VA Medical Center, Kansas City, Missouri

Vicki E. Pollack, Social Science Research Institute, University of Southern California at Los Angeles, Los Angeles, California

Barbara J. Powell, Department of Psychiatry, University of Kansas Medical Center, Kansas City, Kansas; Psychology Service, VA Medical Center, Kansas City, Missouri

Audrey Rice, Psychology Service, Kansas City VA Medical Center, Kansas City, Missouri

Per-Anders Rydelius, Karolinska Istitute, Department of Child and Youth Psychiatry, St. Goran's Children's Hospital, Stockholm, Sweden

Marc A. Schuckit, Director, Alcohol Treatment Program, VA Medical Center, San Diego, California; Professor of Psychiatry, University of California, San Diego

Fini Schulsinger, Psykologisk Institut, Department of Psychiatry, Kommunehospitalet, Copenhagen K, Denmark

James R. Stabenau, Department of Psychiatry, University of Connecticut Health Center, Farmington, Connecticut

George E. Vaillant, Massachusetts Mental Health Center and the Department of Psychiatry, Harvard Medical School, Boston, Massachusetts

Jan Volavka, Manhattan Psychiatric Center, Ward's Island, New York

Meredith Weidenman, Department of Psychiatry, University of Connecticut Health Center, Farmington, Connecticut

Longitudinal Research in Alcoholism

1 A PAEAN TO THE FOLLOW-UP

Donald W. Goodwin

The follow-up is the great exposer of truth, the rock on which fine theories are wrecked and upon which better ones can be built. It is to the psychiatrist what the post-mortem is to the physician.

—P.D. Scott

One reason to believe alcoholism is a real disease—as real as a houseboat or rose bush or double pneumonia—is that it has a natural history. Houseboats have a natural history. Say "houseboat" to someone and he'll probably have a pretty fair idea what it's made of and what will eventually happen to it. A rose has a natural history. A rose is a rose is a rose because it *stays* a rose. It doesn't change into a chrysanthemum. If it does change into a chrysanthemum, it was an unusual rose. It may not have been a rose. It may have been a chrysanthemum that looked like a rose.

Botanists know these things because they have a good system of classification. It permits them to predict the future of plants. From Linnaeus to the present, the secret of success in botany has been the follow-up study.

This is also true of medicine. Long before doctors knew the cause of an illness, they could predict its course and outcome. They could tell which rashes you died from and which you didn't. Double pneumonia was fatal 90 percent of the time regardless of which demon was responsible. "Diagnosis is prognosis" is one of the trustiest axioms in medicine.

The usual sequence in medicine is first to discover the disease, then the cause, then the treatment. It usually doesn't work so well backwards. Polio

1

vaccine did not precede polio. If herpes and syphilis had not been clearly separated before the discovery of penicillin, a lot of penicillin would have been wasted on herpes.

Natural in the term *natural history* means the disease has not been tampered with: it hasn't been treated or it hasn't been treated in a way to alter its "natural" course. The behavioral sciences are lucky in this regard. They deal mainly with conditions for which there are no effective treatments. Drugs may alter the course of schizophrenia (without curing anyone) and thus contaminate its natural history, but in most behavioral disorders, including alcoholism and sociopathy, the natural history remains uncontaminated by treatments destined to win Nobel prizes.

It's widely known that alcoholism has a natural history. "Once a drunk always a drunk" is AA's version. Of course, it's more complicated than that. Just how complicated is demonstrated by the studies in this book. Nevertheless, each study has a premise: if the facts are right, they will permit predictions. That there *is* a natural history (if the facts are right) is an act of faith required of every natural-history investigator.

There may, of course, be several natural histories, or many. Alcohol*isms* may turn out a better word than alcohol*ism*. The answer is not in. In one way or another, all of the studies in this book address the single-versus-many issue, and each advances our knowledge in the process.

A word about the organization of the book: the next five chapters are literally follow-up studies, two from Sweden and three from the United States. These are followed by a review of "high-risk" studies and three specimens of the genre.

A high-risk study is what it says: you study people at high risk for the illness, in this case alcoholism. At particularly high risk for alcoholism are the sons of alcoholics. About one-quarter of them will become alcoholic compared to a prevalence rate of perhaps 3–5 percent of men in the general population. You study them before they start to drink much. If you wait until they drink much, it may be too late: you won't be able to separate the effects of drinking from possible causes. You follow them over sufficient time for some to become alcoholic. You look back at your original data. What did you learn originally that predicts which sons became alcoholic and which did not? Correlations are not the same as causes, but they suggest causes. Specific, effective treatments almost always depend on some knowledge of causes.

A high risk study, in short, is the first stage of a follow-up study. The "typological" studies closing the book are also first stages. The success of a follow-up study depends on whether you ask the right questions to begin with. Deciding in advance whether to lump, split and otherwise organize your material depends on the careful spadework illustrated by these studies.

In the Beginning

The behavioral sciences are still at the Linnaean define-describe-and-follow-up stage of development: still searching for a useful classification. Not everyone appreciates this. Administrators, for example, who talk about "prevention" often do not appreciate this. It is really very hard, preventing a disease before you have gone through the classification stage, before you know whether the rose stays a rose. It's also dreadfully expensive.

Nobody makes this point more eloquently than America's premier physician-essayist, Lewis Thomas.

Thomas says there are three levels of technology in medicine. He calls the first "nontechnology," an endeavor that is impossible to measure "in terms of its capacity to alter either the natural course of disease or its eventual outcome.

> A great deal of money is spent on this. It is valued highly by the professionals as well as the patients. It consists of what is sometimes called 'supportive therapy.' It tides patients over through diseases that are not, by and large, understood. It is what is meant by the phrases "caring for" and "standing by." It is indispensable. It is not, however, a technology in any real sense, since it does not involve measures directed at the underlying mechanism of disease. . . .
>
> It is what physicians used to be engaged in at the bedside of patients with diptheria, meningitis, poliomyelitis, lobar pneumonia, and all the rest of the infectious diseases that have since come under control.
>
> It is what physicians must now do for patients with intractable cancer, severe rheumatoid arthritis, multiple sclerosis, stroke, and advanced cirrhosis. One can think of at least twenty major diseases that require this kind of supportive medical care because of the absence of an effective technology. I would include a large amount of what is called mental disease, and most varieties of cancer, in this category."[1]

The cost of nontechnology is very high and getting higher all the time. Perhaps even more expensive, however, is what Thomas calls "half-way technology." This represents, he says, the kinds of things that must be done to compensate for the incapacitating effects of diseases whose course one is unable to do very much about. "It is a technology designed to make up for disease, or to postpone death." Examples are transplantations of hearts, kidneys, livers and other organs, and the spectacular inventions of artificial organs.

> In the public mind, this kind of technology has come to seem like the equivalent of the high technologies of the physical sciences. The media tend to present each new procedure as though it represented a breakthrough and therapeutic triumph, instead of the makeshift that it really is.

In fact, this level of technology is, by its nature, at the same time highly sophisticated and profoundly primitive. It is the kind of thing that one must continue to do until there is a genuine understanding of the mechanisms involved in disease.

Take kidney disease:

When this level of understanding has been reached, the technology of kidney replacement will not be much needed and should no longer pose the huge problems of logistics, cost, and ethics that it poses today.

Take heart disease:

An extremely complex and costly technology for the management of coronary heart disease has evolved—involving specialized ambulances and hospital units, all kinds of electronic gadgetry, and whole platoons of new professional personnel—to deal with the end results of coronary thrombosis. Almost everything offered today for the treatment of heart disease is at this level of technology, with the transplanted and artificial hearts as ultimate examples. When enough has been learned to know what really goes wrong in heart disease, one ought to be in a position to figure out ways to prevent or reverse the process, and when this happens the current elaborate technology will probably be set to one side. . . .

It is characteristic of this kind of technology that it costs an enormous amount of money and requires a continuing expansion of hospital facilities. There is no end to the need for new, highly trained people to run the enterprise. And there is really no way out of this, at the present state of knowledge. If the installation of specialized coronary-care units can result in the extension of life for only a few patients with coronary disease (and there is no question that this technology is effective in a few cases), it seems to me an inevitable fact of life that as many of these as can be will be put together, and as much money as can be found will be spent. I do not see that anyone has much choice in this. The only thing that can move medicine away from this level of technology is new information, and the only imaginable source of this information is research."

Thomas then describes a third type of technology "so effective that it seems to attract the least public notice."

This is the genuinely decisive technology of modern medicine, exemplified best by modern methods for immunization against diptheria, pertussis, and the childhood virus diseases, and the contemporary use of antibiotics and chemotherapy for bacterial infections. . . .

The point to be made about this kind of technology—the real high technology of medicine—is that it comes as the result of a genuine understanding of disease mechanisms, and when it becomes available, it is relatively inexpensive, relatively simple, and relatively easy to deliver.

Offhand, I cannot think of any important human disease for which medicine possesses the outright capacity to prevent or cure where the cost of the technology is itself a major problem. The price is never as high as the cost of managing the same diseases during the earlier stages of no-technology or halfway technology. If a case of typhoid fever had to be managed today by the best methods of 1935, it would run to a staggering expense. At, say, around fifty days of hospitalization, requiring the most demanding kind of nursing care, with the obsessive concern for details of diet that characterized the therapy of that time, with daily laboratory monitoring, and, on occasion, surgical intervention for abdominal catastrophe, I should think $10,000 would be a conservative estimate for the illness, as contrasted with today's cost of a bottle of chloramphenicol and a day or two of fever. . . .

Pulmonary tuberculosis had similar episodes in its history. There was a sudden enthusiasm for the surgical removal of infected lung tissue in the early 1950s, and elaborate plans were being made for new and expensive installations for major pulmonary surgery in tuberculosis hospitals, and then INH and streptomycin came along and the hospitals themselves were closed up.

It is when physicians are bogged down by their incomplete technologies, by the innumerable things they are obliged to do in medicine when they lack a clear understanding of disease mechanisms, that the deficiencies of the health-care system are the most conspicuous. *If I were a policymaker, interested in saving money for health care over the long haul, I would regard it as an act of high prudence to give high priority to a lot more basic research in biologic science . . .*" (italics added).

Thomas is not a policymaker, alas! The reason I quoted him at length is that maybe someday, somewhere, a policymaker will read Thomas and see the light. But the signs are not auspicious. Consider the following:

The National Institute of Alcohol Abuse and Alcoholism (NIAAA) has just made prevention a high-priority item. In early 1983 the Institute announced that *millions* of dollars would be available in the next few years for "prevention centers." In defining prevention, the Institute said it was not interested in "basic mechanisms" or "studies to determine if particular factors increase the risk of disorder."

In other words, it was not interested in supporting the type of research found in this book, for if there is one theme that dominates the book it is that "particular factors increase the risk of disorder."

The NIAAA policymakers should not be blamed entirely. *Prevention* is a buzz word in the administration and the halls of Congress, and government, after all, pays the bills.

Buzz words have a short half-life. Let us hope the next one is *research*, understood here to include research into the course of illnesses as a step toward understanding mechanisms: truly the most humane and cost-effective thing government can do.

Note

1. The treatment of alcoholism is still at the nontechnology level. Doubters need only look at the list of therapies espoused for the condition: psychoanalysis, transactional analysis, behavior therapy, cognitive therapy, transcendental meditation, poetry therapy, megavitamins, music therapy, tranquilizers, antidepressant medication, primal therapy, lithium, milieu therapy, hypnosis, Alcoholics Anonymous, LSD, disulfirim, religious conversion, biofeedback, and others.

Except for disulfirim, where two controlled studies indicate some efficacy, and Alcoholics Anonymous, supported by a small army of true believers, there is no scientific evidence and not much faith that any of the above helps.

FOLLOW-UP STUDIES

2 RISKS FOR ALCOHOLISM BY AGE AND CLASS AMONG MALES. THE LUNDBY COMMUNITY COHORT, SWEDEN

Leif Öjesjö

Longitudinal studies are particularly useful in ascertaining incidence—the number of new cases that emerge within a specified time interval. When all the cases of the disorder occurring in a defined population are known, it is possible to produce the actual incidence rates of cases in various subgroups and also to give the individual chances. Furthermore, with the prospective method, and with multiple cohorts, it is possible to associate the age-specific rates with the relevant environmental changes during lifetimes of survivors from successive cohorts. Cohort analyses thus offer better chances of distinguishing between nature and nurture, and of correlating changes in the various incidence rates with the social history of the period [1,2].

In view of all the difficulties, it is hardly surprising that such studies are rare. The first major attempts to grasp the size of the problem of alcoholism were made by Klemperer [3], who estimated the lifetime rate of alcoholism to

This study has been supported by Grant No. 71/2 from the Bank of Sweden Tercentenary Foundation, and Grant No. 3474 from the Swedish Medical Research Council. Acknowledgement is given to Olle Hagnell, M.D. and Jan Lanke, Ph.D. for the use of collaborative data and the statistical preparations.

9

be 1.2 percent, and by Fremming [4], who found lifetime rates of 3.5 percent among males and 0.1 percent among females. Helgason [5] has applied similar biological methods for the population of Iceland. Here the crude expectancy of alcoholism, classified as alcohol addiction, habitual excessive drinking and irregular excessive drinking, up to the age of 60 was 9.78 percent for males and 0.50 percent for females. The rates tended to be higher for the well-to-do, findings that Helgason related to the preponderance of rural groups in the sample.

The lifetime rate for alcoholism among males is now generally estimated to be between 3–9 percent depending on the criteria used, and for women the range is between 0.1–1 percent. The onset is likely to take place in the late teens and early twenties, the course is individual, and the alcoholic may not be fully aware of any dependence on alcohol until his thirties. Patterns of pathological drinking are also variable, and one should avoid associating one particular pattern exclusively with 'alcoholism' [6,7].

Apart from the drinking, the leading predictors of problem alcohol intake seem to be various socio-economic dimensions. People in "lower" social positions have the higher rates in most investigations, and they tend to get into trouble out of proportion to the frequency with which they drink [8–14]. Therefore, the study of an "artificial" disease like alcoholism also offers an immanent critique of the particular society within which it flourishes. Fillmore and Caetano [15] suggest that it may be fruitful for future research for the interpretative devices to be turned into hypotheses and tested. Studies that relate the consequences of the drinking to the positions of people within specific social structures would be particularly valuable. One frame of reference is the population at large, using general population surveys or general social statistics. Such studies may, in fact, be the only way of arriving at comparisons of untreated alcohol problem rates in various social contexts, or of answering other questions on relative prevalence and incidence [15].

For the present study the main research questions were the following:

1. What was the incidence for alcoholism in various age and sex groups during the period under study (1957–1972?) What was the expectancy (morbidity risk)?
2. Can the social concept of class be used as a predictor for alcoholism, and can class-specific incidence rates be calculated? If so, which classes, or occupations, are especially associated with the disorder?

Material and Methods

Material

The data have been taken from the Lundby Study, a longitudinal investigation which has been proceeding since 1947. Essen-Möller and co-workers were the first to make a medical-psychiatric census investigation of all the inhabitants (N = 2,550) in the Lundby community, which is situated in a Southern district of Sweden. In 1957 (called "Time 1" for the present purposes) Hagnell added the prospective dimension when he personally reinterviewed the population. The interview drop-out rate was 1 percent in both studies. Information about the deceased was also collected [16,17].

A second follow-up has now been accomplished. The 1,877 probands (952 men, 925 women) from the original cohort still alive in 1972 (Time 2) have been resurveyed during 1972–1974 with similar methods, and the results are now in progress [18,19].

Demographically the number of farmers, farm laborers, and self-employed artisans have declined appreciably since the project started, while factory workers and those employed in service and administration have increased, "as the close-knit self-sufficient provincial village loosened its ties and reached out to take part in the modern world" [20,14]. Post-war Sweden has been characterized by a strong urbanization, and today the majority of the Lundby population (like 80% of Swedish citizens) lives in urban agglomerations. Companies have concentrated at the most important commercial areas at the same time as a depopulation of peripheral regions has taken place [21]. With the development of Sweden into a market-oriented, profit-maximizing society, Swedish industry has gone through a very rapid structural rationalization, not the least in the latter part of the 1960s. In this context it should be borne in mind that the nationalized sector of the economy is smaller and the concentration of economic power in private hands is probably greater in Sweden than in many other countries of Western Europe [22]. With the passage of time the smaller firms either have been forced out of business or have had to merge with the larger ones. These processes have been accompanied by an ever-increasing pressure and insecurity of employment and by difficulties in retaining social and commercial services. The official unemployment rate has been around 6 percent (1.5% unemployed and 4.5% engaged on state financed job training programs) [23]. The sex, age, and education of the labor force are the determining factors in the process of finding jobs, but no doubt the current Swedish class structure is of crucial importance. Advancing age will tend to increase people's problems, while *exclusion from the labor market* and from working life often leads to isolation and other social problems. In sum, the groups at a disadvantage are, above all, the younger generation, the increasingly large group of old people, and the disabled [21].

Methods

In order to collect and evaluate the information the following methods were used:

1. Field notes at Time 1 and Time 2 with anamnesis, social-psychiatric and somatic, taken by research psychiatrists (L.Ö. and O.H.) in face-to-face interviews of about one hour's duration with as many persons as possible from the 1947 cohort, and in most cases including contacts with other family members.
2. Psychiatric status at Time 1 and Time 2 interview.
3. Register information and other objective data collected from key-informants and agencies (psychiatric clinics, Health Insurance Board, Temperance Boards).
4. Final evaluations and classifications made by research psychiatrists (L.Ö. and O.H., where O.H. had also made the Time 1 evaluations).

The collection of data was made as complete as possible. The field work took place independently of the probands' place of residence, i.e. in their homes, at their jobs, in hospitals, prisons, and other institutions. The interviews were of a relatively free, explorative, and open-ended nature, although focused on the psychiatric and medical research questions and on the individuals' life situation (work, family, and home). The method was the one used in clinical situations, particularly with psychiatric outpatients. Mail and telephone surveys probably do not turn out equally well, because of the great importance of probing and reinforcing that only an interviewer can do. The very detailed data that have been collected through the three surveys give an opportunity for an estimation also of the qualitative aspects, at least the broader issues.

Definitions

Alcoholism

The selection of the cases has been based on epidemiologic work defining alcoholism in two gradations, alcohol dependence and alcohol abuse.

1. Alcohol dependence (Diagnostic and Statistical Manual of Mental Disorders (3rd ed.) [DSM III] 303.0) with signs of withdrawal, craving, shakes.
2. Alcohol abuse (DSM III 305.0) with a pattern of heavy pathological drinking and tolerance change.

An individual was included if he or she met the criteria at any time between 1957 (Time 1) and 1972 (Time 2). In addition, a duration of disturbance of at least a year was needed. Consumption data were not registered, but any information about medical complications such as cirrhosis of the liver, brain damage, delirium tremens, convulsions, hallucinations etc., were registered.

Incidence

The incidence of a disease is the number of new cases per year in the population between Time 1 and Time 2. It is given as the annual incidence rate per 100,000. By using the part studied in 1957 (Time 1), who had not developed alcoholism, one escapes the bias inherent in nonprospective studies (i.e. the examiner at Time 1 did not know which of the probands would develop alcoholism up to Time 2). Rates have also been calculated for age and social class subgroups to be compared with the crude incidence baselines and with each other.

Expectancy

Disease expectancy (morbidity risk) is defined as an estimate of the probability that a proband will develop the disease in question at some time during his life, if he survives the period of risk for the disease (the disease expectancy at a very high age is sometimes called the "life expectancy" of acquiring the disease).

Class

Social class was operationally defined from each individual's occupation, type of employment and ownership of the means of production, i.e. from each individual's position in the process of production at Time 1:

1. *Working class* ("blue collar").
2. *Middle strata technicians and administrators* ("white collar").
3. *Petit bourgeoisie* (self-employed businessmen, artisans, and farmers).
4. *Bourgeoisie* (too few in number for separate statistical treatment).

Nonworking dependents were considered to be members of the class of the "bread-winners." For students the father's occupation was used. In the case of the retired the occupation that they had pursued for most of their working lives was used, and if they were unemployed, by the last occupation they had held.

Results

Tables 1 and 2 show the annual age-specific and accumulated risk for developing alcoholism (Alcohol dependence and Alcohol abuse) for the first time for males. Calculations are based on approximately 15000 observation years. New cases among the females were too few for statistical treatment.

The incidence rate for alcoholism among the males was 300 per 100,000 (alcohol dependence, 130 per 100,000).

The estimated morbidity risk (expectancy) measured as accumulated probability, i.e. the percentage of men who have developed alcoholism or who will develop it sometime during their lives, was 19.3 (alcohol dependence, 8.7).

Incidence rates were the highest in the younger age groups as it was found that 61 percent of the probability of developing an alcoholism was manifested before age 30, and that 78 percent of the probability was manifested before age 40; there was a risk also after age 40, which remained up to very high age.

Tables 3, 4, 5, 6 and 7, figures 2, 3, and 4 show the risk of developing alcoholism in relation to the social dimensions of class and education. Alcohol dependence and alcohol abuse were handled as a unity in these tabulations because of the relatively small numbers, and as division into different degrees of severity would have provided figures too small for statistical treatment.

Table 2-1. The Incidence and Risk for Men in a Total Population of Becoming Alcoholic (Lundby Cohort 1957–1972)

Age Interval	Observation Years Under Risk	Cases	Annual Incidence Rate	Cumulative Probability of Developing an Alcoholism
00–09	.0	0	— (—)	— (—)
10–19	1049.4	7	.0067 (.0025)	.065 (.024)
20–29	2421.0	14	.0058 (.0015)	.117 (.026)
30–39	2578.6	10	.0039 (.0012)	.151 (.027)
40–49	2281.1	5	.0022 (.0010)	.169 (.028)
50–59	2481.2	2	.0008 (.0006)	.176 (.028)
60–69	1904.1	2	.0011 (.0007)	.184 (.028)
70–79	995.6	1	.0010 (.0010)	.193 (.029)
80+	564.4	0	.0000 (.0000)	.193 (.029)
0+	14275.4	41		
Age standardized			.0030 (.0005)	

Table 2-2. The Incidence and Risk for Men in a Total Population of Becoming a Dependent Alcoholic (Lundby Cohort 1957–1972)

Age Interval	Observation Years Under Risk	Cases	Annual Incidence Rate	Cumulative Probability of Developing an Alcoholism
00–09	.0	0	— (—)	— (—)
10–19	1064.3	2	.0019 (.0013)	.019 (.013)
20–29	2527.0	10	.0040 (.0013)	.057 (.017)
30–39	2751.4	4	.0015 (.0007)	.070 (.018)
40–49	2434.5	3	.0012 (.0007)	.082 (.019)
50–59	2600.4	0	.0000 (.0000)	.082 (.019)
60–69	2033.6	1	.0005 (.0005)	.086 (.020)
70–79	1111.1	0	.0000 (.0000)	.086 (.020)
80+	597.0	0	.0000 (.0000)	.086 (.020)
0+	15119.3	20		
Age standardized			.0013 (.0003)	

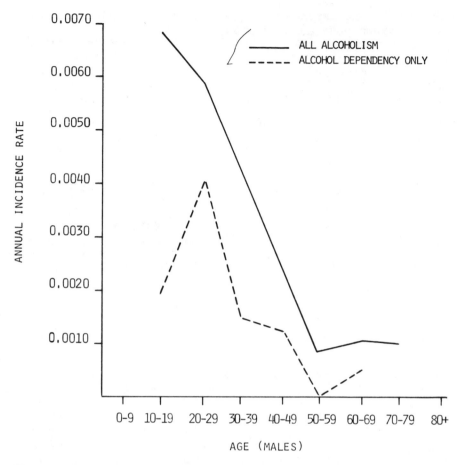

Figure 2-1. Annual Incidence Rate by Age and Sex (Male) of Developing Alcoholism in the Lundby General Population Cohort Based on Data from the Prospectively Observed 15–Year Period 1957–1972

Working class ("blue collar") had the highest incidence (340 per 100,000) and the highest expectancy (35.2%). Middle strata administrators and technicians ("white collar") had a lower risk (incidence 190 per 100,000, life expectancy 9.6%). The petit bourgeois aggregate of businessmen, artisans and farmers had risks somewhere in between (incidence 230 per 100,000, life expectancy 16.0%).

Differences between various educational groups are probably also highly related to class. Those with elementary school background showed a

Table 2-3. The Incidence and Risk for Working-Class Men of Becoming an Alcoholic (Lundby Cohort 1957–1972)

Age Interval	Observation Years Under Risk	Cases	Annual Incidence Rate	Cumulative Probability of Developing an Alcoholism
00–09	.0	0	—	—
10–19	140.1	4	.0286	.248
20–29	753.6	4	.0053	.287
30–39	1073.2	5	.0047	.320
40–49	864.1	2	.0023	.335
50–59	953.7	1	.0010	.342
60–69	698.2	1	.0014	.352
70–79	318.8	0	.0000	.352
80+	142.0	0	.0000	.352
0+	4943.7	17	.0034	—

Table 2-4. The Incidence and Risk for Middle Strata Men of Becoming an Alcoholic (Lundby Cohort 1957–1972)

Age Interval	Observation Years Under Risk	Cases	Annual Incidence Rate	Cumulative Probability of Developing an Alcoholism
00–09	.0	0	—	—
10–19	10.7	0	.0000	.000
20–29	199.6	1	.0050	.049
30–39	432.8	1	.0023	.071
40–49	356.2	1	.0028	.096
50–59	287.1	0	.0000	.096
60–69	217.0	0	.0000	.096
70–79	72.3	0	.0000	.096
80+	12.4	0	.0000	.096
0+	1588.1	3	.0019	—

Table 2-5. The Incidence and Risk for Self-Employed Men of Becoming an Alcoholic (Lundby Cohort 1957–1972)

Age Interval	Observation Years Under Risk	Cases	Annual Incidence Rate	Cumulative Probability of Developing an Alcoholism
00–09	.0	0	—	—
10–19	42.2	0	.0000	.000
20–29	507.2	4	.0079	.076
30–39	991.9	4	.0040	.112
40–49	1040.1	2	.0019	.129
50–59	1201.9	1	.0008	.136
60–69	960.3	1	.0010	.145
70–79	599.0	1	.0017	.160
80+	410.0	0	.0000	.160
0+	5752.6	13	.0023	—

significantly higher risk than those with some further education. The estimated morbidity risk measured as cumulated probability of developing alcoholism among the elementary school group was 20.3 percent (alcohol dependence 9.2%) compared with the much lower 6.9 percent risk for those with any further education (alcohol dependence 2.5%).

Discussion

Reichenbach [24] has said that it is the concept of probability that constitutes the scientific evidence. However, although the risks can be calculated on samples of almost any size, their precision in the prediction of future risks is low, if the number of subjects is small. The reader has already been forwarned that categories and subcategories of the Lundby sample are sometimes very sparsely represented. Another problem is that longitudinal studies, by the time they are brought to some point of completion, may provide results valid only about a time or circumstance that might never recur [25]. If, for example, a condition begins to rise in incidence among new cohorts of later birth-date, then the rise will be reflected in the cross-section curves, tending to create age peaks in the newly affected younger age groups, but without raising the rates among the old [26].

What constitutes "knowledge" here must be explained and understood in the light of the social formation and the historical period in which it emerges.

In this report the tabulated morbidity risks are the chances conditional on reaching a certain age (80+) during a certain period (1957–1972). In the majority of the cases alcoholism had begun at a relatively young age, before

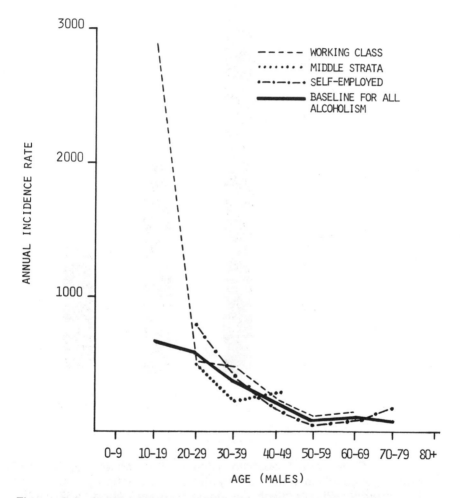

Figure 2-2. Annual Incidence Rate by Age, Sex (Male), and Class of Developing Alcoholism in the Lundby General Population Cohort Based on Data from the Prospectively Observed 15-Year period 1957–1972

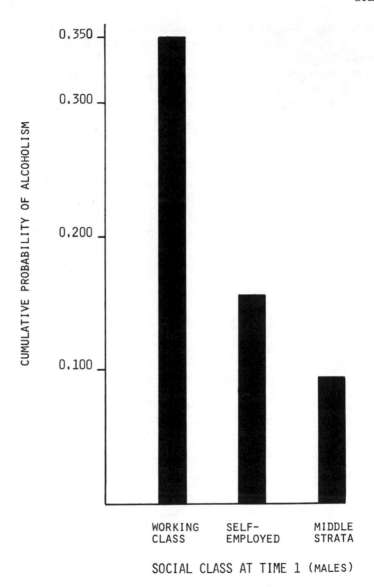

Figure 2-3. Cumulative Probability Rate by Sex (Male) and Class of Developing Alcoholism in the Lundby General Population Cohort Based on Data from the Prospectively Observed 15–Year Period 1957–1972

Table 2-6. The Incidence and Risk for Men with Only Elementary School of Becoming an Alcoholic (Lundby Cohort 1957–1972)

Age Interval	Observation Years Under Risk	Cases	Annual Incidence Rate	Cumulative Probability of Developing an Alcoholism
00–09	.0	0	—	—
10–19	1008.1	7	.0069	.067
20–29	2106.8	14	.0066	.127
30–39	2182.8	9	.0041	.162
40–49	2064.0	4	.0019	.178
50–59	2378.1	2	.0008	.185
60–69	1820.8	2	.0011	.194
70–79	946.5	1	.0011	.203
80+	555.0	0	.0000	.203
0+	13062.1	39	.0030	—

Table 2-7. The Incidence and Risk for Men with Further Education of Becoming an Alcoholic (Lundby Cohort 1957–1972)

Age Interval	Observation Years Under Risk	Cases	Annual Incidence Rate	Cumulative Probability of Developing an Alcoholism
00–09	.0	0	—	—
10–19	41.3	0	.0000	.000
20–29	314.2	0	.0000	.000
30–39	395.9	1	.0025	.025
40–49	217.0	1	.0046	.069
50–59	103.1	0	.0000	.069
60–69	83.3	0	.0000	.069
70–79	49.1	0	.0000	.069
80+	9.4	0	.0000	.069
0+	1213.3	2	.0016	—

30 in about 60 percent, and before 40 in about 80 percent of the cases. The results are similar to Segal's [28] findings that the incidence of alcoholism after age 35 drops sharply, while—on the other hand—the search for medical help increases.

When the class-specific rates were considered, the risk was found to be highest for the working class (expectancy 35%), versus petit bourgeois businessmen, artisans and farmers (expectancy 16%), and versus the middle strata, "white collar" groups of technicians, administrators, and office employees (expectancy 10%). The results support the earlier suggestion that "class creates alcoholics in different rates through their general class situations." Class is obviously an important predictor of an alcoholic outcome, where indeed the source of the "problem" may lie in the specific hardships the classes meet with over time, and that is related to their positions in the social and economical structure. It is noted that industrial workers are prone to escape-drinking because their badly paid, monotonous, dead-end, and exhausting work gives them little satisfaction and self-esteem, and because they have no resources for enriching their leisure time with high-quality cultural activities [29,13,15,14].

Research has often neglected the social features of the larger society, such as unemployment, and living cycles from which escape is improbable, and that in turn are shaped by a form of social organization under capitalism that determines both the form and the content of the isolated variables. Much conventional research therefore generates a *theoretical bias* rather than simply a researcher bias, that fails to reveal the social contradictions and corresponding social and structural tensions of the social order. Western societies with fast changes in their economy brought about by increases in the size of firms and scale of production (often multinational) place new demands upon local resources and labor markets. In response, families and social networks begin to change the ways they relate to individual members, changes that cause individuals to become more directly vulnerable to the stresses and strains generated. The result is that dysfunction, as manifest in the incidence and prevalence of various pathologies, increases with both ups and downs in the economy. Only future research can discover how much such results change from one situation to another. Particularly needed is a social epidemiology that can explain how a factor such as economic change is converted into individual stressors as it moves through a social network (30).

To sum up: at one level one may seek to establish the population facts concerning alcoholism. It is quite another matter to explain the multiple causal mechanisms involved [31].

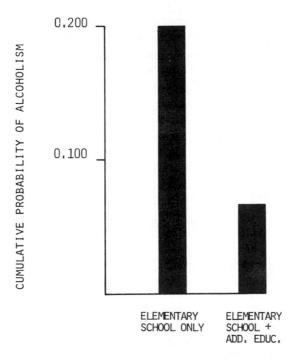

TYPE OF EDUCATION AT TIME 1 (MALES)

Figure 2-4. Cumulative Probability Rate by Sex (Male) and Education of Developing Alcoholism in the Lundby General Population Cohort Based on Data from the Prospectively Observed 15–Year Period 1957–1972

The first level demands surveys and statistics and is based on the extensive design; the second demands biochemistry and physiology as well as qualitative family, life-style, and life-history data, and is based on the intensive design. It implies the deep and detailed investigation of the mediating processes involved, and of single cases treated as typical of the category of cases to be studied. To truly appreciate the strengths and limitations of this particular approach to social epidemiology, linking economic structure with individual well-being, Sclar [30] argues that it is necessary to consider each individual manifestation of dysfunction on a case-by-case basis. This is because the meaning of the individual data has a range of complexity which is too easily lost in attempts to generalize the approach to a range of problems. It is only with increased conceptual sophistication that it will be possible to pull together the myriad of contradictory findings that fill the literature. The validity of the results (qualitative or quantitative) depends on a confluence or correlation with other findings. Indeed, sometimes it is the *atypical* use of alcohol, i.e. the use against any demographic odds, that implies the greatest need for an individual [32].

References

1. Morris, J. N. *Uses of Epidemiology*. Edinburgh and London: E. and S. Livinstone, 1970.
2. Chafetz, M. E., Blane, H. T., and Hill, M. J. *Frontiers of Alcoholism*. New York: Science House, 1970.
3. Klemperer, J. Zur Belastungsstatistik der Durchschnitts-bevölkerung. *Z. Neurol.* 146:277, 1933.
4. Fremming, K. H. Sygdomsrisikoen for sindslidelser. (Risk calculations for mental illnesses). (In Danish). Dissertation. Copenhagen, 1947.
5. Helgason, T. Epidemiology of mental disorders in Iceland. *Acta Psych. Scand.* [*Suppl.*] 173, 1964.
6. Woodruff, R. A., Goodwin, D. W., and Guze, S. B. *Psychiatric Diagnosis*. New York: Oxford University Press, 1974.
7. Winocur, G. and Tsuang, M. T. Expectancy of alcoholism in a Midwestern population. *J. Stud. Alcohol* 39:1964, 1978.
8. Kornhauser, A. and Reid, O. M. *Mental Health of the Industrial Worker. A Detroit Study*. New York: Wiley, 1965.
9. Cahalan, D. and Room, R. Problem drinking among American men. Monographs of the Rutgers Center of alcohol studies, No. 7. New Haven: College and University Press, 1974.
10. Pearlin, L. I. and Radabaugh, C. W. Economic strains and the coping functions of alcohol. *Am. J. Sociol.* 82:652, 1976.
11. Plant, M. Alcoholism and occupation: cause or effect? A controlled study of recruits to the drink trade. *Int. J. Addict.* 13:626, 1978.
12. Smart, R. Drinking problems among employed, unemployed and shift workers. *J. Occup. Med.* 21:731, 1979.
13. Parker, D. A. and Brody, J. A. Risk Factors for Occupational Alcoholism and Alcohol Problems. In: *Alcoholism in the Workplace*. Research Monograph Series. National Institute on Alcohol Abuse and Alcoholism. Rockville, Md., 1980.
14. Öjesjö, L. The relationship to alcoholism of occupation, class and employment. *J. Occup. Med.* 22:657, 1980.
15. Fillmore, K. and Caetano. R. Epidemiology of occupational alcoholism. Paper presented at the National Institute of Alcohol Abuse and Alcoholism's workshop on alcoholism in the workplace, Reston, Virginia, May 22, 1980.
16. Essen-Möller, E. Individual traits and morbidity in a Swedish rural population. *Acta Psychiatr. Scand.* [*Suppl.*] 100, 1956.

17. Hagnell, O. *A Prospective Study of the Incidence of Mental Disorder*. Lund: Svenska Bokförlaget, 1966.
18. Hagnell, O. and Öjesjö, L. A prospective study concerning mental disorders of a total population investigated 1947, 1957 and 1972. *Acta Psychiatr. Scand.* [*Suppl.*] 263:1, 1975.
19. Hagnell, O. and Öjesjö, L. Prevalence of male alcoholism in a cohort observed for 25 years. *Scand. J. Soc. Med.* 8:55, 1980.
20. Leighton, D. C., Hagnell, O., Leighton, A. H., et al., Psychiatric disorders in a Swedish and a Canadian community. An exploratory study. *Soc. Sci. Med.* 5:189, 1971.
21. Royal Ministry of Foreign Affairs *The Biography of People. Past and Future Population Changes in Sweden. Conditions and Consequences*. Stockholm: Allmänna Förlaget, 1974.
22. Korpi, W. Poverty, Social Assistance and Social Policy in Sweden 1945–72. In Scase, R. (ed.), *Readings in the Swedish Class Structure*. Oxford: Pergamon, 1976.
23. Fry, J. A. Introduction. In Fry, J. A. (ed.), *Limits of the Welfare State: Critical Views on Post-War Sweden*. Hants, England: Saxon House, Teakfield, 1979.
24. Reichenbach, H. *Experience and Prediction*. Chicago: The University of Chicago Press, 1957.
25. Block, J. and Haan, N. *Lives Through Time*. Berkeley: Bancroft Books, 1971.
26. Susser, M. W. and Watson, W. *Sociology in Medicine* (2nd ed.). New York: Oxford University Press, 1975.
27. Epidemiology of Alcohol Abuse and Alcoholism in Occupations. In *Occupational Alcoholism*: A Review of Research Issues. NIAAA, Rockville, Md. pp 21–88, 1982.
28. Segal, B. M. The effect of the age factor on alcoholism. In Sexias, F. A. (ed.), *Currents in alcoholism*. Vol. 2. New York: Grune and Stratton, 1977.
29. Honkasalo, M. L. Työ ja alkoholijuomien käyttö-katsaus anglosaksisessa ja skandinaavisessa kirjallisuudessa käsiteltyyn problematiikkaan. (In Finnish). (Work and drinking habits—a review of Anglo-Saxon and Scandinavian literature). *Alkoholikysymys* 46:35, 1978.
30. Sclar, E. D. Community economic structure and individual well-being. A look behind the statistics. *Int. J. Health Serv.* 10:563, 1980.
31. Harré, R. The notion of causality. *Br. J. Psychiatry* 137:578, 1980.
32. Robins, L. N., Davis, D. H. and Wish, E. Detecting predictors of rare events: demographic, family and personal deviance as predictors of stages in the progression toward narcotic addiction. In Strauss, J. S., Babigian, H. M., and Roff, M. (eds.), *The Origins and Course of Psychopathology*. New York: Plenum Press, 1977.

3 CHILDREN OF ALCOHOLIC FATHERS— A LONGITUDINAL PROSPECTIVE STUDY

Per-Anders Rydelius

As a result of various longitudinal prospective studies done in recent decades in different fields, such as psychiatry and child psychiatry, it has become possible to discern certain patterns in the development of mental illness, of the abuse of drugs and alcohol, and of criminality in adults [11]. Although our total understanding to date probably covers only a minute portion of "the true reality," the experience gained so far should serve as an alarm bell for those who are active in psychiatric care programs, perhaps prompting a rethinking of older perspectives and initiating efforts to construct new therapeutic programs. It should be obvious to all who are engaged in work with children and young people that although a good deal of theoretical knowledge is readily available, it is a far from simple matter to apply this knowledge in practice for the benefit of especially vulnerable groups. This is clearly demonstrated in Joan McCord's follow-up studies of a therapeutic program run in the U.S.A. [4], and in the Swedish follow-up studies, reported by Nylander and Curman, of children who had received psychiatric care and various supportive social measures [12]. The difficulty in achieving successful therapeutic results in these groups can doubtlessly be explained in a number of ways. However, it is possible that an effective therapeutic program giving lasting results must include continuous follow-up controls and the

27

provision of help and support to children living in particularly risk-fraught environments, right from the time of their birth until they reach adulthood.

Insecure Children in Sweden

The first professorship in Sweden in the discipline of "Child and Youth Psychiatry" was created in 1958 at the Karolinska Institute. The chair was originally sited at Kronprinsessan Lovisa's Children's Hospital, from which it was transferred in 1970 to St. Göran's Children's Hospital, both in Stockholm. Professor emeritus Sven Ahnsjö and the present head of department, Professor Ingvar Nylander, have been responsible for a considerable amount of important pioneer work at St. Göran's Hospital, having directed the interests of child psychiatric research at an early stage toward the group of "children who suffer."

Around the middle 1950s, Ingvar Nylander was engaged as a child psychiatric consultant at a major pediatric medical and surgical clinic. In the course of this work, he observed that in children with so-called psychosomatic symptoms—physical symptoms such as headache, stomachache, "growing pains", etc.—for which no underlying physical cause could be found, there were often very noticeable insecurity factors in the children's immediate environment—mental disease in the parents, addiction in the parents, problems with intimate relations in the family such as harrowing divorce situations, and so forth. The observations that were collected and described in the publication "Physical symptoms and psychogenic etiology. An investigation of a consultation material" [13], can be said to have formed the foundation for the child psychiatric research developments that ensued at the clinic, and were, in addition, the constituent basis for the present prospective study of children from environments characterized by the abuse of alcohol. One of the aims of this study was, in fact, to clarify whether there was evidence to prove that children living in an insecure environment with serious familial stress factors (in this instance, grave alcoholism in the father) really did react by developing symptoms of a psychosomatic nature.

The Study of Children from Alcoholic Homes

In searching for a group of children for whom it could be said that their environments contained emotional stress factors, it was found that children whose fathers had extreme problems with alcohol fulfilled this particular requirement. During the 1950s, there was a clinic in Stockholm called the "Maria Polyclinics" that handled alcoholics. Individuals suffering from alcoholism were sent to the clinic for treatment, often forcibly remitted by welfare authorities in charge of temperance care. Men with children were selected from the clientele at the Maria Polyclinics for the study. These fathers had, as a rule, a long history of alcoholism, often more than 10 years, and while in the throes of a bout they frequently became violent and aggressive and beat up other members of the family, usually the wives in the first instance. Very often, the men also had criminal backgrounds and, in addition, could not support their families either because they were undisciplined at their places of work or because they were unable to attend work regularly as a result of their abuse of alcohol.

As a result, the wives of these alcoholics were constantly under a considerable strain and often had an enormous burden of work as they were not only responsible for the upbringing of the children, possibly all on their own, but were also responsible for earning the money needed to support the family. It is hardly to be wondered at that nearly one-third of the alcoholic wives, and mothers of a large group of children, were mentally exhausted, as well as being in a poor mental and physical state otherwise.

The fathers who received treatment at the Maria Polyclinics at the end of the 1950s had a total of almost 1,000 children. However, in many cases, the fathers no longer had any contact whatsoever with their children as the mothers had managed to break away from the bonds of a marriage that was hurtful. In other cases, the children were the result of a temporary extramarital relationship and there was never any contact at all between father and child. Nevertheless, in a couple of hundred families, the father and mother were living together and there were children in the family. This group comprised the material from which families with children between the ages of 4–12 were selected, resulting in a total of 229 children (113 boys and 116 girls) from 141 different families.

The Control Group

To evaluate the symptoms shown by the children of alcoholic fathers, a control group was selected with great care according to the principle of matched social twins. This was done in order to be able to check all "external environmental factors" so that any differences observed between the test material and the control group could quite definitely be attributed to the "internal environment of the family," i.e., constitutional factors and psychodynamic relationships prevailing inside the family unit as a consequence of the father's alcoholism and the secondary effects of these conditions on the mental status of the mother. A control group could thus be selected which provided a matched control child for every proband, paired according to sex, age, district of residence in Stockholm, conformity of paternal social class affiliation, and in the case of school children, even school class and intellectual capacity. The control material was honed down so that in the final count all the control cases in which paternal alcoholism was suspected or confirmed were eliminated. The resultant control group comprised 163 matched social twins, 83 boys and 80 girls.

The Primary Study

The primary investigation of the material took place in 1958, and revealed considerable negligence in the care of the children belonging to families with alcoholic fathers, who often exhibited signs of physical neglect and also, to a large extent, symptoms of mental insufficiency. In contrast to the control children, they even showed symptoms of a "physical nature," i.e., symptoms such as headaches, stomachaches, heart trouble and "growing pains," which were the initial reasons for contacts between these children and doctors and hospitals giving them treatment for physical illnesses. It is possible that the medical staff treating the children did not realize that there was some underlying psychological or psychiatric reason for the physical symptom shown, and very often extensive medical examinations were carried out, which could even include X-rays and laparotomies, although no underlying physical disease could be found that would explain the severe and disabling symptoms sometimes displayed by the children.

Half of the group of probands also experienced considerable problems of adjustment at school where they were unable to keep up with the rest of the class despite being of normal intelligence, the reasons for falling behind being their restlessness, were hyperactivity, and lack of concentration. As many as 75 percent of the 7–9-year-old boys, the youngest group of schoolboys, were regarded as problem children at school for these reasons. The girls from alcoholic home environments exhibited symptoms of mental insufficiency to the same extent as the boys and had similar problems of adjustment at school.

The investigation material was presented in 1960 in the first doctoral thesis in child psychiatry to be published in Sweden. The author was Ingvar Nylander and the work was entitled "Children of Alcoholic Fathers" [14].

Alcohol Policies in Sweden

The negative effects of alcohol on the mental and physical health of Swedes born and living during the 1800s resulted in the growth of a "strict alcohol-political movement" in Sweden at the beginning of the 1900s. Special laws governing the care of persons addicted to alcohol were passed by parliament and general restrictive regulations were introduced to control the consumption of alcohol. Right up until 1955, the sale of spirits in Sweden was regulated by restrictions that permitted adult males who were steady and hard-working to purchase a certain maximum quantity of liquor each month, the quantity being reduced if they became less "conscientious." During a long stretch of time while these restrictions were in force, women were not permitted to buy alcohol at all.

Probably because of this extremely restrictive alcohol policy, and in association with a very active temperance movement, alcoholism in Sweden was almost totally confined to the male population and was hardly ever found in Swedish women and never in children or youths.

When the first study was carried out at the end of the 1950s, the group termed "children of alcoholics" therefore comprised only a small group in the Swedish community, which might explain why the report was considered to be of very little importance when it was published in 1960. When studying the conditions under which these children were living, it was found that the efforts made by society to help, insofar as any efforts were made, were not coordinated by the various authorities and that it was often difficult to establish any basis for cooperation with the families as the parents were frequently suspicious and could not cope with the effort of "opening up their intimate lives to strangers." Another effect of the alcohol policies of that time was that only a very few of the mothers in the study were abusers of alcohol. Despite the lamentable conditions under which the mothers were living, only two of them were actually alcoholics.

The Dilemma with Prospective Studies

When the primary investigation was concluded, the study material was put aside with the intention of using it as the basis for a prospective longitudinal study of the life-situation of the children when they had reached adulthood. The plans for the future work included the use of a blind procedure, i.e. no personal contact was to be taken with either probands or controls; rather, data collection drew on the resources offered by the Swedish community, which are rather special in that 1) each separate municipality keeps its own records of persons registered for addiction, social maladjustment, etc., and that 2) hospitals and health insurance offices keep records of illnesses, the former as case histories stored in the hospital archives and the latter as records showing the amount of insurance money paid out when evidence of sickness is presented.

The children of alcoholic parents were followed up for a period of 20 years, and their social adjustment and their illnesses during that time were traced. It is a matter of debate whether—or the extent to which—the results of a longitudinal study such as this can be transferred to the situation prevailing in society today. It is quite possible that a variable that was being studied once may lose its topicality owing to changes that take place in the social scene and therefore perhaps no longer has exactly the same importance as it had at the time of the original study [16]. An example of this can be given: the increasing consumption of alcohol in Sweden has meant that alcoholism can now be found in both women and young people. Furthermore, the wives of alcoholic men are themselves often alcoholics in Sweden today, implying that the children in such families are subject to risks that are new today and were unknown at the time of the original study. However, there is no reason to believe that children in alcoholic families in which both parents are alcoholics are in any way better off than children in families in which only the father is an alcoholic, and it can therefore be said that a prospective study of the type that has now been carried out will at least show the minimum risks that children in such a situation will be likely to run. In reality, it would be necessary to run two successive and identical longitudinal studies at different times in order to clarify the effects of changes in the social scene on the results obtained from the studies [16].

As shown in the following section, it is not possible to arrive at any general conclusion from this study on children of alcoholic fathers by the author and postulate that it is applicable to children from all alcoholic families. One of the conclusions that can be drawn is that the results are primarily applicable to children growing up in families in which the father is gravely alcoholic, socially maladjusted and shows criminal tendencies.

For this reason, another study has been carried out in which children from alcoholic families with a good economic and social status are compared to children from alcoholic families with a poor economic and social status. This was a retrospective study and was concerned with children from Sweden of the 1960's. However, the results have shown that children from homes considered to be "good environments" run more or less the same risk of developing problems of social maladjustment and of addiction as the children who come from unsatisfactory environments. This study is also mentioned in a later section of this article [15].

The Follow-up Study

The results of the 20-year follow-up study are presented in the form of a doctoral thesis written by the present author and entitled: "Children of alcoholic fathers—their social adjustment and their health status over 20 years" [17].

The procedure employed for this study was blind, data concerning the probands being obtained from registers maintained by the various Swedish authorities: the Social Welfare Register, the Temperance Register and the Criminal Register, as well as from the records kept by the Health Insurance Office relating to periods of illness, and also by collecting and collating data from case histories stored in hospital archives relating to the mental and physical status of the person in question.

At the time of the 20-year follow-up study, the children had become adults aged 24–32 years. One sex-related difference had become apparent during the observation period. Boys from alcoholic homes had not managed to run their lives nearly as well as the boys from the control families, whereas the girls from alcoholic homes had managed to run their lives just as well as the girls from the control families.

The proband boys had a greater need of social assistance than the control boys, and had, in addition, developed their own alcohol problems, made their debuts in crime, been more ill more often and required more treatment for both mental and physical illnesses than the controls. They were also in greater need of surgery because of accidents of different kinds, frequently injuries resulting from fights or their abuse of alcohol or drugs. When visiting hospitals or polyclinics for treatment, the probands were often identified by the staff as being alcoholics or drug addicts and they were quite often intoxicated on these occasions. The main reasons noted for dispensing psychiatric treatment to these boys were mental symptoms arising from the misuse of alcohol or drugs, whereas psychiatric treatment was needed only very rarely by the control boys.

Concerning the proband girls, it was established that they had had a greater need of sick care at gynecological departments than the control girls and they were also registered more often at hospitals and polyclinics because of their abuse of alcohol and drugs. Further, they tended to have a greater need of social assistance in the form of financial help and they had given birth to a larger number of children than the control girls.

Sex-Related Differences

There are, without doubt, a number of different explanations for the sex-related differences observed. One possible explanation might be that the wives of the alcoholics in 1958 served as better identification models for the daughters than the alcoholic fathers did for the sons. Another explanation might be that the variables studied were of a type that measures "male adjustment problems" more comprehensively than "female adjustment problems." Other Swedish researchers who have followed up boys and girls coming from problem environments have also noted that girls tend to adjust socially relatively well when they grow up but they also tend to succumb to "women's illnesses" (i.e., gynecologic troubles) more frequently than girls from better backgrounds [2]. One more explanation might be the time factor. The social adjustment criteria studied here might possibly occur later for women than they do for men. This has been indicated in other studies run in Sweden: women are older when they make their debut, perhaps older than 40 years, but their problems associated with social adjustment will then develop very rapidly and lead to a serious degree of rejection by society [1,5–10].

Help Given by the Authorities

As a result of this longitudinal study, it has become apparent that the children who developed social adjustment problems, when they became adults, could be identified at an early age by the authorities. Those who were registered with the Child Welfare Committee offices during adolescence for asocial behavior were later in life involved in criminal acts, or became addicted to alcohol or drugs, were often ill and, in addition, were often registered at hospitals and polyclinics where they received treatment for their addictions. Although these observations were recorded in the official registers, the individuals concerned have seldom been the recipients of any consistent, coordinated, long-term supportive measures. Any help that has been made available to them has often been in the form of stopgap measures.

Specially Vulnerable Groups

An attempt was also made to elucidate whether any predictions could be made relating to future maladjustment problems and addiction on the basis of certain items of data collected in 1958 that were connected with the situation of the father, the mother and the child, and with the mental status of the family members. In this instance, the data obtained indicated that the boys who reacted to their situations by "acting-out" and who were physically neglected and whose fathers were especially seriously addicted to alcohol constituted the most vulnerable group. Other data indicated that the group of proband boys whose behaviour was characterized by more "ingoing" anxiety symptoms, such as headaches, heart trouble, etc., were inclined to adjust relatively well socially when they reached adulthood.

Criminality in the City

It can be established that 25 percent of the control boys were noted in the Criminal Register during the observation period. This is a surprising finding since the control group in the 1950s consisted of Class 3 families that functioned satisfactorily and in which only a few of the fathers and mothers were in poor mental health. It is therefore possible that the environment of a large town or city might in itself have a potentiating effect on criminality since the results of other studies dealing with people living in Stockholm also indicated that criminality in Stockholm boys was twice as high in the 1970s as it was in the 1950s [3].

Children of Alcoholic Fathers
from Good Social Environments

When the research material gathered until 1979 was being analyzed, the results obtained gave rise to the question of how children belonging to the upper social stratum, whose fathers were alcoholics, adjusted to society later in life. In an attempt to find an answer to this question, Ingvar Nylander and the present author did an investigation of the children of male alcoholics who had registered for treatment for their alcoholism at a particular alcohol polyclinic in Stockholm between the years 1962–1967. The men registering at this clinic, at Karolinska Hospital, were mainly people whose alcoholism was "concealed," and they were not tainted by criminality nor were they "rejects" of the labor market. Two groups were selected for studies from this patient material, one consisting of the children of fathers from a very high social level with an excellent economic status (higher academics, upper echelon officers, doctors, dentists, managers, higher civil servants, and so forth), and a comparison group consisting of children from working class homes during an equivalent period of time, but the fathers of these families were not nearly as afflicted as the fathers who had received treatment for their alcoholism in 1958 at the Maria Polyclinics in Stockholm. This was a retrospective study but in other respects the same procedures were employed as in the main follow-up investigation, i.e., the children were traced through the Social Welfare Register, the Temperance Register and the Criminal Register. The results obtained indicated that children from alcoholic homes with a good social and economic external environment are just as likely to develop problems of criminality and abuse in adulthood as the children from alcoholic homes with a poor social and economic status.

Conclusions

The investigations dealing with children living in homes characterized by alcoholism that have been carried out by Ingvar Nylander and the present author, have thus shown that children—primarily boys—from families in which the fathers are alcoholics run a considerable risk of developing social maladjustment problems (including alcoholism, drug addiction, and criminality) in adulthood, regardless of whether the economic and social standard of the external environment is satisfactory or not. Owing to a lack of experience, we do not know how best to help these vulnerable children so that they do not become social "rejects" later in life, but in all probability it will be necessary to set up supportive programs for them that will have to be put into effect at a very early age, perhaps even from or before birth.

References

1. Dahlgren, L. Female alcoholics. A psychiatric and social study. Stockholm: Thesis from the Department of Clinical Alcohol and Drug Research, Karolinska Hospital, Karolinska Institute, 1979.
2. Jonsson, G. *Girls on the Skid. A Study of Female Oppression.* Stockholm: Tiden/Folksam, 1977. (In Swedish)
3. Kühlhorn, E. The increase of social problems among adolescents. *Brarapport* 1978; 1:3. (In Swedish)
4. McCord, J.: A thirty-year follow-up of treatment effects. *Am. Psychol.* 33:284, 1978.
5. Medhus, A. Morbidity among female alcoholics. *Scand. J. Soc. Med.* 2:5, 1974.
6. Medhus, A. Conviction for drunkenness-A late symptom among female alcoholics. *Scand. J. Soc. Med.* 3:23, 1975.

7. Medhus, A. Veneral diseases among female alcoholics: *Scand. J. Soc. Med.* 3:29, 1975.
8. Medhus, A.: Criminality among female alcoholics. *Scand. J. Soc. Med.* 3:45, 1975.
9. Medhus, A.: Mortality among female alcoholics. *Scand. J. Soc. Med.* 3:111, 1975.
10. Medhus, A.: Female alcoholics and public assistance. *Scand. J. Soc. Med.* 3:143, 1975.
11. Mednick, S. A. and Baert, A. E. (eds.) Prospective Longitudinal Research: An empirical basis for the primary prevention of Psychosocial Disorders. New York: Oxford University Press, 1981.
12. Nylander, I. A 20-year prospective follow-up study of 2164 cases at the Child Guidance Clinics in Stockholm. *Acta Paediatr. Scand.* [*Suppl.*]276, 1979.
13. Nylander, I. Physical symptoms and psychogenic etiology. An investigation of consultation material. *Acta Paediatr. Scand.* [*Suppl.*]48:69, 1959.
14. Nylander, I. Children of alcoholic fathers. *Acta Paediatr. Scand* [*Suppl.*]49:121, 1960.
15. Nylander, I. and Rydelius, P. A. A comparison between children of alcoholic fathers from excellent versus poor social conditions. Acta Paediatr. Scand. 71: 809, 1982.
16. Rydelius, P. A. *A Longitudinal Prospective Study of the Children of Alcoholic Fathers: A Methodological Study and a Description of the Life Situations of the Children After 15 Years.* A research report from the Child Psychiatric Clinics of the Karolinska Institute, St. Göran's Hospital, Stockholm, 1980. (In Swedish)
17. Rydelius, P. A.: Children of alcoholic fathers—their Social Adjustment and Their Health Status over 20 Years. Acta Paediatr. Scand. [*suppl.*]286:1981.

4 THE LONGITUDINAL COURSE OF ALCOHOLISM AMONG WOMEN CRIMINALS: A SIX-YEAR FOLLOW-UP

Ronald L. Martin
C. Robert Cloninger
Samuel B. Guze

To date, little has been reported concerning the longitudinal course of alcoholism in criminal women. Glueck and Glueck [5], in their study of 500 delinquent girls, found that 40 percent "drank to excess" when followed-up as adults. Nineteen women were included in Maddocks' [9] study of untreated psychopaths. A third of these women used alcohol "to excess" at a five-year follow-up. Maddocks generalized that many "psychopaths" (both men and women) eventually "drifted into" alcoholism, implying that alcoholism was a rather late complication in this group. Neither study, however, included the detailed longitudinal data necessary to evaluate the course of alcoholism in criminal women.

A group of 66 convicted female felons were first studied by members of our group in 1969 [2], and followed-up five to six years later. As reported previously, a high rate of alcoholism was found both at the initial and follow-up evaluations [11]. To date, however, the longitudinal course of alcoholism in these women has not been reported in detail. This will be the focus of this chapter.

The authors gratefully acknowledge the cooperation of Mr. Vearl Harris and the staff of the Missouri State Board of Probation and Parole, and Eunice Henry for her assistance. This investigation was supported in party by UPHS Grant AA00209 and Research Scientist Development Award MH-00048.

39

Method and Subjects

The Index Study

Methods of subject selection, interviewing, record assessment, and diagnosis were reviewed in detail previously [2].

The index group of 66 female criminals represented the entire caseload of District 8 of the Missouri State Board of Probation and Parole on July 1, 1969, plus new cases added in July and August. All of the women were convicted felons.

Assessment of each women was based on a 2–4 hour structured interview as well as review of criminal justice and medical records. The interview protocol has been published in full elsewhere [8].

Lifetime psychiatric diagnoses were made according to well-studied, published criteria [10]. These criteria were subsequently incorporated with little change into the "Feighner criteria" [4]. For most analyses women with definite and probable or questionable diagnoses were considered together. The terms antisocial personality and sociopathy were used interchangeably.

Alcoholism was diagnosed on the basis of symptomatic drinking leading to alcohol-related problems in three of the following four groups: (Group 1) tremors or other manifestations of withdrawal, "blackouts," binges and benders, other medical complications; (Group 2) inability to stop drinking, attempts to control by allowing drinking only under certain circumstances, drinking before breakfast, drinking nonbeverage alcohol; (Group 3) arrests, traffic difficulties, trouble at work, fighting; (Group 4) feeling they drank too much, family objected to their drinking, loss of friends, feeling guilty about drinking. Questionable alcoholism was diagnosed in the presence of symptoms in two of the four groups.

The occurrence of any of these drinking-related problems was referred to as "alcohol abuse." Alcoholism was considered in remission if an alcoholic woman had not abused alcohol for six months prior to the evaluation.

The Follow-up Study

Methods of the follow-up study in general were published in detail previously [10]. In brief, five years following the index interviews attempt was made to contact and reinterview all 66 women. The interviewer at follow-up (R. L. Martin) remained blind to the original interviews (performed by C. R. Cloninger) until all interviews, diagnoses, and other assessments were completed.

In addition to interview information, current Missouri Highway Patrol and FBI records were obtained on all women. Medical records were obtained whenever possible. Information obtained in the process of tracing the women (such as reports from spouses, relatives, friends, and employers) were recorded. In women not contacted or not cooperative with an interview as much information as possible was obtained from these sources. Follow-up assessment and diagnosis was based on all of these sources of information.

Data Analysis

Means appear with standard errors of the mean $\bar{x} \pm$ SEM). Sample means were evaluated using the two-tailed t-test (t) for independent samples. Proportions were evaluated using two-tailed chi-square tests with one degree of freedom with Yates correction for continuity, except where sparse frequencies (any expected value less than five) required use of Fisher's exact probability test. In all cases "significant" or "significance" were used in the statistical sense denoting probabilities $<.05$. "Trends" denoted probabilities $>.05$ but $<.10$.

Results

Alcoholism at Index

Lifetime Prevalence. Alcoholism was diagnosed in 31 (47%) of the 66 women criminals on the basis of the index evaluation. Thus, alcoholism was the most frequent psychiatric disorder after antisocial personality (diagnosed in 65%). The alcoholism diagnoses were definite in 28 women, questionable in three.

An additional woman was considered an alcohol abuser at the index evaluation, but did not fulfill criteria for alcoholism. On the basis of interview and other information obtained at follow-up the woman had clearly minimized the extent of her drinking problems at index and would have fulfilled criteria for alcoholism had she been candid. Since sufficient symptoms to warrant a diagnosis of alcoholism had antedated the index interview she was included with the index alcoholics for purposes of follow-up.

Two other women were considered alcohol abusers at the index evaluation. Since no information was obtained indicating that criteria for alcoholism were fulfilled at the time of the index interview they were included with the nonalcoholics.

Active Alcoholism. At the time of the index crime, alcoholism was remitted in (34%) of the 32 alcoholic women. At the index evaluation, five (16%) were in remission (for 1–12 years). The other 27 (84%) had abused alcohol during the six months prior to interview.

General Characteristic of the Alcoholics. Basic demographic data comparing the 32 alcoholic and 34 nonalcoholic women is presented in table 4-1. The mean age of the alcoholics (29.2 ± 1.6 years) did not differ from that of the nonalcoholics, and the two groups did not differ as to racial composition. Approximately half of the whites and half of the blacks were alcoholic, and there was one alcoholic and one nonalcoholic American Indian. Only two (6%) of the alcoholic women were married and with their spouses compared with 12 (35%) of the other women. This was a significant difference ($p < .01$).

The alcoholic and nonalcoholic women are compared on the basis of criminality in table 4-2. A disproportionate number of the alcoholic women had a history of arrest (nontraffic offenses) prior to the index offense compared with the nonalcoholic women (72% vs 41%). The two groups did

Table 4-1. Index Demographic Variables, Alcoholics vs. Nonalcoholics

Index Variable	Alcoholics (N = 32)	Nonalcoholics (N = 34)
Age, year		
Range	17–54	18–53
Mean $\pm$ SEM	29.2 ± 1.6	29.4 ± 1.6
Race		
White, f (%)	16 (50%)	18 (53%)
Black, f (%)	15 (47%)	15 (44%)
American Indian, f (%)	1 (3%)	1 (3%)
Marital Status		
Married, f (%)	2 (6%)*	12 (35%)*
Divorced or Separated, f	18	15
Widowed, f ⎤ f (%)	5 ⎤ 30 (94%)	1 ⎤ 22 (65%)
Never Married, f	7	6

*Difference in proportion alcoholics vs. nonalcoholics significant: $p < .01$

Table 4-2. Index Criminality Variables, Alcoholics vs. Nonalcoholics

Index Variable	Alcoholics (N = 32)	Nonalcoholics (N = 34)
Record		
Prior arrest, f (%)	23 (72%)*	14 (41%)*
Prior felony conviction, f (%)	5 (16%)	8 (24%)
Index Crime		
Against person:		
Homicide, f	6 ⎤	8 ⎤
Robbery, f ⎤ f (%)	3 ⎬ 11 (34%)	2 ⎬ 10 (29%)
Assault, f ⎦	2 ⎦	0 ⎦
Against property:		
Burglary, f ⎤	3 ⎤	5 ⎤
Larceny, f ⎥	4 ⎥	7 ⎥
Forgery, f ⎥ f (%)	8 ⎥ 21 (66%)	3 ⎥ 24 (71%)
Embezzlement, f ⎥	1 ⎥	2 ⎥
Auto theft, f ⎥	0 ⎥	1 ⎥
Drug violations, f ⎥	4 ⎦	6 ⎦
Driving while intoxicated, f ⎦	1 ⎦	0 ⎦
Parolee, f (%)	15 (47%)	18 (53%)
Probationer, f (%)	17 (53%)	16 (47%)

*Difference in proportion alcoholics vs nonalcoholics significant at the $p < .05$ level.

not differ as to prior felony convictions with less than a quarter of each group having such a history. The two groups did not differ as to whether the index crime was against person (approximately one-third of each group) or against property. Both groups consisted of approximately one-half parolees and one-half probationers.

The presence of other psychiatric disorders among the alcoholics and nonalcoholics is presented in table 4-3. All of the alcoholics had additional diagnoses. A disproportionate number of alcoholics were also antisocial (81% vs. 51%) and homosexual (31% vs. 9%) compared with non-alcoholics. From another perspective 60 percent of the sociopaths were alcoholic as were 77 percent of the homosexual women.

Age of Onset of Alcoholism. The first drinking-related problems were reported to have occurred from age 12 to age 50, with the mean first occurence at age 21.4 ± 1.3 years. Four (13%) of the 32 alcoholic women reported their first drinking problems prior to age 16, 14 (44%) prior to age

Table 4-3. Other Psychiatric Disorders at Index, Alcoholics vs. Nonalcoholics

Index Psychiatric Disorders*	Alcoholics (N = 32)	Nonalcoholics (N = 34)
Antisocial personality, f (%)	26 (81%)[†]	17 (50%)[†]
Anxiety neurosis, f (%)	3 (9%)	4 (12%)
Drug dependence, f (%)	10 (31%)	7 (21%)
Homosexuality, f (%)	10 (31%)[†]	3 (9%)[†]
Hysteria, f (%)	14 (44%)	13 (38%)
Mental deficiency, f (%)	1 (3%)	3 (9%)
Primary depressive disorder, f (%)	0	2 (6%)
Schizophrenia, f (%)	0	1 (3%)

*Total number of disorders is greater than 66 because most women received more than one diagnosis.

[†] Difference in proportion, alcoholics vs. nonalcoholics, significant at the $p < .05$ level.

20, and 27 (90%) prior to age 30. Four reported an onset between age 30 and 35, and one alcoholic woman first had problems at age 50.

Onset of Alcoholism Relative to the Onset of Criminality. Seventeen alcoholic women reported that alcohol problems preceded their first criminal behavior, while 15 reported the precedence of criminality. The reported onsets of alcohol abuse and criminal problems were within two years of each other in 13 (41%) of the 32 alcoholic women.

Duration of Alcoholism. The duration of alcoholism among the 32 alcoholics (the number of years from the onset of alcohol abuse until remission or until the index interview for those still active) ranged from 1 to 34 years with a mean duration of 6.8 ± 1.2 years. The mean duration for the 27 active alcoholics was 6.9 ± 1.9 years, for the alcoholics in remission at index, 4.8 ± 2.3 years.

Alcoholism During Follow-up

Reevaluation of the Index Alcoholics. Of 32 index alcoholics, 24 (75%) were adequately evaluated at follow-up to ascertain the course of their alcoholism. Twenty-three of these women were alive at the follow-up evaluation occurring at a mean of $5.8 \pm .2$ years after the index evaluation. One of the index alcoholics died two years after the index evaluation.

Alcohol Abuse During Follow-up. Thirteen (54%) of the 24 index alcoholics had alcohol problems during follow-up. This included one of the two reevaluated alcoholics in remission at the index evaluation.

The alcoholic woman who died continued to abuse alcohol until her death at age 40. The cause of death was attributed to congestive heart failure. She died during a drinking binge. She had neglected medical advice regarding the management of hypertension and the need to cease alcohol abuse.

Another alcoholic woman suffered serious medical complications of alcohol abuse. At the follow-up evaluation this 52-year-old woman was in an after-care hospital awaiting transfer to a nursing home. She suffered from hepatic cirrhosis, hepatic failure, and moderate dementia. She abused alcohol until hospitalized with hepatic coma and congestive heart failure. She had been hospitalized previously (at age 49) for hepatic coma and was warned then to cease drinking entirely. This advice was heeded for three days after discharge.

Remission at Follow-up. At the six-year follow-up evaluation a total of 13 women (54% of the 24 reevaluated index alcoholics) were free of alcohol abuse for at least six months. This included two women who had some alcohol problems during follow-up but were in remission by the end of the period.

Predictors of Continued Alcohol Abuse. Table 4-4 compares the 11 women who continued to abuse alcohol at follow-up to the 13 remitted alcoholics. There was a trend ($.05 < p < .10$) for the nonremitted alcoholics to have had a longer duration of alcoholism at index (10.1 ± 2.8 years vs. 4.2 ± 1.0 years). There were no significant differences or trends as to the other variables shown although the nonremitters were on the average older at index than the remitters, and twice the rate of blacks compared with whites, and twice the rate of those whose index crime was against person compared with those whose crime was against property were active alcoholics. The presence or absence of index diagnoses of antisocial personality, hysteria, drug dependence, or homosexuality did not predict the course of alcoholism.

Correlates of Continued Alcohol Abuse. As shown in table 4-5 only one of six alcoholics who were married at follow-up continued to abuse alcohol, compared with 10 (56%) of 18 nonmarried alcoholics. This difference was a trend ($.05 < p < .10$). The nonremitters were on the average older at follow-up than the remitted alcoholics (38.2 ± 2.9 vs. 32.4 ± 2.5 years of age), but this difference was not significant.

Continued alcohol abuse was not correlated with continued criminality nor continued drug abuse. Half of the alcoholic women who were criminally

Table 4-4. Index Variables and Nonremitted Alcoholism at Follow-up

Index Variable	Nonremitters (N = 11)	Remitters (N = 13)
Age at index, year		
Range	22–52	17–54
Mean ± SEM	32.5 ± 2.8	26.9 ± 2.6
Alcoholism, age onset, year		
Range	13–35	14–50
Mean ± SEM	21.5 ± 1.9	22.2 ± 2.5
Alcoholism, duration at index, year		
Range	1–34	1–15
Mean ± SEM	10.1 ± 2.8*	4.2 ± 1.0*
Race		
White, f (row %)	4 (31%)	9 (69%)
Black, f (row %)	6 (60%)	4 (40%)
American Indian, f (row %)	1 (100%)	0
Marital Status		
Married, f (row %)	0	2 (100%)
Not married, f (row %)	11 (50%)	11 (50%)
Criminal record		
Prior arrest, f (row %)	8 (47%)	9 (53%)
Prior felony conviction, f (row %)	2 (67%)	1 (33%)
Type of index crime		
Against person, f (row %)	6 (67%)	3 (33%)
Against property, f (row %)	5 (33%)	10 (67%)
Other psychiatric disorders		
Antisocial personality	10 (53%)	9 (47%)
Hysteria	4 (40%)	6 (60%)
Drug dependence	3 (38%)	5 (63%)
Homosexuality	5 (50%)	5 (50%)

*Differences in proportion, nonremitted vs. remitted alcoholics, a trend ($.05 < p < .10$).

recidivist and half of those who abused drugs during follow-up were nonremitted.

Incidence of Alcoholism During Follow-up. One new case of alcoholism developed during the six-year follow-up. This woman was diagnosed at index (age 27) with antisocial personality and drug dependence. She abused heroin from age 23 until age 32 when she was advised that any continued use would destroy her kidneys. She abruptly ceased heroin use and began drinking at least 12 beers daily. She had no prior history of alcohol abuse. She felt that she was drinking too much but was unable to quit or limit her consumption. She drank through the day having her first drink upon awakening. After one year with this drinking pattern she developed a nephrotic syndrome and was placed on renal dialysis three times weekly. She ceased all alcohol consumption at that point and was abstinent when interviewed at follow-up at age 34.

Onset of Other Psychiatric Disorders Among the Alcoholics. One woman suffered the onset of schizophrenia, another of dementia during follow-up.

The woman who developed schizophrenia began showing signs of psychosis at age 25, a few months after her evaluation at index when she was diagnosed with hysteria and alcoholism. She was subsequently hospitalized twice for psychotic episodes and was receiving depot fluphenazine every other week at the time of the follow-up evaluation. She was not very communicative at the follow-up interview and it was necessary to obtain most of the information concerning her follow-up course from interviews of family members and review of medical records. Alcohol abuse as well as criminal activities and excessive somatic complaints ceased with the onset of her psychotic illness.

As previously discussed, one alcoholic woman became moderately demented during follow-up, showing progressive mental decline along with hepatic failure and at least two episodes of hepatic coma.

Table 4-5. Follow-up Correlates of Nonremitted Alcoholism

Follow-up Variable	Nonremitters (N = 11)	Remitters (N = 13)
Age at follow-up, year		
Range	26–60	26–59
Mean ± SEM	38.2 ± 2.9	32.4 ± 2.5
Marital status		
Married, f (row %)	1 (17%)*	5 (83%)*
Not married, f (row %)	10 (56%)	8 (44%)
Continued criminality, f (row %)	5 (50%)	5 (50%)
Drug abuse in follow-up, f (row %)	2 (50%)	2 (50%)

*Difference in proportion, nonremitted vs. remitted alcoholics, a trend (.05 < p < .10).

Three alcoholic women not diagnosed drug dependent at the initial evaluation were so diagnosed at follow-up. However, this did not represent new cases of drug dependence. All three women had extensive histories of drug abuse antedating the index evaluation but minimized or denied this abuse at the initial interview.

Nine (38%) of the 24 index alcoholics were considered to have secondary unipolar affective disorders at the follow-up evaluation. Although these women were not diagnosed with depression at index this was attributable, at least in part, to the diagnostic procedure. At index women with hysteria who reported affective syndromes were not given an additional diagnosis of a secondary affective disorder whereas they were at follow-up. Seven (all but two) of the alcoholic women with secondary depressions diagnosed at follow-up were index hysterics.

Discussion

High Prevalence of Alcoholism Among Female Criminals

Nearly one-half of a sample of 66 convicted women felons were diagnosed alcoholic at the initial evaluation. This is in marked excess of the rate of 1 percent estimated for the general female population [6]. It is even in marked excess of the rate of 5 percent heavy drinkers found among women in a large national survey [1].

Early Onset of Alcoholism

Nearly half of the alcoholic felons began their alcohol abuse before the age of 20. In contrast, an average onset of problem drinking in the early thirties has been reported in several studies of noncriminal alcoholic women [3].

Which Comes First, Alcoholism or Criminality?

Contrary to the implication of Maddocks [9] that alcoholism was a rather late complication of "psychopathy," over half of the alcoholic women in this study abused alcohol prior to the onset of criminality. Nearly half reported the onset of both alcohol and criminal problems within two years of each other. Thus, alcoholism and criminality appear more as highly correlated conditions than as one developing as a consequence of the other.

Alcoholism, Homosexuality, and Drug Dependence

Alcoholism was significantly associated with homosexuality in this sample. Over 75 percent of the homosexual women were alcoholic. Only about 20 percent of the felons were homosexual but they composed nearly a third of the alcoholics. This supports the recent report by Lewis, Saghir, and Robins [16] of a high prevalence (in their study 28%) of alcoholism among homosexual women. As with the association of alcoholism and sociopathy, it is difficult to move from the observation of a correlation to any causative hypothesis.

Nearly 60 percent of the drug dependent felons were also alcoholic but the two forms of substance abuse were not statistically correlated in this sample. The one woman who became alcoholic during follow-up did so upon the cessation of heroin abuse. As was discussed in a previous report [12], however, such a "switch" only occurred in one case. Thus, substitution of alcohol for abandoned drug abuse did not appear to be a regularly occurring phenomenon as has been reported in other populations of drug addicts [14]. None of the alcoholics developed drug abuse when they ceased to abuse alcohol.

Course of Alcoholism Similar to Course
Among Noncriminal Women

It was possible to evaluate the course of alcoholism in 75 percent of the index alcoholics during the six-year follow-up. Remission, based on the absence of any alcohol abuse for six months prior to the follow-up evaluation, occurred in slightly over half. This remission rate is similar to that reported in a three-year follow-up of a psychiatrically hospitalized group of women alcoholics reported by Schuckit and Winokur [13]. Their follow-up was at three years rather than at six, but it is argued that the two studies are still comparable. All but two of the remitting alcoholics in the present study had done so by three years.

The female felon alcoholics had similar medical complications as have been reported in other female alcoholic populations [13,15]. One alcoholic women died during follow-up. Her death was attributable, at least in part, to neglect of a medical problems and continued alcohol abuse. Another women developed hepatic cirrhosis, hepatic failure, and dementia. Too few women were affected, however, to make any statistical comparisons.

One alcoholic felon (also diagnosed with hysteria at index) developed schizophrenia during follow-up. No studies relating to the risk of schizophrenia among alcoholic women are known to the authors. Interestingly, alcohol abuse, as well as criminal behavior and excessive somatic complaining, ceased with onset of psychosis in this woman.

Prediction of Continued Alcohol Abuse?

Continued alcohol abuse was associated (at least as a trend) with the duration of alcoholism at the index evaluation but not with age at index, the age of onset of alcohol abuse, marital status, prior criminal record, or intercurrent psychiatric disorders. There was some suggestion that blacks as opposed to whites, and those whose index crimes were against person rather than property fared worse, but those relationships did not reach statistical significance. Schuckit and Winokur [13] also found a positive correlation between poor outcome and the duration of alcoholism in their sample of female alcoholics. They also found that poor outcome and early age of onset of alcoholism were associated.

Correlates of Continued Alcohol Abuse

Unmarried felons (including those divorced, separated, and widowed) tended to continue alcohol abuse more often than married women. Although the association was only a trend, alcoholism failed to remit in only one alcoholic woman who was married at follow-up. Thus, alcoholism in criminal women appears to have a similar association with unsuccessful marital adjustment as has been reported in other populations.

Continued alcohol abuse was not correlated with continued criminality. Half of the alcoholic women who remained criminally active continued to abuse alcohol, half did not. This contrasts to findings in men criminals where continued alcohol abuse was highly correlated with continued criminality [7].

Overall Summary and Clinical Implication

Alcoholism was extremely prevalent in a group of women felons. The onset of alcoholism was much earlier in this group than has been observed in other groups of alcoholic women. The longitudinal course of alcoholism, however, was very similar to that reported in noncriminal women.

Rather than occurring as a late complication of sociopathy [9], alcoholism and criminality, in most cases, both began early in life, often in close temporal relation with one another.

Alcoholism often continued after criminality had been abandoned. Thus, alcoholic women criminals should be monitored for alcohol abuse even after they are no longer criminally active.

References

1. Cahalan, D., Cisin, I., and Crossley, H. M. *American Drinking Practices*. New Haven: College and University Press, 1969.
2. Cloninger, C. R. and Guze, S. B. Psychiatric illness and female criminality: the role of sociopathy and hysteria in the antisocial woman. *Am. J. Psychiatry* 127:303, 1970.
3. Corrigen, E. M. *Alcoholic Women in Treatment*. New York: Oxford University Press, 1980.
4. Feighner, J. P., Robins, E., Guze, S. B., et al. Diagnostic criteria for use in psychiatric research. *Arch. Gen. Psychiatry* 26:57, 1972.
5. Glueck, S. and Glueck, E. T. *Five Hundred Delinquent Women*. New York: Kraus Reprint, 1965.
6. Goodwin, D. W. and Guze, S. B. Heredity and alcoholism. In B. Kissin and H. Begleiter (eds.), *Biology of Alcoholism*, Vol. 3, New York: Plenum Press, 1974.
7. Guze, S. B., Goodwin, D. W., and Crane, J. B. Criminal recidivism and psychiatric illness. *Am. J. Psychiatry* 127:832, 1970.
8. Guze, S. B. *Criminality and Psychiatric Disorders*. New York: Oxford University Press, 1976.
9. Maddocks, P. D. A five-year follow-up of untreated psychopaths. *Br. J. Psychiatry* 116:511, 1970.
10. Martin, R. L., Cloninger, C. R., and Guze, S. B. The evaluation of diagnostic concordance in follow-up studies: II. a blind, prospective follow-up of female criminals. *J. Psychiatr. Res.* 15:107, 1979.
11. Martin, R. L., Cloninger, C. R., and Guze, S. B. Alcoholism and female criminality. *J. Clin. Psychiatry* 43:400, 1982.
12. Martin, R. L., Cloninger, C. R., and Guze, S. B. The natural history of somatization and substance abuse in women criminals: a six-year follow-up. *Comprehensive Psychiatry* 23:528, 1982.
13. Schuckit, M. A. and Winokur, G. A short-term follow-up of women alcoholics. *Dis. Nerv. Syst.* 33:672, 1972.
14. Willis, J. H. and Osbourne, A. B. What happens to heroin addicts? A follow-up study. *Br. J. Addict.* 73:189, 1978.

15. Wilkerson, P. Sex Differences in Morbidity of Alcoholics. In O. J. Kalant (ed.), *Alcohol and Drug Problems in Women*. New York: Plenum Press, 1981.
16. Lewis, Saghir, and Robins, Drinking patterns in Homosexual and Heterosexual Women. *J. Clin. Psychiatry, 43*, 277, 1982.

5 NATURAL HISTORY OF MALE ALCOHOLISM: PATHS TO RECOVERY

George E. Vaillant
Eva S. Milofsky

Our understanding of alcoholism is hampered both by the dearth of long-term follow-up studies of treatment and by the absence of studies of the natural history of alcoholism. Until we possess such studies, intelligent evaluation of treatment will be impossible; yet the acquisition of such studies is not easy.

First, we cannot understand the natural history of alcoholism by drawing samples from clinic populations. Alcoholics with the most benign prognoses often never come to clinical attention. As is the case with patients afflicted with other chronic illnesses, alcoholics who attend clinics tend to be more ill, to be more psychologically impaired, and, unless great care is taken in sample selection, to reflect previous treatment failures.

Second, not only must community samples be studied for many years, but attrition must also be avoided. In disorders that can last for decades, attrition of even 1 percent a year soon becomes unacceptable. We never know if alcoholics who disappear from treatment follow-up studies do so because their clinical course has been so benign or so malignant.

This investigation was supported in part by research grant AA-01372 from the National Institute of Alcoholism and Alcohol Abuse, by the Grant Foundation, Inc, and by the Spencer Foundation. We are grateful to the *Archives of General Psychiatry* for permission to republish this article from the February 1982, issue.

Third, to understand the role of treatment in the recovery process, controlled studies are desirable, but in a chronic illness like alcoholism such studies are extremely difficult. Alcoholics assigned to control groups cannot be forbidden to seek treatment elsewhere. With the continued passage of time, the variety of different treatments that a relapsing alcoholic may experience steadily increases. Therefore, an alternative strategy is to let each alcoholic serve as his or her own control. If each individual is followed up for decades, the "treatment" experience that occurs at the time of recovery may be regarded as possibly effective, and previous "treatment" experiences that have failed can be regarded as possibly ineffective.

Fourth, to evaluate efficacy of intervention, premorbid factors become extremely important. Just as in schizophrenia inadvertent selection for certain premorbid factors accounted for the illusory efficacy of insulin coma, so Costello [1,2] and Baekland et al. [3] have demonstrated that much of the treatment success attributed to disulfiram, group therapy, aversion techniques, and long hospital stays can in fact be explained by differences in premorbid status.

Finally, to understand the recovery process in alcoholism, the study should be so designed as to maximize the elucidation of natural healing processes as well as that of effective clinical intervention. Indeed, there is extensive literature, reviewed by Edwards and co-workers [4,5] suggesting the recovery process in alcoholism may depend almost entirely on factors other than specific treatment interventions.

The present study describes an effort to understand naturalistically the recovery process in alcoholism. A cohort of 456 nondelinquent inner-city schoolboys, demographically at high risk for alcoholism, were prospectively followed up at multiple points in time until age 47 [6,7,8,9]. Attrition was kept to 0.25 percent per year. Six questions that often arouse controversy in the field of alcoholism were asked: What proportion of a selected cohort of alcoholics can be expected to be in remission by age 47? What were the important premorbid predictors? what were the important treatment factors? Is return to social drinking the exception or the rule? Is reliance by remitted alcoholics on Alcoholics Anonymous (AA) the exception or the rule? Are abstinent alcoholics psychosocially better off than those who continue to drink?

Methods

Sample

The sample included the 456 early adolescents studied by the Gluecks [6,7] between 1940 and 1963 as a control group for their well-known studies of juvenile delinquents. In more recent follow-ups, [8,9] this group has been called the Core City sample. In terms of IQ, ethnicity, and residence in high-crime neighborhoods, this sample had been carefully matched with 456 Boston youths who had been remanded to reform school. Their average IQ was 95 ± 12, and they had attended the same inner-city school as the delinquents. Although there were no blacks in the Gluecks' study, one or both of the parents of 61 percent of the boys had been born in a foreign country. Only 11 percent of the parents but 51 percent of the subjects in middle life fell in social classes I, II, and III. Although at age 14 ± 2 years, the youths had been chosen for nondelinquency, eventually 19% spent time in jail. Only 33 percent of their parents even attended high school; 48 percent of the subjects graduated from high school.

At the time of original study, the boys, their parents, and their teachers were individually interviewed. For all first-degree relatives, public records were searched for evidence of alcoholism, criminal behavior, and mental illness. More than 90 percent of surviving subjects were reinterviewed at ages 25 and 31 [7]. At these interviews, alcohol abuse (or its absence) was specifically recorded. At age 47, a two-hour semistructured interview with a detailed 23-item section on problem drinking was used to reinterview 84% of the surviving subjects. Most of these interviews were performed by individuals with two or more years' experience in alcohol clinics. In addition to the serial interviews, psychiatric, medical, and arrest records were obtained on most subjects over the 33-year follow-up period. These records helped to confirm that the subjects were reliable informants and to identify additional alcohol-related problems.

Clinical Ratings

Early Life Ratings.   Clinicians, blind to all information after adolescence, on the basis of a search of social service records and interviews with the boy, his parents, and his teacher, rated the men on the following scales:

Childhood Environmental Strengths.   This is a 20-point scale described in detail elsewhere [10] that rated the men by a clinical judgment of childhood environmental strengths. Rater reliability among three raters ranged from .70 to .89.

Childhood Environmental Weaknesses.   This is a 50-point scale [9] based on 25 concrete criteria that reflected the Gluecks' more clinically defined Delinquency Prediction Scale [6]. The scale included five objective items reflecting gross lack of family cohesion and ten items reflecting inadequate parental supervision and affection. Rater reliability ranged from .91 to .94. If ten or more items were present, the boy was said to belong to a multiproblem family.

Boyhood Competence or Success at Erikson's Stage 4 Tasks. This was an 8-point scale [9] assessing the extent to which the subjects at entrance into the study had mastered Erikson's fourth stage of industry—"doing things beside and with others." It was intended as a crude assessment of ego strength. Rater reliability ranged from .70 to .91.

Outcome Ratings. Clinicians blind to all data gathered before age 31, on the basis of a two-hour interview at ages 31 and 47 and recent public records, rated the men on the following scales:

Health Sickness Rating Scale (HSRS). HSRS is described in detail elsewhere [11,12]. With 34 case illustrations serving as guides, the scale places individuals along a 100-point continuum that ranges from total institutional dependency (0 to 10) to the exhibition of multiple manifestations of positive mental health (90 to 100). Rater reliability was .89.

Sociopathy Scale. This was based on the 19 criteria used by Robins [13] for the diagnosis of sociopathic personality. Presence of five or more criteria led to a dignosis of sociopathic personality.

Social Competence (Object Relations). For the Core City sample, this was an 8-point scale [8] summing up each individual's relative success in accomplishing eight different tasks of adult object relations excluding marriage; one task each reflected enjoyment of children, family or origin, and workmates; three tasks reflected friendship network; and two tasks reflected participation in group activities.

Alcoholism Ratings. These were obtained in the same manner as the outcome ratings, except for the fact that since evidence for problem drinking was made by consensus, rater reliabilities were not obtained.

Alcohol Dependence (n = 71). This definition was that of the American Psychiatric Association's *DSM-III*, i.e., evidence of pathologic alcohol use and impairment of social or occupational functioning for one month or more, and tolerance or withdrawal symptoms from alcohol. (The *DSM-III* scale was applied only to the 400 completed cases.)

Problem Drinking Scale (PDS) [14]. The PDS was an equally weighted 16-item scale devised to combine the emphasis on the *DSM-III* on physiological dependence and the emphasis of the Cahalan scale [15] on social deviance. The scale depended on objective alcohol-related problems (e.g., blackouts, arrests, medical complications of alcohol abuse) and gave double weights for alcohol problems that occurred frequently. Extensive discussion of reliability and discriminant function analysis of the items are presented elsewhere [16]. (In this article, only the 400 completely studied cases will be discussed.)

The PDS was used to classify as social drinkers 260 men (240 of completed cases) with zero to one item on the PDS and as alcohol abusers 120 men (110 of the completed cases) with four or more items. This definition of alcohol abuse was stricter than that of the *DSM-III*; only 68, however, of the 110 "alcohol abusers" defined by the PDS met the *DSM-III* criteria for dependence.

Of the remaining 76 men, 14 could not be classified because of insufficient data. Sixty-two men (50 of the completed cases) manifested two or three different alcohol-related PDS items during their adult lives, but spent most of their lives as asymptomatic drinkers.

Abstinence. Consuming less than a drink (one shot of whiskey, 360 ml of beer) a month for 12 consecutive months, or remaining totally abstinent for 24 months except for a single drinking bout of less than seven days' duration, was defined as abstinence.

Return to Social Drinking. These men in the past had met the criteria for alcohol abuse and now drank more often than once a month, but had gone for 12 months without any identified alcohol-related problems on the PDS.

Results

Of the 456 junior high school students originally studied by the Gluecks, all have been accounted for, either by confirmed evidence of death or by positive evidence of survival and geographic location after age 40. Eighty-four percent of the surviving men were reinterviewed at age 47; in most cases, if a man was not personally reinterviewed at ages 25, 31, and 47, a close relative was interviewed [7,8]. Complete drinking histories from ages 20–47 were obtained for 400 men; the drinking practices of only 14 men, most of whom died young, were completely unknown. The 56 incomplete cases included

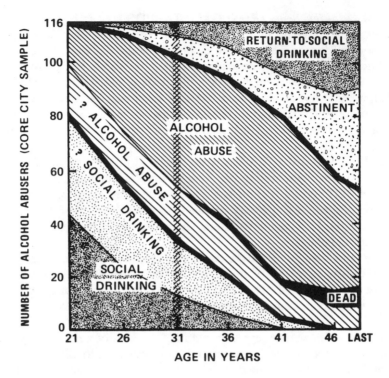

Figure 5-1. Proportion of 116 Core City Men Who Evidenced Multiple Symptoms of Problem Drinking at Any Given Age.

arbitrary exclusion of the 19 men who died before age 40, 29 (8%) who withdrew from the study, and eight who could not be located at age 47.

Of the 400 complete cases, there were 110 men who met the criteria for alcohol abuse—four or more symptoms on the PDS [14,16]. This report focuses on these 110 men. Seventy-one (18%) of the 400 men also met the *DSM-III* criteria for alcohol dependence, and 70 men manifested seven or more problems on the more sociologically oriented Cahalan PDS [15]. All but four of the men in these latter categories also met the criteria for alcohol abuse on the PDS.

Figure 5-1 depicts the lifetime pattern of alcohol use or abuse in the Core City men who at some point in their lives met the criteria for alcohol abuse. (The figure also includes six men known to be alcohol abusers but who died prior to interview.) By age 31, more than half of the 110 Core City men who were ever classified as alcohol abusers had already manifested four or more alcohol-related problems. By age 47, more than half of the Core City alcohol abusers, however, had become abstinent or had returned to asymptomatic drinking, defined as "social drinking" in the "Methods" section.

As table 5-1 suggests, not all the men who in fig 5-1 were classed as abstinent in a given year remained abstinent during subsequent years. Of the 400 men for whom complete data were available, 110 met the arbitrary definition of alcohol abuse; of these, 49 men became abstinent for one year or more. Eleven of the 49 abstinent men were abstinent for at least a year, but relapsed to chronic alcohol abuse. The remaining 38 men will be termed "currently abstinent." In terms of number of alcohol-related problems, these currently abstinent men had been just as symptomatic as the men who currently met the *DSM-III* criteria for alcohol dependence. Twenty-one of these currently abstinent men—termed "securely abstinent"—were those alcoholics who achieved three or more years of abstinence (average, ten years).

Eighty percent of the 49 ever abstinent men met the *DSM-III* definition of alcohol dependence. In contrast, only a third of the 18 alcohol abusers who resumed asymptomatic drinking for two years or more (average, ten years) met the *DSM-III* definition of alcohol dependence, and only half of the men

Table 5-1. Definitions of Abstinence Among 110 Alcohol Abusers in the Core City Sample

Definition	No. of Men (N = 110)
Never abstinent (for 1 yr)	61
Ever abstinent (for at least 12 consecutive months)	49
Relapsed to intermittent alcohol abuse	5
Relapsed to "progressive" alcohol dependence	6
Currently abstinent (for at least the preceding 12 months)	38
Abstinent for 4 years in a nursing home	1
Abstinent for more than 3 years, but have engaged in > 1 binge per year or periods of controlled drinking	3
Abstinent in the community, but for less than 3 years	13
Securely abstinent (for at least the preceding 36 months; mean, 10 years)	21

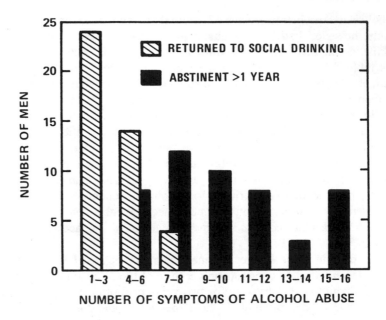

Figure 5-2. Number of Men at Any Symptom Level on Problem Drinking Scale Who Either Became Abstinent or Resumed Social Drinking for More than One Year.

who at age 47 still met the definition for alcohol abuse met the *DSM-III* definition of alcohol dependence. In other words, being alcohol dependent and/or having many alcohol-related problems appeared to be associated with eventual sustained abstinence.

Figure 5-2 makes this point differently. Many of the men who in the past had experienced five or fewer problems on the PDS currently meet the definition for return to social drinking, but none stopped drinking for a year or more. In contrast, only four of the 72 men with more than six problems on the PDS ever returned to controlled or "social" drinking, but 43 became abstinent for a year or more.

At last follow-up, 35 of the 110 men classified as alcohol abusers continued to abuse alcohol and exhibited the progressive course described by Jellinek [18]. These are termed "progressive alcoholics." Yet, as table 5-2 illustrates, blindly assessed childhood functioning did not differentiate these most chronic alcohol abusers from those who achieved the most favorable outcome—the securely abstinent. The childhood variables that were most important in predicting mental health [9] were IQ, maternal supervision, boyhood competence, and childhood environmental strengths and weaknesses. Yet these variables could not differentiate even the 20 progressive alcoholics who have exhibited the most social deterioration from the 21 securely abstinent men. In other words, childhood variables that are predictive of lifelong mental health did not seem to affect even the most extreme outcomes in alcohol addiction.

Table 5-2 also contains the three childhood variables that most clearly predict alcoholism: family history of alcoholism, premorbid antisocial behavior, and absence of southern European ethnicity. These variables, too, however, failed to predict remission.

Table 5-3 examines the reported treatment experiences encountered by the 49 Core City men who achieved at least a year of abstinence during that year. Specific clinical interventions seemed to be relatively unimportant. Only four of the abstinent men received psychotherapy, two disulfiram, and three help from a halfway house. A similar number of abstinent men had received these same treatments in the past without success. Indeed, only 15 of the 49 men who achieved a year of abstinence reported receiving any kind

Table 5-2. Comparison of Premorbid Values in Securely Abstinent and Progressive Alcoholics

Premorbid Variables	Social Drinker (N = 260)	Securely Abstinent (N = 21)	Progressive Alcoholic (N = 35)
Adequate maternal supervision (top third)	30%	38%	34%
Boyhood competence			
Top quartile	28	29	20
Bottom quartile	15	24	14
Few strengths in childhood	23	33	37
Many weaknesses in childhood (multiproblem family membership)	11	14	11
IQ < 90	28	29	29
Clear family history of alcoholism	32*	62	57
Southern European ethnicity	45*	10	17
Truancy or antisocial behavior in junior high school	2*	19	3

*These premorbid variables distinguished the 110 alcohol abusers from the 260 social drinkers ($p < .001$; χ^2 test). Using Student's t test, no significant differences between the abstinent alcoholics and the progressive alcoholics were detected for any of the variables in Table 5-3.

Table 5-3. Treatment Experiences Associated With Abstinence

"Treatment" Experience	Ever Abstinent (N = 49)	Securely Abstinent (N = 21)
Psychotherapy	8%	5%
Disulfiram (Antabuse)	4	5
Halfway house	6	0
Alcohol clinic/hospital	30	20
Alcoholics Anonymous	37	38

of professional assistance with their alcoholism during that year. Rather, in a community sample of alcoholics, self-help appeared more useful than clinical treatment. Eighteen men involved themselves in AA during the year they first became abstinent, and only three of the men who became abstinent had tried AA in the past and failed.

Forty-one percent of the abstinent men attributed their remission to "willpower," but table 5-4 illustrates that many nonspecific therapeutic factors appeared to underlie what the subjects, themselves, perceived as willpower. First, almost half of the men who achieved a year or more of abstinence found a substitute for alcohol; some found more than one. These substitute dependencies varied from candy binges (five men) to diazepam (Valium) and chlordiazepoxide (Librium) (five men); from marijuana (two men) to mystical belief, prayer, and meditation (five men); from compulsive work or hobbies (nine men) to compulsive gambling (two men); and from compulsive eating (three men) to chain smoking (seven men). In addition, the increased involvement of some of the men with religion and AA could be interpreted as a substitute dependency. Indeed, a little reflection discloses that AA, if regularly attended, provides all of the "nontreatment factors" described in table 5-4.

Second, although none of the Core City men received behavior modification as a result of deliberate clinical treatment, about half of the men experienced some kind of "naturalistic" behavior modification, by which we mean that their drinking behavior resulted in immediate negative consequences. For two men, the consequences were the result of disulfiram therapy. For 24 men, a disturbing medical complaint (e.g., ulcer, insomnia, hypertension, epilepsy) compelled them to be conscious of excess drinking. For some men, the behavior modification was through compulsory supervision by the courts or their employer.

A third factor that was associated with remission in more than half of the men was the discovery of a stable source of increased hope and self-esteem.

For six men, this was increased religious involvement, and for 18 men this was involvement in AA. Although such involvement—20 to more than 1,000 visits to AA, with a mean of 300 visits—by no means prove that AA causes abstinence, such a high proportion of men using AA suggests that, at least in Boston, AA may reach a greater fraction of the alcoholic population than do alcohol clinics.

The fourth factor associated with the first year of abstinence was the acquisition by 16 men of a new close relationship uncontaminated by the old injuries, resentments, and guilts that alcoholics inflict on those who care about them. For many, this relationship was a new wife or a special relationship with a nonprofessional helping person or mentor; for others, it was learning to help others who were as troubled as themselves; and for still others, this relationship appeared to result from internalizing a loved person who had recently died.

The 24 men in the Core City sample who used AA extensively (14 men made 75 visits or more, and the mean was 300 visits) were different from the 30 men who achieved a year or more of abstinence without AA. Alcoholic Anonymous tended to be a treatment of last resort. The men who used AA tended to be binge drinkers and far more symptomatic ($p < .01$) than those who became abstinent by other means. Alcoholic Irish-Americans did not enjoy a better prognosis than other ethnic groups, but they were more likely both to be very symptomatic and to achieve abstinence through AA. Of special interest was the observation that besides ethnicity, the absence of

Table 5-4. Nontreatment Factors Associated With Abstinence

Nontreatment Factors	Ever Abstinent (N = 49)	Securely Abstinent (N = 21)
Substitute dependency	53%	67%
Behavior modification		
Compulsory supervision or sustained confrontation	24	0
Medical consequences	49	48
Hope/self-esteem		
Increased religious involvement	12	19
Alcoholics Anonymous*	37	38
Social rehabilitation		
New love relationship	32	38

*A little reflection discloses that Alcoholics Anonymous, if meetings are frequently attended, may also be viewed as a substitute dependency, a behavior modification, *and* a source of social rehabilitation.

maternal neglect and the presence of a warm childhood were the most powerful premorbid predictors of AA utilization ($p < .05$). This was in spite of the fact that parental alcoholism was associated positively both with neglect during childhood and later use of AA ($p < .05$). As measured by the Wechsler Intelligence Scale for Children, high verbal intelligence was only weakly associated with AA attendance. In the present study, childhood emotional problems, social competence in childhood or adult life, social class, and number of sociopathic symptoms were not associated with AA attendance.

Tables 5-5 and 5-6 illustrate that abstinence from alcohol was closely correlated with social recovery. The first four variables in table 5-5 illustrate that the men who achieved secure abstinence had been nearly as symptomatic in terms of their alcohol abuse, psychopathology, and antisocial behavior as those men who are currently seriously abusing alcohol. At the time of the most recent follow-up, however, the 21 securely abstinent men seemed nearly as free from psychosocial pathology as those men for whom alcohol abuse had never been a problem.

Table 5-5. Comparison of Current Adult Adjustment in Securely Abstinent and Progressive Alcoholics

	Social Drinker (N = 240*)	Securely Abstinent (N = 21)	Progressive Alcoholic (N = 35)
≥ 7 symptoms (Cahalan scale)	0%	71%	74%
Ever alcohol dependent (*DSM-III*)	0	71	74
Psychiatric diagnosis for nonalcoholic-related problem (ever)	23	33	45
≥ 5 symptoms of sociopathy (ever)	0.4	24	32
Dead	3	5	14
Current social competence in top 40%	46	30	21
Currently enjoys his children	25	43	11
Enjoys a current marriage	55	52	9
Current annual earned income	$17,000	$15,000	$9,000†
Health Sickness Rating Scale score of < 70	24	29	72

*This number varied slightly since completeness of data sets varied slightly for each subject.

†Current income was known for only 28 of the 35 progressive alcoholics, but since the less well-studied men tended to be having even more trouble with their lives, the progressive alcoholics' average income may well be even lower.

Table 5-6. Relative Mental Health of Alcoholics Achieving Abstinence

Health Sickness Rating Scale and Gerard and Colleagues [17] Terminology*	Gerard and Colleagues [17] Abstinent Alcoholics (N = 50)	Core City Sample			
		Social Drinker (N = 227†)	Securely Abstinent (> 3 yr) (N = 20)	Currently Abstinent (< 3 yr) (N = 12†)	Progressive Alcoholic (N = 29†)
0–60 (overtly disturbed)	54%	8%	0%	25%	38%
61–70 (inconspicuous inadequacy)	24	16	30	33	34
71–80 (Alcoholics Anonymous)	12	29	40	25	28
81–100 (independent success)	10	47	30	17	0

*Correlating Luborsky's [11] terminology with that of Gerard and colleagues [17] is admittedly arbitrary.

† Thirteen of the social drinkers, six of the progressive alcoholics, and three of the abstinent alcoholics were less than completely interviewed, and thus Health Sickness Rating Scale ratings could not be confidently ascertained.

Table 5-6 contrasts our assessment of abstinent alcoholics from a community sample with that by Gerard et al. [17] of a public clinic sample. The distribution of mental health ratings (HSRS scores) for the recently abstinent men resembled that for the progressive alcoholics, and the distribution of HSRS scores for the securely abstinent, who had been abstinent for an average of ten years, resembled that of the social drinkers. Childhood variables known to predict adult HSRS scores did not distinguish any of the four groups in Table 5-6. The implications of this table are twofold. Gerard and colleagues' clinic alcoholics exhibited more psychopathology than our community sample, thereby exaggerating the psychopathology of their abstinent alcoholics. Nevertheless, Core City men who are abstinent for only one to three years appear to experience considerable psychiatric disability.

Comment

Like the definition of alcoholism, the definition of abstinence is relative. Since alcoholism, like hypertension, represents a continuum [16], not a yes-no phenomenon, and since remissions and relapses are common, the characteristics of abstinence must be carefully defined—especially in a longitudinal study. Always, it must be kept in mind that the classification of a subject as abstinent is a labeling process carried out by an observer; it is a clinical judgment in which the available evidence, often incomplete and occasionally conflicting, is used to place each subject in a defined category.

Many recent studies [5,19,20] have demonstrated that achieving one or even six months of abstinence is predictive of very little in the way of stable abstinence. In our study, relapse after even a year of stable abstinence was not at all uncommon. Nevertheless, the recovery process in alcoholism is ongoing. Over the short term, alcohol dependence often resembles a remitting but progressive illness like multiple sclerosis; over the long term, among those who survive alcoholism often resembles a self-limiting illness. Thus, the proportion of Core City men that over time could be placed in the abstinent and return to social drinking categories in fig. 5-1 are impressive.

Although much of our information came retrospectively from the subjects, the mean length of stable abstinence and for return to asymptomatic drinking was ten years. Their socioeconomic adjustment and our search of public records confirmed the men's accounts. Paradoxically, alcoholics who were most severely afflicted often achieved the most stable recoveries. For example, among the Core City men, there were 25 alcohol abusers who manifested five or more symptoms on the Robins' sociopathy scale [13]. Of these men, 48 percent are currently abstinent. In contrast, there were 40 alcohol abusers with no antisocial symptoms except their drinking, and only 28 percent are currently abstinent.

The prognostic findings of Fig. 5-1 are consistent with those of the authors of the "Rand report" [19,20] resumption of asymptomatic drinking is not at all uncommon among former alcohol abusers. However, severity of symptoms appeared to be the limiting factor. Figure 5-2 makes it clear that, for our sample, return to asymptomatic drinking appeared possible only for those who have been a "little bit" alcoholic—five or fewer symptoms on the PDS. In contrast, only alcohol abusers with six or more symptoms ever came to clinical attention [16].

The finding that premorbid childhood factors were not predictive of long-term outcome in alcoholism is consistent with the failure of studies that have employed a prospective design [14,21–23] to confirm psychodynamically based theories of the causation of alcoholism. In contrast, the prognosis of psychiatric conditions such as juvenile delinquency [7], schizophrenia [24], and reactive depression [25] are powerfully affected by good premorbid social and psychological adjustment. In reviews of the short-term response to treatment of alcoholism, factors associated with social stability [3,26] especially occupational and marital stability, account for most of the explained variance in response to treatment [1,2]. These social variables, however, may be more useful in determining how compliant an individual is to a middle-class, medical-model intervention over the short term than they are in determining the lifetime course of alcoholism [27].

In conformity with table 5-3, a recent international symposium [4] on the efficacy of treatment in alcoholism suggested that conventional clinical treatment may do relatively little to alter the natural history of alcoholism. In understanding why this should be so, it is well to remember that alcoholism is not only an illness, it is also a habit. Deciding on the factors relevant to recovery from any intractable habit is at best an uncertain process, and recovery from alcoholism is no exception.

One approach to understanding "spontaneous" remission is to ask ex-alcoholics what they thought made the difference. Using this approach, the answer is often "willpower" and "hitting bottom." Such explanations may reflect the failure of both interviewer and subject to identify important contingencies associated with changes in habit.

A second approach, the one employed in this study, was to disregard what the patient initially said and to study temporally related contingencies. For justification, this approach depends on the theory that addiction is largely maintained by conditioning and by "chains" of reinforcers of which the patient is not conscious; recovery, too, will depend on factors of which the habituated individual may not be aware. Among the Core City alcoholics, a key to recovery seemed to be their recognition that they were no longer consciously in charge of their drinking and that their use of alcohol was no longer under voluntary control. This self-discovery appeared to be a highly personal process, but one mediated by forces that can be understood by social scientists and harnessed by health professionals. Indeed, 17 of the 21 securely abstinent men had manifested at least two of the four factors in table 5-4 during their recovery. The remaining four men who had achieved stable abstinence by what appeared—at least in retrospect—to be willpower had been far less symptomatic in their alcohol abuse. Thus, once identified, all of the four factors in table 5-4—"behavior modification," substitute dependencies, increased religious involvement, and new relationships—make sense. Although we cannot prove that these variables had not often occurred before the subjects' lives and had gone unnoticed, the four factors are embodied in many other particularly successful alcohol treatment programs [28] and are also relevant in recovery from heroin addiction [29].

In understanding table 5-4, it is important to appreciate that a major source of help in changing involuntary habits may come from increased religious involvement. Only recently have investigators like Frank [30], Bean [31], and Mack [32] begun to elucidate the nature of this process. Alcoholics and victims of other incurable habits feel defeated, bad, and helpless; invariably they suffer from impaired morale. For recovery, powerful new sources of self-esteem and hope must be discovered. Equally important is the fact that religious involvement facilitates deployment of the defense of reaction formation, wherein an individual abruptly rejects and hates what he once cherished and loved, or vice versa. Reaction formations are essential to abstinence, and they are often stabilized by surrendering commitments to one set of desires up to a "higher power" that dictates the exact opposite.

At the present time in the United States, AA reaches an estimated 650,000 individuals, as many or more as are reached by medical clinics and practitioners combined [3,33]. Besides embodying the four therapeutic factors in table 5-4 and facilitating reaction formation, AA also transforms two other defenses of the alcoholic. First, the alcoholic's tendency to project his problems onto the outside world is transformed into a credo of assuming responsibility for all of his problems. Second, the denial of the alcoholic is transformed into public, almost exhibitionistic insistence on "I am an alcoholic."

Alcoholics Anonymous is not better than clinical intervention; rather, it is different. An individual's relationship to a community-based self-help organization is intrinsically different from his relationship to a clinic in the medical model. He belongs to the first; he only visits the latter. One visit to an alcohol clinic is undoubtedly more effective than a single visit to AA, but AA involvement, if it develops, is usually measured in hundreds of visits spread over years.

In the absence of careful follow-up studies, the insistence of both AA and the National Council on Alcoholism on abstinence as the only treatment of alcoholism has led thoughtful scientists to call the concept of abstinence into question [34]. Pattison [35] and Gerard et al. [17] have suggested that alcohol abuse may actually reflect a means of buffering psychiatric symptoms. However, if Gerard et al. [17] found an enormous amount of psychopathology in their follow-up of 50 abstinent clinic patients, they found still more psychopathology in the individuals in their study who continued drinking. The many laboratory studies reviewed by Mello and Mendelson [36] uniformly concur that, unlike opiates, heavy ingestion of alcohol enhances anxiety, depression, and low self-esteem. In other words, alcohol is a poor tranquilizer or buffer to psychopathology.

Van Dijk and Van Dijk-Koffeman [37] studied the physical health, "mental condition," housing, social adjustment, and family, work, and financial situation of 50 patients who became abstinent or returned to social drinking. Over a two-year period, they compared these 50 patients with 80 patients from the same treatment cohort who continued to engage in frequent alcohol abuse. Sixty percent of those who continued to abuse alcohol, but none of the abstinent, actually became worse on the six adjustment variables that Van Dijk and Van Dijk-Koffeman studied; 70 percent of the abstinent improved, as contrasted to 5 percent of the continued alcohol abusers.

The field of alcoholism has been plagued by oversimplification, and abstinence per se must certainly represent an oversimplified treatment goal. As table 5-6 illustrates, release from stable bondage, however painful, rarely brings instant relief. As in returning prisoners of war [38,39], depression and divorce are common in the early stages of abstinence; cognitive function and occupational stability are poor. Perhaps, as table 5-5 and 5-6 suggest, it is not that abstinence is good, but that abuse of alcohol is painful. Abstinence must remain a means, not an end. It is justified as a treatment goal only if moderate drinking is not a viable alternative and only if the real goal, social rehabilitation, is kept in view.

This article has addressed four discrepancies that may exist between the actual natural history of alcoholism and clinician's preconceptions about that natural history. Clinicians' preconceptions may be biased by studying only alcoholics who come to clinics, by studying them retrospectively, and by studying them for too short a time.

First, the syndrome of alcoholism may have a relatively good prognosis, but clinicians do not usually meet recovered alcoholics in their clinics and emergency rooms. Second, return to asymptomatic drinking is a common outcome for many alcohol abusers, but these are rarely the very symptomatic alcohol abusers who seek help in clinics; nor are they, once recovered, those who speak out on public issues in alcohol education. Third, prospective study suggests that alcoholics become anxious and depressed because they have lost control of their use of alcohol more often than the anxious and depressed become alcoholic [14,23]. Thus, abstinence alone may often be enough to lead to substantial improvement in psychopathology. Fourth, the relative ineffectiveness of clinic treatment in producing abstinence does not mean that clinicians should despair. Rather, in alcoholism, the success of natural healing processes should encourage us to pay the same kind of attention to these forces that William Withering paid to *Digitalis purpurea*.

References

1. Costello, R. M. Alcoholism treatment and evaluation: In search of methods. *Int. J. Addict.* 10:251, 1975.
2. Costello, R. M. Alcoholism treatment effectiveness: slicing the outcome

variance pie, in Edwards G., Grant M. (eds), *Alcoholism Treatment in Transition*. London: Croom Helm Ltd, 1980.

3. Baekland, F., Lundwall, L., and Kissin, B. Methods for the treatment of chronic alcoholism: a critical appraisal. In Gibbins, R. J., Israel, Y., Kalant, H. et al. (eds), *Research Advances in Alcohol and Drug Problems*. New York: Wiley, 1975, vol. 2.

4. Edwards, G., Grant, M. (eds), *Alcoholism Treatment in Transition*. London: Croom Helm Ltd, 1980.

5. Orford J., Edwards, G. *Alcoholism*. Oxford: Oxford University Press, 1977.

6. Glueck, S. and Glueck E. *Unraveling Juvenile Delinquency*. New York: The Commonwealth Fund, 1950.

7. Glueck, S. and Glueck E. *Delinquents and Nondelinquents in Perspective*. Cambridge, Mass.: Harvard University Press, 1968.

8. Vaillant G. E. and Milosky, E. S. Natural history of male psychological health: IX. Empirical evidence for Erikson's model of the life cycle. *Am. J. Psychiatry*, 137:1348, 1980.

9. Vaillant G. E., Vaillant C. O. Natural history of male psychological health: X. Work as a predictor of positive mental health. *Am. J. Psychiatry,* 138:1433, 1981.

10. Vaillant G. E. The natural history of male psychological health: II. Some antecedents of healthy adult adjustment. *Arch. Gen. Psychiatry*, 31:15, 1971.

11. Luborsky, L. Clinicians' judgment of mental health. *Arch. Gen. Psychiatry*, 7:407, 1962.

12. Luborsky, L., Bachrach H. Factors influencing clinicians' judgments of mental health. *Arch. Gen. Psychiatry*, 31:292, 1974.

13. Robins, L. N. *Deviant Children Grown Up: A Sociological and Psychiatric Study of Sociopathic Personality*. Baltimore, Williams & Wilkins Co, 1966.

14. Vaillant G. E. Natural history of male psychological health: VIII. Antecedents of alcoholism and 'orality.' *Am. J. Psychiatry*, 137:181, 1980.

15. Cahalan D. *Problem Drinkers:* A National Survey. San Francisco: Jossey-Bass, 1970.

16. Vaillant G. E., Gale, L., Milofsky, E. S. Natural history of male alcoholism: II. Is alcoholism a bad habit, disease or a continuum? *J. Stud. Alcohol.,* in press.

17. Gerard, D. L., Saenger, G., Wile, R. The abstinent alcoholic. *Arch. Gen. Psychiatry*, 6:83, 1962.

18. Jellinek, E. M. *The Disease Concept of Alcoholism*. New Haven, Conn.: Hillhouse Press, 1960.

19. Polich, J. M., Armor, D. J., Braiker, H. B. *The Course of Alcoholism*. New York, Wiley, 1981.

20. Armor D. J., Polich, J. M., Stanbul, H. B. *Alcoholism and Treatment*. New York: Wiley, 1978.

21. McCord W. and McCord J. *Origins of Alcoholism*. Palo Alto, Calif.: Stanford University Press, 1960.

22. Kammeier, M. L., Hoffmann, H., Loper, R. G. Personality characteristics of alcoholics as college freshmen and at time of treatment. *Q. J. Stud. Alcohol.*, 34:390, 1973.
23. Vaillant, G. E. Milofsky, E. S. Natural history of male alcoholism: III. Etiology *Am. . Psychol.* in press.
24. Vaillant, G. E. Prospective prediction of schizophrenic remission. *Arch. Gen. Psychiatry*, 11:509, 1964.
25. Brown, G. W., Harris, T. *Social Origins of Depression.* London: Tavistock Publications Ltd, 1978.
26. Gibbs, I. Flanagan, J. Prognostic indicators of alcoholism treatment outcome. *Int. J. Addict.* 12:1097, 1977.
27. Bromet, E., Moos, R., Bliss, F. et al. Post-treatment functioning of alcoholic patients: Its relation to program participation. *J. Consult. Clin. Psychol.*, 45:829, 1977.
28. Vaillant, G. E. The doctor's dilemma, in Edwards, G. Grant, M. (eds): *Alcoholism Treatment in Transition.* London: Croom Helm Ltd, 1980.
29. Vaillant, G. E. A 12-year follow-up of New York addicts: IV. Some determinants and characteristics of abstinence. *Am. J. Psychiatry.* 123:573, 1968.
30. Frank, J. D. *Persuasion and Healing: A Comparative Study of Psychotherapy.* Baltimore: Johns Hopkins University Press, 1961.
31. Bean, M. Alcoholics Anonymous. *Psychiatr. Ann.*, 5:5 1975.
32. Mack J. Alcoholism, A. A., and the governance of the self, in Bean, M. H. and Zinberg, N. E. (eds): *Dynamic Approaches to the Understanding and Treatment of Alcoholism.* New York, Glencoe, Ill.: Free Press, 1981.
33. Hingson, R., Scotch, N., Day, N. et al. Recognizing and seeking help for drinking problems. *J. Stud. Alcohol.* 41:1102, 1980.
34. Blane, H. T. Half a bottle is better than none. *Contemp. Psychol.* 23:396, 1978.
35. Pattison, E. M. A critique of abstinence criteria in the treatment of alcoholics. *Int. J. Soc. Psychiatry*, 1968.
36. Mello, N. K. Mendelson, J. H. Alcohol and human behavior, in Iversen, L. L. Iversen, S. D. Snyder, S. H. (eds): *Handbook of Psychopharmacology: XII. Drugs of Abuse.* New York: Plenum Press, 1978.
37. Van Dijk, W. K. and Van Dijk-Koffeman, A. A follow-up study of 211 treated male alcoholic addicts. *Br. J. Addict.* 68:3, 1973.
38. Hall, R. C. W., Malone, P. T. Psychiatric effects of prolonged Asian captivity: A two-year follow-up. *Am. J. Psychiatry*, 133:786, 1973.
39. Sledge, W. H., Boydstun, J. A., Rabe, A. J. Self-concept changes related to war captivity. *Arch. Gen. Psychiatry*, 37:430, 1980.

6 CAUSAL MODELS OF PERSONALITY, PEER CULTURE CHARACTERISTICS, DRUG USE, AND CRIMINAL BEHAVIORS OVER A FIVE-YEAR SPAN

George J. Huba and Peter M. Bentler

Since before the advent of the scientific study of drug use, there has been continuing social interest in determing how patterns of drug use may affect "deviant" or possibly criminal behaviors [see 3, for an illuminating historical perspective spanning millenia]. In this chapter we use latent variable causal models to explore the relationships between such constructs while recognizing that since we only have measures of self-reported deviance collected in the final year of our study, our results about the pattern of causality must be interpreted with caution.

As a construct, deviance is one of the more difficult to define unambiguously within the scientific literature [16]. Psychologists and sociologists have discussed this concept in a variety of different ways. Other social scientists have eschewed the concept of "deviance" entirely while using

This research was partially supported by Grant No. DA-01070 from the National Institute on Drug Abuse. The authors wish to thank Suong Luong and Norma Chapman for production assistance. Portions of this work are reprinted from Huba and Bentler [6] with the permission of the publisher.

73

alternate constructs such as "disruptive behavior patterns," "criminal acts," or "problem behaviors" [10]. Throughout our work, we have taken a pragmatic approach and clustered a set of actions together under the label of "deviance" merely because it is traditional to do so. Our use of the term is one of convenience; our analyses treat these actions as *behaviors*. Our study has focused upon the set of 16 mildly and seriously criminal and disruptive activities selected by Johnston, O'Malley, and Eveland [11] in their important work on the relationship of drug use and deviance. In our earlier work [6] we studied this set of 16 single-item indicators of the times an individual had performed each behavior. The behaviors examined ranged from such mildly disruptive ones as fighting or arguing with one's parents to carrying a deadly weapon, engaging in gang fights, or undertaking vandalism. We determined that the varied set of indicators could be conceived of as manifestations of four latent tendencies toward criminal action. The first factor was one of Confrontations, the second was Theft, the third was Property Crimes, and the fourth was Automobile Theft. The four latent variables were intercorrelated at moderately high levels, and we concluded that at the next higher order of abstraction, there was a single factor of generalized deviance.

In this chapter we use the previous results on the appropriate measurement model for the domain to study how drug use latent variables predict deviance four years later. We also examined how the deviance indicators relate to two stable individual difference characteristics of nonabidance with the law and positive self regard as well as to general involvement with the peer culture and the perception during junior high school that many of one's friends engage in acts of minor "deviance" within an achievement-oriented school culture. Thus, we will be considering the effects of drug-taking upon latent proclivities toward deviance within the context of other psychosocial factors which may also serve to explain drug-taking and deviance. While we study latent proclivities toward classes of actions, we have not systematically contrasted theories that these latent variables are primarily caused by personality tendencies (primary deviance models) with secondary deviance models arguing that society stigmatizes certain behaviors and fosters patterns of cooccurrence.

Causal Models for Theory Testing

Different patterns of interrelationships among major constructs in the personality, intimate support, drug use, and deviance domains are studied in this chapter through the use of latent variable causal models. Since this chapter and much of our other published work on drug-taking and psychosocial behaviors [see 5,6,8] uses the nonstandard statistical technique of latent variable causal modeling, it seems desirable to introduce the conceptual logic of the modeling procedures we employ. Technical issues are reviewed by Bentler [1]. As a method of theory testing with correlational data, causal modeling represents a set of statistical techniques for investigating sample data in light of hypothesized population models about the influence of certain variables upon others. In general, a model represents a simultaneous series of statements about the regressions of particular variables on various other ("causal," explanatory) variables. The most popular form of causal modeling, path analysis, is thus a sophisticated type of simultaneous multiple correlation or regression analysis, whereas recent developments in causal modeling embed factor analysis into a path-analytic type of framework. In such a framework, the regressions are at the level of the unmeasured latent variables or factors, and the factors themselves are interrelated by factor-analytic assumptions to the observed, manifest variables. Whenever possible, it is desirable to make such regressions at the level of latent variables where measurement error is explicitly estimated so that it cannot bias estimates of the size and sign of causal influences. The goals of causal modeling include both the testing of a proposed model against data and the development of models that adequately account for the data in hand. In this chapter we will address both of these goals by asking whether certain causal linkages hypothesized by different individuals are indeed necessary for our longitudinal data, and then asking how much of the variation in our dependent measures is accounted for by the proposed theoretical scheme. An additional feature is that when certain conditions of "nesting" are satisfied, it is possible to compare and contrast alternate theoretical models proposed to account for the same relationships. We will make use of this feature to contrast certain theoretical models that do not contain certain theoretical paths with some formulations that do contain these same paths.

Although causal models should be evaluated by a variety of criteria including meaningfulness, they can be tested statistically using well-known principles for adequacy in explaining the observed data. A statistical assessment of the goodness-of-fit of a model is afforded by a large-sample chi-square test: The hypothesis that the sample variances and covariances are drawn from a population having the hypothesized causal structure is evaluated against the alternate null hypothesis that the variables are simply correlated. If the chi-square value is large relative to degrees of freedom, the proposed causal structure must be rejected because the observed sample data would be extremely unlikely to be obtained if the hypothesized model were true in the population. Although the chi-square statistic provides a formal statistical means of assessing the goodness of fit for models when the assumptions are met, in very large samples of observations, trivial departures of the observed data from the hypothesized model can lead to the statistical rejection of the formulation. Therefore we supplement our decision-making procedures with the normed and nonnormed fit indices developed by Bentler and Bonett [2]. The normed fit coefficient ranges from zero (indicating poor model fit) to unity (indicating perfect model fit) but is not corrected for the size of the model, while the nonnormed coefficient is corrected for the size of the model and assumes similar values to the normed coefficient but can be slightly smaller than zero and slightly larger than unity. Of course, there are always alternate ways to parameterize certain portions of complex mathematical models, but many of these variants are trivial in their differences from one another.

It is important to recognize that this chapter makes certain scientific assumptions about the constructs assessed and then uses appropriate statistical methods for the assumptions. The most important assumption that is made is that we are interested in relating error-free constructs from our different systems to one another rather than interrelating error-prone indicators. Consequently we use methods that explicitly make use of multiple indicators of deviance, peer culture characteristics, and personality dimensions. We study how the construct variance common to several alternate, fallible measured indicators of a construct points toward models of how different constructs are interrelated to one another. Thus the models of this chapter try explicitly to eliminate potentially contaminating sources of error variance which might serve to bias the types and amounts of relationship between constructs that are inferred.

Introduction to the UCLA Study of Adolescent Growth

The UCLA Study of Adolescent Growth, from which the data for this chapter are derived, is a five-year, cohort-sequential study that has thus far collected four waves of data at annual or biannual intervals. Three grade (7th, 8th, 9th) cohorts were used and, beginning in 1976, data were collected in Project Years I, II, IV, and V. A comprehensive treatment of the many different facets of the UCLA Study is given by Huba and Bentler [6].

In the initial wave of data collection, self-reports were collected from the 1,634 young adolescents on aspects of their personality, perceptions of the peer culture, drug use patterns, intentions to use drugs in the future, and general school adjustment. Similar information was collected at the follow-ups. In the last wave we also obtained information about the patterns of "deviant" or criminal behavior engaged in by the adolescents.

For the present analyses we have used data collected from the two youngest grade cohorts in the first and fifth years of the study. The oldest cohort was not utilized since they had graduated from school by the time of the final assessment wave, and thus their behaviors may be qualitatively different in certain of the domains. In the first year the individuals were in either the seventh or eighth grades while in the final year they were in the eleventh or twelfth grades. Of these 688 individuals, 229 (33.6%) were male and 459 (66.4%) were female while 372 (54.1%) were in the youngest cohort and 316 (45.9%) were in the middle cohort. These individuals did not appear to be initially different from the total sample [see 6, chap. 6 and 7].

Selection of Indicators for the Causal Models

Ideally, the appropriate quasi-experimental design for unambiguously showing that drug use and patterns of deviance are not correlated, or that patterns of youthful drug use do not increase the levels of performing deviant behaviors, would be one in which there were "pretest" or "initial" measures of deviance as well as measures at the final time, or "outcome" variables. Such designs examining changes from an initial time to a final time are the strongest ones for imputing causality, since the results are somewhat ambiguous if we show strong effects without such controls when alternate explanations based on differences in initial levels of deviant behavior might be invoked. Such an argument was used by Johnston et al. [11] in their analysis of the relationship of drug use and deviance. On the other hand, if we make partial, but not perfect, controls for differences in predisposing deviance tendencies, it can be argued that a lack of effect is a relatively good argument that there is not a *strong* influence of drug use on deviance, unless such an effect is a "suppressor" or paradoxical one running counter to our expectations.

Given that our five-year longitudinal study assessed deviance only in Year V, it seems desirable to use a premeasure of a relatively enduring tendency toward performing deviant behaviors. As such a dispositional measure we chose the latent construct of nonabidance with the law (rebelliousness or little Law Abidance) which our earlier work [5–6, chap. 11] has shown to be strongly predictive of drug-use behaviors. Low Law Abidance tendencies are presumably also related to the performance of criminal behaviors when the opportunity arises for such expression. The construct is a broad one that encompasses facets of disregard for authority, nontraditional political beliefs, and a lack of allegiance to traditional religious and moral standards. Of the many different constructs available to us, it seemed that the single most appropriate initial control variable was this latent construct. Law Abidance was assessed by three separate four-item indicators in our study: scales of Law Abidance, (non) Liberalism, and Religious Commitment were used. Internal consistency reliability coefficients (α) in our full sample of 1,634 adolescents were .58, .26, and .77 for the three scales respectively [6, chap. 6].

Another latent variable from the personality system that was selected for analysis here consists of the factor of Positive Self Concept. While Huba and Bentler [6, chaps. 11, 40] have found that this factor does *not* strongly predict changes in drug use over time, it does specifically seem to influence changes in patterns of Hard Drug Use. We also felt that there have been sufficient indications in the theoretical literature that this factor may be an important precursor of multiple modes of deviance [see, for instance, 14]. In our first-year battery, we assessed three indicators of this factor: a four-item scale of Self-Acceptance; a four-item scale of Attractiveness; a six-item scale of Clothes-consciousness. The internal consistency (α) coefficients for the three scales were .75, .71, and .63 in the full sample (N = 1634). Note, by the way, that the Clothes-consciousness scale for this age group seems to indicate carefulness in one's self-presentation mode while the remaining scales measure positive self-regard about one's lifestyle and social attractiveness.

In our studies of adolescents [5–7] we identified about a dozen factors as parts of a generalized domain of social support systems. In the theoretical model, this set of influences has been collectively referred to as the Intimate Support System [5–7]. For the present purposes, we selected two factors for intensive study in relationship to drug use and deviance. The first dimension is Peer Culture Involvement as measured by items of how often the respondent drives around with friends, listens to records with friends, and goes to parties with friends. These items mark this factor in several different waves of the study data [see 6, chaps. 12, 15, 24 for extensive factor-analytic evidence] and Kandel's [13] theory places great importance upon this factor. A second dimension selected for intensive study was one of Friends Poor School Performance. This factor is hypothesized to be one of having friends who perform acts that are at least somewhat deviant for seventh and eighth grade students in a school environment. Three items used as indicators of the factor are: the number of friends perceived to cut class, to cheat on exams, and who potentially will quit school. In our study we find that this primary factor is an indicator of a second-order factor of peer culture deviance [6, chap. 24].

In Year V, we asked the respondents how often they had committed each of 16 acts ranging from minor fights to major acts of vandalism during the previous six months. Confirmatory factor analyses revealed four major latent variables of Confrontations, Theft, Property Crimes, and Automobile Theft. Since the item distributions were strongly skewed, we formed scores for three of these factors by summating the number of times an event of that type occurred. For the scale of Confrontations, we summated the number of times the individual got into serious fights, got into gang fights, caused a serious injury, and carried a knife: coefficient α for this scale was .61. For the scale of Theft we summed items for the number of times the individual had stolen something worth less than $50, stolen something worth more than $50, or shoplifted: coefficient α for the scale is .67. For the scale of Property Crimes we summed items of how often the individual trespassed, committed vandalism at school, committed vandalism at work, and committed arson: coefficient α for this scale was .41. In the current analyses we consider a general factor of Deviance presumed to cause all three of these scales.

In the first year of the study we assessed cumulative frequency of using 13 substances on a five-point anchored rating scale. Nine available indicators— cigarettes, beer, wine, liquor, marijuana, hashish, amphetamines, tran- quilizers, hallucinogenics—were chosen on the basis of confirmatory factor analyses [7]. In the fifth year of the study we also measured frequency-of-use in the last six months for 26 substances and for these analyses selected nine items parallel to those of the first year including cigarettes, beer, wine, liquor, marijuana, hashish, amphetamines, minor tranquilizers, and LSD. Addi- tionally in the fifth year we also assessed cigarettes smoked per day, drinks of alcohol typically consumed, and marijuana "joints" usually smoked: we refer to these latter three indicators as "quantity" indices.

For drug use, six latent variables were hypothesized on the basis of the confirmatory factor analyses of Huba, Wingard, and Bentler [7]. The first factor was first-year Alcohol Use and had loadings for the first-year variables of beer, wine, liquor, and cigarettes. The second first-year factor was Cannabis Use and had loadings for marijuana, hashish, and cigarettes. The third first-year factor was Hard Drug Use and had loadings for ampheta- mines, tranquilizers, and hallucinogenics, and secondarily for liquor, and hashish. Note that the first-year drug use factors are not independent cluster ones: individual manifest drug indicators sometimes load on more than one latent variable. On the other hand, we expect the largest and major loadings to be for those drugs usually associated with the name assigned.

We also hypothesized three major factors or latent variables for fifth year drug use corresponding to those of the first year. Since we had available measures of the quantity of various substances used, it was possible to restrict our attention to the latent variables common to both quantity and frequency. The fifth-year factors were accordingly parameterized in the manner parallel to that used for the first-year factors with the exception that the quantity measures were hypothesized to load on the appropriate dimensions. Accordingly, there were hypothesized loadings on the fifth-year Alcohol Use factor for the frequency of using beer, wine, liquor, and cigarettes as well as alcohol quantity and cigarette quantity. The fifth-year Cannabis Use factor was hypothesized to have loadings for the frequency of using marijuana, hashish, and cigarettes as well as the number of marijuana and tobacco cigarettes typically smoked. The fifth-year Hard Drug Use factor was hypothesized to have loadings for the frequency of using amphetamines, minor tranquilizers, LSD, and secondarily liquor and hashish. A major feature of the measurement model was that we hypothesized that all repeatedly measured indicators would have correlated residual terms.

In the initial model, the hypothesized structural regression coefficients among the drug use factors were as follows. First-year Cannabis Use was influenced by first-year Alcohol Use. First-year Drug Use was hypothesized to be influenced by first-year Cannabis Use and Alcohol Use. Fifth-year Alcohol Use was considered to be a function of first-year Alcohol Use. Fifth-year Cannabis Use was a function of first-year Alcohol Use, first-year Cannabis Use, and fifth-year Alcohol Use. Fifth-year Hard Drug Use was hypothesized to be a function of first-year Hard Drug Use, first-year Cannabis Use, first-year Alcohol Use, fifth-year Cannabis Use and fifth-year Alcohol Use. This initial set of structural regression parameters is what would be expected in an "escalating" simplex pattern of involvement [12]. That is, if we hypothesize that drug use initiation goes through progressive stages of Alcohol Use to Cannabis Use, and then to Hard Drug Use, we would believe that there would be a "step-forward" pattern among the latent variables. On the other hand, if we do not believe that such a hierarchical progression exists, the present model will not be a reasonable one for the data. Huba and Bentler [6, chap. 26], using latent variable causal modeling methods, established that only the paths described above are necessary to explain these data. (Huba and Bentler [6, chaps. 10, 48] also replicated this latter conclusion using alternate log-linear models which do not make such strong distributional assumptions.) The major question addressed here is how the current psychosocial predictor latent variables describe and modify the patterns of causation among the latent variables of drug use.

In the initial model we also hypothesized a direct path from each first-year psychosocial latent variable to each drug factor. Furthermore, we hypothesized that there would be paths from each first-year psychosocial latent variable to General Deviance. Finally, we predicted a path from each first-year drug use factor to the fifth-year General Deviance factor. Time was used to order the effects from first-year drug use to the fifth-year general Deviance latent variable. However, since we do not believe that it is now possible to posit unambiguously a unidirectional causal flow from drug use to Deviance or vice versa, we did not allow one-way causation among the fifth-year factors of drug use and the fifth-year Deviance factor assessed contemporaneously: we specified that there would be a correlation of the residuals (or the parts of the variation in the latent variables not attributable to the first-year factors).

A final characteristic of the initial model is that we permitted 35 correlated uniqueness terms (minor parameters) among the 21 drug-use variables based upon the previous work using these data by Huba and Bentler [6, chap. 26]. We did not permit any correlated uniquenesses initially between psychosocial and deviance variables or between drug use and these two domains.

In an attempt to maintain simplicity in our presentation, we show the initial causal model for the data in summary form in figures 6-1 and 6-2. Figure 6-1 shows the measurement structure for the model without the paths hypothesized to interconnect the constructs. Not shown in this figure are correlated uniqueness terms. In figure 6-2 we show the latent constructs and the paths hypothesized to exist among these factors. In the figures we employ the now-standard pictorial conventions that large circles are latent variables and rectangles represent manifest or measured variables. Single-headed arrows represent presumed causal paths while double-head arrows represent patterns of covariation. In figure 6-1, small circles have been used to represent measurement errors (in causal modeling we usually estimate the variances of these sources) while in figure 6-2, small circles have been used to represent prediction errors (of which we again estimate the variance). That is, in figures 1 and 2 small circles represent "prediction" errors: in figure 6-1 the measurement error is that part of the observed variable not "predicted" by the factors while in figure 6-2 the prediction error is that part of the construct not "caused" by the other factors.

Results

The statistical chi-square goodness-of-fit index for the initial model was 823.18 with 499 degrees of freedom. This chi-square was sufficiently large

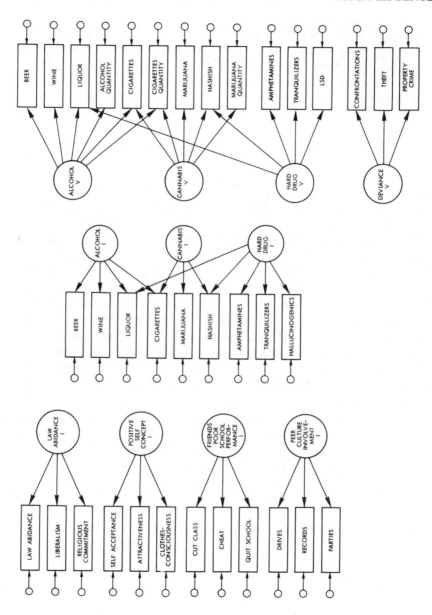

Figure 6-1. Initial Causal Model

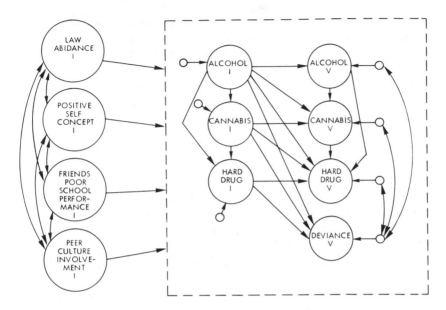

Figure 6-2. Latent Constructs and Hypothesized Paths Between Factors

An arrow to the dashed area denotes a hypothesized causal paths to all latent variables inside the dashes.

that we had to conclude that the model was not fully adequate, as initially parameterized, to describe fully all of the observed interrelationships. On the other hand, the values for the normed (.910) and nonnormed (.938) fit coefficients were large and it seemed to us that the models were good ones for explaining the data, with minor modifications permitting the representation to fit the data adequately.

Modifications were made by including correlated errors of measurement terms. That is, we permitted correlations between selected pairs of the "unique" or "error variance" parts of the manifest indicators. Including such minor parameters is a now-standard way of fitting initial theoretical models more closely to empirical data (see 6, chap. 9, for a discussion of this strategy and its utility). After including 46 additional *minor* parameters, the modified model adequately fits the data: chi-square was 503.92 with 453 degrees of freedom ($p = .05$) and the normed fit index was .945 while the non-normed fit index was .992. The second representation fits the data significantly better than the first ($x^2 = 319.26$, d.f. $= 46$, $p < .001$).

In this summary chapter we do not present all parameter estimates obtained under the final model as modified from that pictured in figures 6-1 and 6-2. Specifically, since the factor loadings, error variances, and error covariances assumed values consistent with that hypothesized, we do not show those parameter estimates: a complete set of all parameter estimates is given by Huba and Bentler [6, chap. 40].

For the purposes of determining how the latent constructs "cause" one another, the most important parameters in the model are those which are shown in figure 6-2, as "path" or structural regression coefficients among latent variables. Table 6-1 summarizes the values of the path coefficients under both the initial and final models (we present both sets of coefficients so that the reader can ascertain that fitting the model to the data does not change the overall pattern of coefficients inferred to be significant). In table 6-1, we show the unstandardized coefficients (B), standardized coefficients (β), and finally critical ratios (z) for the unstandardized coefficients which are z-scores for testing the significance of the regression weights.

As shown in table 6-1, virtually the same conclusions are drawn about the pattern of causation from the initial and final formulations of the model. To quantify the similarity under the two formulations we calculated three kinds of correlation coefficients for the two sets of unstandardized weights, standardized weights, and critical ratios. The 43 different coefficients were treated as observations and while the resulting correlations cannot be tested for significance, their size provides a quantitative description of the overall pattern of similarity. For the sets of unstandardized weights the product-moment correlation is .994, Mosteller-Tukey's [15] biweighted symmetric-robust correlation is .991, and the Spearman rank-order correlation is .992. For the sets of standardized weights, the product-moment correlation is .990, the symmetric-robust correlation is .993, and the Spearman rank correlation is .991. Finally, for the sets of critical ratios, the product-moment correlation is .994, the robust correlation is .990, and the rank correlation is .998.

To simplify discussion we prepared figure 6-3 showing the final model significant paths using as a criterion a .95 one-tailed level of significance. The numbers which are shown in figure 6-3 are the standardized structural regression (path) weights.[1,2]

Summarizing the figure, the following paths are statistically significant. First, low levels of Law Abidance lead to high levels of first-year Alcohol Use. Friends' Poor School Performance leads to low levels of Alcohol Use: the path represents a paradoxical one opposite in sign to that which might be expected. First-year Cannabis Use is a positive function of first-year Alcohol Use, a negative function of first-year Law Abidance, and a positive function of Peer Culture Involvement. First-year Hard Drug Use is a positive function of Cannabis Use and Friends Poor School Performance, but a negative function of first-year Alcohol Use and Positive Self Concept. Fifth-year Alcohol Use is a positive function of first-year Alcohol Use, and a negative

Table 6-1. Structural Regression Coefficients and Critical Ratios Under Initial and Final Formulations

Dependent Latent Variable	Independent Latent Variable	Initial Model*			Final Model*		
		B	β	z	B	β	z
Alcohol Use I	Law Abidance I	-.96	-.71	-5.89	-.99	-.72	-5.76
Alcohol Use I	Positive Self Concept I	.14	.10	1.60	.14	.10	1.59
Alcohol Use I	Friends Poor School Performance I	-.28	-.20	-2.33	-.32	-.24	-2.73
Alcohol Use I	Peer Culture Involvement I	.18	.13	1.63	.19	.14	1.59
Cannabis Use I	Alcohol Use I	.21	.22	2.65	.20	.21	2.49
Cannabis Use I	Law Abidance I	-.42	-.32	-2.82	-.46	-.35	-2.85
Cannabis Use I	Positive Self Concept I	.01	.01	.15	.04	.03	.45
Cannabis Use I	Friends Poor School Performance I	.04	.03	.35	.03	.02	.26
Cannabis Use I	Peer Culture Involvement I	.29	.22	2.88	.25	.19	2.27
Hard Drug Use I	Alcohol Use I	-.17	-.19	-2.21	-.18	-.22	-2.50
Hard Drug Use I	Cannabis Use I	.51	.56	6.31	.50	.55	6.27
Hard Drug Use I	Law Abidance I	.12	.10	.83	.06	.05	.42
Hard Drug Use I	Positive Self Concept I	-.25	-.20	-3.20	-.18	-.15	-2.28
Hard Drug Use I	Friends Poor School Performance I	.16	.13	1.63	.19	.16	1.91
Hard Drug Use I	Peer Culture Involvement I	.00	.00	-.02	-.05	-.04	-.43
Alcohol Use V	Alcohol Use I	.14	.17	1.90	.15	.17	2.02
Alcohol Use V	Law Abidance I	-.44	-.38	-3.10	-.43	-.37	-2.96
Alcohol Use V	Positive Self Concept I	.08	.07	1.21	.07	.05	.87
Alcohol Use V	Friends Poor School Performance I	-.26	-.23	-2.73	-.27	-.23	-2.78
Alcohol Use V	Peer Culture Involvement I	.20	.17	2.21	.19	.16	1.93
Cannabis Use V	Alcohol Use I	-.16	-.15	-2.26	-.15	-.14	-2.16
Cannabis Use V	Cannabis Use I	.38	.34	5.49	.37	.33	5.49
Cannabis Use V	Alcohol Use V	.68	.54	9.95	.69	.55	10.26

(continued next page)

Table 6-1 (continued)

Dependent Latent Variable	Independent Latent Variable	Initial Model*			Final Model*		
		B	β	z	B	β	z
Cannabis Use V	Law Abidance I	-.29	-.20	-1.93	-.23	-.16	-1.47
Cannabis Use V	Positive Self Concept I	.04	.03	.62	.04	.02	.45
Cannabis Use V	Friends Poor School Performance I	-.11	-.07	-1.12	-.07	-.05	-.74
Cannabis Use V	Peer Culture Involvement I	-.07	-.05	-.77	-.06	-.04	-.57
Hard Drug Use V	Alcohol Use I	.13	.13	1.84	.14	.14	1.96
Hard Drug Use V	Cannabis Use I	-.05	-.05	-.61	-.05	-.04	-.53
Hard Drug Use V	Hard Drug Use I	-.03	-.02	-.43	-.03	-.02	-.44
Hard Drug Use V	Alcohol Use V	.13	.11	1.82	.12	.10	1.76
Hard Drug Use V	Cannabis Use V	.56	.60	7.43	.58	.61	7.68
Hard Drug Use V	Law Abidance I	.05	.04	.33	.09	.07	.57
Hard Drug Use V	Positive Self Concept I	-.12	-.08	-1.56	-.14	-.10	-1.83
Hard Drug Use V	Friends Poor School Performance I	.06	.05	.64	.05	.03	.48
Hard Drug Use V	Peer Culture Involvement I	-.09	-.06	-.94	-.07	-.05	-.65
Deviance V	Alcohol Use I	-.09	-.11	-1.07	-.06	-.07	-.67
Deviance V	Cannabis Use I	.12	.15	1.51	.15	.18	1.83
Deviance V	Hard Drug Use I	-.10	-.10	-1.46	-.12	-.13	-1.83
Deviance V	Law Abidance I	-.51	-.47	-2.80	-.45	-.41	-2.32
Deviance V	Positive Self Concept I	.09	.08	1.02	.08	.07	.85
Deviance V	Friends Poor School Performance I	-.05	-.04	-.47	.01	.01	.07
Deviance V	Peer Culture Involvement I	-.11	-.10	-1.01	-.18	-.17	-1.53

*B is the symbol used for the unstandardized structural regression weight; β is the symbol used for the standardized structural regression weight; z is the symbol used for the critical ratio.

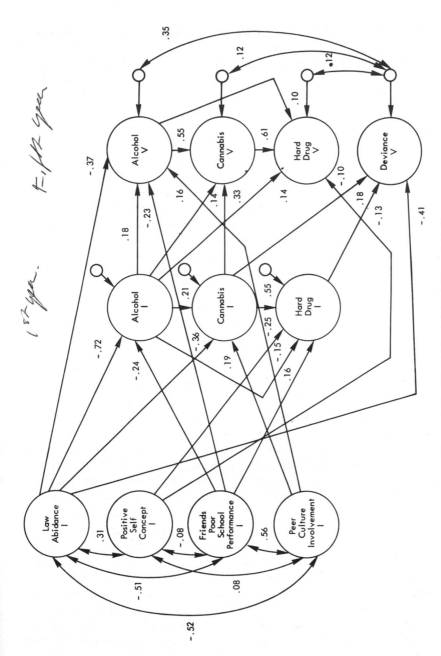

Figure 6-3. Final Model Significant Paths

function of first-year Law Abidance and Friends Poor School Performance as well as a positive function of Peer Culture Involvement. Fifth-year Cannabis Use is a negative function of first-year Alcohol Use, but a positive function of first-year Cannabis Use and fifth-year Alcohol Use. Hard Drug Use V is a positive function of first-year Alcohol Use, Alcohol Use V, and Cannabis Use V as well as a negative function of Positive Self Concept.

The latent variable of primary interest here—general Deviance—is a positive function of first-year Cannabis Use and there is a suppressor (negative) effect of the Hard Drug Use factor upon Deviance. Of the psychosocial factors, Law Abidance exerts a negative direct effect.

Another important piece of information to consider in interpreting the models is the correlations implied among latent variables. Table 6-2 shows these values (a function of the data, model parameterization, and estimates) under both initial and final formulations. The values under the two formulations are virtually identical and when minor numerical discrepancies occur, the same conclusions as to approximate degree and sign of relationship would be made. Examining the final model estimates, note than even across five years, Alcohol Use I (.21) and Cannabis Use I (.24) are quite related to Deviance V as is Law Abidance I (−.34). All contemporaneously measured latent variables are related to Deviance V with the correlations being .50, .49, and .47 for Alcohol Use V, Cannabis Use V, and Hard Drug Use V.

Thus far we have only been concerned with what might be called direct effects or paths which go directly from one latent variable to another. However, when we consider the values in table 6-2, we can see that frequently there are correlations among latent variables not connected by direct paths. How can this be so? Correlations between latent variables arise from sources which might be called "causal" and "spurious." Spurious correlations occur because causal and noncausal factors are correlated while causal correlations occur because one construct causes another either directly (as shown in table 6-1 and figure 6-3) *or* because there is indirect causation through another variable. For instance, while first-year Law Abidance does not directly affect fifth-year Cannabis Use, Law Abidance does affect Alcohol I, Alcohol V, and Cannabis I which themselves "cause" not only each other, but also Cannabis V. Thus, Law Abidance I has an indirect effect upon Cannabis V. All of the other possible indirect effects can also be traced through the model by seeing how the causes of a particular latent variable are themselves generated by one or more factors. Table 6-3 presents a tabular summary of the total tracing process and shows how latent variables influence one another directly and indirectly. It can be seen that the influences on Deviance V are virtually all direct, with indirect effects being

Table 6-2. Latent Variable Correlations Implied Under Initial and Final Formulations*

		I	II	III	IV	V	VI	VII	VIII	IX	X	XI
I	Alcohol Use I	1.00	.52	.06	.42	.35	.32	.21	-.65	.00	.23	.36
II	Cannabis Use I	.51	1.00	.45	.30	.49	.30	.25	-.58	-.01	.36	.47
III	Hard Drug Use I	.06	.45	1.00	.05	.18	.08	.00	-.20	-.20	.25	.18
IV	Alcohol Use V	.43	.30	.05	1.00	.65	.50	.49	-.44	.04	.10	.29
V	Cannabis Use V	.34	.48	.19	.65	1.00	.66	.47	-.47	.00	.14	.27
VI	Hard Drug Use V	.32	.30	.09	.51	.67	1.00	.42	-.35	-.08	.09	.14
VII	Deviance V	.21	.24	.00	.50	.49	.47	1.00	-.37	.00	.13	.11
VIII	Law Abidance I	-.64	-.59	-.24	-.43	-.45	-.34	-.34	1.00	.18	-.51	-.46
IX	Positive Self Concept I	-.08	-.08	-.18	-.04	-.06	-.14	-.06	.31	1.00	-.03	.17
X	Friends Poor School Performance I	.20	.35	.27	.08	.14	.08	.13	-.51	-.09	1.00	.56
XI	Peer Culture Involvement I	.40	.47	.18	.30	.29	.16	.09	-.53	.08	.56	1.00

*Values for initial model are above diagonal while the values for the final model are below the diagonal.

almost zero. The total of these two sources is the total "causal" or "nonspurious" correlation accounted for by the model. The difference between the total correlation estimates of table 6-2 and the total estimates shown here for pairs of latent variables represents the spurious correlation. Note that effect estimates are given both for the initial model without minor parameters and for the final model, and that the estimates under both formulations are exceedingly similar.

Discussion

We examined how six latent variables of drug use and four psychosocial functioning latent variables relate to a latent construct of deviance. While this chapter is limited in length and thus we cannot discuss all ramifications of the causal model in detail, major results are summarized below. More detailed explanations as well as additional, more refined analyses of these models are given by Huba and Bentler [6, chaps. 26, 29, and 40].

In the drug use portion of our causal model we show a stepwise progression from Alcohol Use to Cannabis Use to Hard-Drug Use occurring over time. The negative (suppressor) paths found mean that usage of a specific type which is not sustained across the five years will not lead to an escalating pattern at the end of the five years. Initial levels of low Law Abidance have important implications, both in the first year and in changes over time, for explaining patterns of Alcohol and Cannabis Use. Low levels of Positive Self Concept help to explain Hard Drug Use both in the first and fifth years. Thus, while there appears to be a transition into Alcohol and Cannabis Use because of initial patterns of rebelliousness, low levels of Positive Self Concept seem to influence transitions into patterns of Hard Drug Use including amphetamines, tranquilizers, and LSD consumption.

Two different peer culture latent variables—Peer Culture Involvement and Friends Poor School Performance—have inconsistent patterns of causation in exerting influence upon the drug use factors. Note that the effects of Friends' Poor School Performance are negative: this latent variable is correlated to too small a degree with the drug use factors given its correlation with other psychosocial factors (notably low Law Abidance) which have profound effects on drug-taking factors. Heightened levels of Peer Culture Involvement are important for understanding levels of using Alcohol and Cannabis.

When we consider the fifth-year General Deviance latent variable, we find a strong tendency for low levels of Law Abidance to explain this construct. Within that context, there are only *marginally* significant effects for Cannabis and Hard Drug Use to change levels of Deviance over and beyond

Table 6-3. Direct, Indirect, and Total Effects Under Initial and Final Formulations

Dependent Latent Variable	Independent Latent Variable	Initial Model			Final Model		
		Direct	Indirect	Total	Direct	Indirect	Total
Alcohol Use I	Law Abidance I	-.71	.00	-.71	-.72	.00	-.72
Alcohol Use I	Positive Self Concept I	.10	.00	.10	.10	.00	.10
Alcohol Use I	Friends Poor School Performance I	-.20	.00	-.20	-.24	.00	-.24
Alcohol Use I	Peer Culture Involvement I	.13	.00	.13	.14	.00	.14
Cannabis Use I	Alcohol Use I	.22	.00	.22	.21	.00	.21
Cannabis Use I	Law Abidance I	-.32	-.16	-.48	-.35	-.15	-.50
Cannabis Use I	Positive Self Concept I	.01	.02	.03	.03	.02	.05
Cannabis Use I	Friends Poor School Performance I	.03	-.04	-.02	.02	-.05	-.03
Cannabis Use I	Peer Culture Involvement I	.22	.03	.25	.19	.03	.22
Hard Drug Use I	Alcohol Use I	-.19	.12	-.07	-.22	.11	-.10
Hard Drug Use I	Cannabis Use I	.56	.00	.56	.55	.00	.55
Hard Drug Use I	Law Abidance I	.10	-.13	-.03	.05	-.12	-.06
Hard Drug Use I	Positive Self Concept I	-.20	-.00	-.21	-.15	.00	-.15
Hard Drug Use I	Friends Poor School Performance I	.13	.03	.16	.16	.03	.19
Hard Drug Use I	Peer Culture Involvement I	.00	.12	.11	-.04	.09	.05
Hard Drug Use I	Alcohol Use I	.17	.00	.17	.17	.00	.17
Alcohol Use V	Law Abidance I	-.38	-.12	-.49	-.37	-.12	-.50
Alcohol Use V	Positive Self Concept I	.07	.02	.09	.05	.02	.07
Alcohol Use V	Friends Poor School Performance I	-.23	-.03	-.26	-.23	-.04	-.27
Alcohol Use V	Peer Culture Involvement I	.17	.02	.19	.16	.02	.18
Cannabis Use V	Alcohol Use I	-.15	.17	.02	-.14	.16	.03

(continued next page)

Table 6-3 (continued)

Dependent Latent Variable	Independent Latent Variable	Initial Model			Final Model		
		Direct	Indirect	Total	Direct	Indirect	Total
Cannabis Use V	Cannabis Use I	.34	.00	.34	.33	.00	.33
Cannabis Use V	Alcohol Use V	.54	.00	.54	.55	.00	.55
Cannabis Use V	Law Abidance I	-.20	-.32	-.52	-.16	-.34	-.50
Cannabis Use V	Positive Self Concept I	.03	.04	.07	.02	.04	.06
Cannabis Use V	Friends Poor School Performance I	-.07	-.12	-.19	-.05	-.13	-.18
Cannabis Use V	Peer Culture Involvement I	-.05	.17	.12	-.04	.16	.12
Hard Drug Use V	Alcohol Use I	.13	.02	.15	.14	.03	.17
Hard Drug Use V	Cannabis Use I	-.05	.19	.14	-.04	.19	.15
Hard Drug Use V	Hard Drug Use I	-.02	.00	-.02	-.02	.00	-.02
Hard Drug Use V	Alcohol Use V	.11	.32	.43	.10	.34	.44
Hard Drug Use V	Cannabis Use V	.60	.00	.60	.61	.00	.61
Hard Drug Use V	Law Abidance I	.04	-.44	-.40	.07	-.44	-.37
Hard Drug Use V	Positive Self Concept I	-.08	.07	-.01	-.10	.06	-.04
Hard Drug Use V	Friends Poor School Performance I	.05	-.17	-.13	.03	-.17	-.14
Hard Drug Use V	Peer Culture Involvement I	-.07	.09	.03	-.05	.10	.05
Deviance V	Alcohol Use I	-.11	.04	-.07	-.07	.05	-.02
Deviance V	Cannabis Use I	.15	-.06	.09	.18	-.07	.11
Deviance V	Hard Drug Use I	-.10	.00	-.10	-.13	.00	-.13
Deviance V	Law Abidance I	-.47	.01	-.45	-.41	-.03	-.44
Deviance V	Positive Self Concept I	.08	.01	.09	.07	.02	.09
Deviance V	Friends Poor School Performance I	-.04	.00	-.04	.00	-.01	-.00
Deviance V	Peer Culture Involvement I	-.10	.01	-.09	-.17	.02	-.14

those predicted by initial rebelliousness tendencies. The influence of Cannabis is positive: greater Cannabis Use leads to marginally greater levels of General Deviance. On the other hand, low levels of initial Hard Drug Use is associated with Deviance in the fifth year; this latter finding, however, is not especially disturbing to us since youthful experimentation with Hard Drug is not stable from the first to the fifth years. There is moderate residual covariation between the fifth-year General Deviance factor and those parts of fifth-year drug use not explained by first drug use and psychosocial factors. In all cases the residual correlations are positive indicating associations between fifth-year General Deviance and the fifth-year drug-taking factors which cannot be explained by the different first-year psychosocial and drug use factors. If one espoused a strong causal theory, these positive correlations could be translated into additional positive direct effects of drug use on deviance.

The present causal model represents an attempt to study the inter-relationships between the domain of General Deviance and drug taking using latent variable causal models. Of particular importance we find that there are patterns of causation across five years attributable to several personality and peer culture factors. Indirect effects, as well as total ones, have been specified and estimated using state-of-the-art methods.

Notes

[1] It might also be asked if the paths not shown in figure 3 (and not seen to be significant in table 1) are collectively, as a group, able to be eliminated from the model. To make such a test we eliminated all paths in the final formulation which did not have an absolute critical ratio of at least 1.64 (the one-tailed .05 significance level) *except* those among the drug use factors. The chi-square value for the effect of eliminating 17 causal paths is 16.09 (d.f. $= 17, p > .50$) which allows us to conclude that collectively the coefficients are not statistically necessary.

[2] We also split the sample into males and females and fit the final model to the two groups separately. The chi-square goodness-of-fit statistic for the males was 638.41 (d.f. $= 453$, $p < .001$) and the chi-square goodness-of-fit statistic for the females was 556.33 (d.f. $= 453$, $p < .001$). Note that the model did not fit as well in the two subgroups studied individually; we attribute this result to the fact that the distributional assumptions are only partially met and that the result of isolating different subgroups is to exacerbate any nonlinearities and peculiarities which might inflate the chi-square statistic artificially. Slightly different patterns of correlated uniquenesses permit the solutions to fit the data. Within the context of the final models fit separately to the covariance matrices of each group we also calculated an approximate z-test for the difference between corresponding structural regression coefficients (using the estimate for females minus the estimate for males divided by the pooled standard error which is defined as the square root of the sum of the squared standard errors). Using such a statistic, none of the differences had a critical ratio with an absolute value exceeding 1.96 that is the two-tailed .05 significance level. The only result which is even marginally significant is that Cannabis Use across five years appears to be slightly more stable for males than females ($z = 1.93$).

References

1. Bentler, P. M. Multivariate analysis with latent variables: Causal modeling. *Ann. Rev. Psych.* 31:419, 1980.
2. Bentler, P. M., & Bonett, D. G. Significance tests and goodness of fit in the analysis of covariance structures. *Psych. Bull.* 88:588, 1980.
3. Brecher, E. M. *Licit and Illicit drugs.* Boston: Little, Brown, 1972.
4. Duncan, O. D. *Introduction to Structural Equation Models.* New York: Academic, 1975.
5. Huba, G. J., and Bentler, P. M. A developmental theory of drug use: Derivation and assessment of a causal modeling approach. In P. B. Baltes & O. G. Brim, Jr., (eds.), *Life-span Developmental and Behavior.* New York: Academic, in press. (1986)
6. Huba, G. J., & Bentler, P. M. *Antecedents and Consequences of Adolescent Drug Use: A Longitudinal Study of Psychosocial Development Using a Causal Modeling Approach.* New York: Plenum, in press.
7. Huba, G. J., Wingard, J. A., and Bentler, P. M. Beginning adolescent drug use and peer and adult interaction patterns. *J. Consult. Clin. Psych.* 47:265, 1979.
8. Huba, G. J., Wingard, J. A., and Bentler, P. M. Framework for an Interactive Theory of Drug Use. In D. J. Lettieri, M. Sayers, and H. W. Pearson (eds.), *Theories on Drug Abuse.* Rockville, Md.: National Institute on Drug Abuse, 1980.
9. Huba, G. J., Wingard, J. A., and Bentler, P. M. Comparison of two latent variable theories for adolescent drug use. *J. Pers. Soc. Psych.* 40:180, 1981.
10. Jessor, R. and Jessor, S. L. *Problem Behavior and Psychosocial Development.* New York: Academic, 1977.
11. Johnston, L. D., O'Malley, P. M., and Eveland, L. K. Drugs and Delinquency: A Search for Causal Connections. In D. B. Kandel (ed.), *Longitudinal Research on Drug Use.* Washington, D.C.: Hemisphere, 1978.
12. Kandel, D. B. Stages in adolescent involvement in drug use. *Science* 190:912, 1975.
13. Kandel, D. B. Convergence in Prospective Longitudinal Surveys of Drug Use in Normal Populations. In D. B. Kandel (ed.), *Longitudinal Research on Drug Use: Empirical Findings and Methodological Issues.* Washington, D.C.: Hemisphere, 1978.
14. Kaplan, H. B. *Deviant Behavior in Defense of Self.* New York: Academic, 1980.
15. Mosteller, F. and Tukey, J. W. *Data Analysis and Regression.* Reading, Mass: Addison-Wesley, 1977.
16. Segal, B., Huba, G. J., and Singer, J. L. *Drugs, Daydreaming and Personality: A Study of College Youth.* Hillsdale, N.J.: Lawrence Erlabum Associates, 1980.

II HIGH-RISK STUDIES

7 STUDIES OF FAMILIAL ALCOHOLISM: A GROWTH INDUSTRY

Donald W. Goodwin

In 1940, Jellinek [1] proposed a diagnostic category called "familial alcoholism" characterized by early age of onset and a particularly severe course. Neglected for nearly 40 years, the concept of familial alcoholism has recently awakened new interest. The impetus for the revival has been a number of twin and adoption studies indicating a possible genetic predisposition to alcoholism. Two kinds of research have evolved from these studies: (1) comparisons of familial and nonfamilial alcoholics, and (2) comparisons of children of alcoholics with children of nonalcoholics (high-risk studies).

A number of centers are pursuing these lines of research, with the findings just beginning to appear in the literature. Before reporting what has been learned so far, I will briefly review the twin and adoption data which stimulated the two new lines of research.

Twin Studies

There have been two major twin studies of alcoholism. One, in Sweden, found that identical twins more often were concordant for alcoholism than were fraternal twins [2]. The more severe the alcoholism, the greater the discrepancy between concordance rates in identical versus fraternal twins.

Another study, in Finland, found that identical twins were more concordant for quantity and frequency of drinking but not for adverse consequences of drinking [3]. There was a trend for younger identical twins to be more concordant for adverse consequences.

Other twin studies [4] indicate genetic control over the metabolism of alcohol, but varying rates of metabolism probably have no relevance to alcoholism.

The Danish Adoption Studies

Another approach to separating "nature" from "nurture" is to study individuals separated from their biological relatives soon after birth and raised by nonrelative adoptive parents.

Beginning in 1970, I and my colleagues started a series of adoption studies in Denmark to investigate the possibility that alcoholism in part has genetic roots [5]. The studies involved interviewing four groups of subjects, all children of alcoholics. The first group consisted of sons of alcoholics (average age, 30 years) raised by nonalcoholic foster parents. The second group consisted of sons of alcoholics (average age, 33 years) raised by their alcoholic biologic parents. The third and fourth groups consisted, respectively, of daughters of alcoholics (average age, 37 years) raised by nonalcoholic foster parents and daughters of alcoholics (average age, 32 years) raised by their alcoholic biologic parents. Paired with each group was a control group matched for age and, in the adopted samples, circumstances of adoption. All adoptees were separated from their biologic parents in the first few weeks of life and adopted by nonrelatives. The interviews were conducted by Danish psychiatrists "blind" to the overall purpose of the study and the identity of the interviewees—whether they were children of alcoholics or controls. The results were as follows:

Sons of alcoholics were about four times more likely to be alcoholic than were sons of nonalcoholics, *whether raised by nonalcoholic foster parents or raised by their own biological parents*. They were no more likely to be "heavy" drinkers or have other psychiatric or personality disorders.

Of the adopted daughters of alcoholics, 2 percent were alcoholic and 2 percent more had serious problems from drinking. In the adopted control group, 4 percent were alcoholic. Of the nonadopted daughters, 3 percent were alcoholic and 2 percent were problem drinkers. None of the nonadopted control women was alcoholic. Thus, both in the proband and control female groups, a higher-than-expected prevalence of alcoholism was found. Nothing was known about the biologic parents of the controls other than they did not have a hospital diagnosis of alcoholism (the alcoholic parents of the probands were identified because they had been hospitalized with this diagnosis). Possibly some of the biologic parents of the alcoholic controls were alcoholics. However, this could not be demonstrated one way or the other, and the findings from the daughter adoption study are inconclusive.

In both the adopted and nonadopted daughter groups there were low rates of heavy drinking. About 8 percent of the subjects were heavy drinkers, as compared to nearly 40 percent of the male subjects. Therefore, of women who met the criteria for heavy drinking, a substantial number developed serious problems from drinking, requiring treatment.

As with the male adoptees, the adopted-out daughters of alcoholics and controls did not differ with regard to other variables such as depression or drug abuse. There has been speculation, based on family studies, that female relatives of alcoholics are prone to be depressed while male relatives are subject to alcoholism [6]. Indeed, 30 percent of daughters *raised* by alcoholics had been treated for depression by age 32, compared to about 5 percent of the controls. Apparently, growing up with an alcoholic parent increases the risk of depression in women but not in men, a susceptibility that does not exist if daughters are raised by nonalcoholic foster parents. This does not deny the possibility of a genetic predisposition to depression in female relatives of alcoholics, since many genetic disorders require an environmental "trigger" to become clinically apparent.

Summarizing the results of the Danish studies:

1. Children of alcoholics are particularly vulnerable to alcoholism, whether raised by their alcoholic parents or by nonalcoholic foster parents.
2. The vulnerability is specific for alcoholism and does not involve increased risk for other psychopathology, including abuse of other substances.
3. Alcoholism is not on a continuum with "heavy drinking" or even with "problem drinking" (defined as heavy drinking that results in problems but does not justify the term *alcoholism* as defined in these studies).
4. More definitive conclusions could be drawn from studies of the sons of alcoholics than of the daughters because the female control adoptees also had a higher rate of alcoholism than would be anticipated from the estimated prevalence in the general population.
5. The men in the study were relatively young to be diagnosed as alcoholic. Where they met the criteria for alcoholism, they almost always had received treatment, suggesting they had a severe form of alcoholism. The

women alcoholics also had a severe form of alcoholism, requiring treatment, but were somewhat older.

Other Adoption Studies

Four other adoption studies have been conducted, two of them after the Danish studies.

In the early 1940s, Roe [7] obtained information about 49 foster children in the 20- to 40-year age group, 22 of normal parentage and 27 with a biological parent described as a "heavy drinker." Neither group had adult drinking problems. Roe concluded there was no evidence of hereditary influences on drinking.

This conclusion can be questioned on several grounds. First, the sample was small. There were only 21 men of "alcoholic" parentage and 11 of normal parentage. Second, the biologic parents of the probands were described as "heavy drinkers," but it is not clear how many were alcoholic. Most had a history of antisocial behavior; none had been treated. All of the biological parents of the proband group in the Danish study received a hospital diagnosis of alcoholism and at a time when this diagnosis was rarely employed in Denmark.

In 1972, Schuckit et al. [8] also studied a group of individuals reared apart from their biologic parents who had either a biologic parent or a "surrogate" parent with a drinking problem. The subjects were significantly more likely to have a drinking problem if their biologic parent was considered alcoholic than if their surrogate parent was alcoholic.

More recently, Bohman [9] studied 2,000 adoptees born between 1930 and 1949 by inspecting official registers in Sweden for notations about alcohol abuse and criminal offenses in the adoptees and their biological and adoptive parents. There was a significant correlation between registrations for abuse of alcohol among biologic parents and their adopted sons. Registered criminality in the biologic parents did not predict criminality or alcoholism in the adopted sons.

Cadoret and Gath [10] studied 84 adult adoptees separated at birth from their biological relatives and having no further contact with them. Alcoholism occurred more frequently in adoptees whose biologic background included alcoholism than it did in other adoptees. Alcoholism was not correlated with any other biologic parental diagnosis.

The above studies produced results similar to those found in the Danish adoption studies: alcoholism in the biologic parents predicted alcoholism in their male offspring raised by unrelated adoptive parents but did not predict other psychiatric illness.

Familial Alcoholism

Further studies tend to support the idea that "familial alcoholism" may be a valid diagnostic category. Separating alcoholics into familial versus non-familial types, studies indicate that familial alcoholism should include at least the first three of the following four features.

A Family History of Alcoholism

If an alcoholic reports having one close relative who is alcoholic, he often reports having two or more.

Early Onset of Alcoholism

The sons of alcoholics in the Danish study (5) were alcoholic by their late 20s; usually male alcoholics are in their mid- or late 30s before they are identified as alcoholics. In the Finnish twin study [3], younger identical twins more often were concordant for alcoholism than older twins. In five separate reports [11–15], younger alcoholics more often have alcoholic relatives than do older alcoholics, or there is other evidence that familial alcoholism has a relatively early age of onset.

Severe Symptoms, Requiring Treatment at an Early Age

The alcoholic biologic parents in the Danish studies had been identified because they had received the diagnosis in a Danish hospital. As noted, it is customary in many Danish hospitals to avoid the diagnosis of alcoholism when another diagnosis is available, eg, a personality disorder. Therefore, it can safely be assumed that the alcoholic parents were severely alcoholic and this may explain why their offspring were so clearly alcoholic at a young age. In the twin study of Kaij [2] the concordance rate for alcoholism in identical twins rose as a function of the severity of the alcoholism. Another study [16] reported that "essential" alcoholism more often is associated with a family history of alcoholism than "reactive" alcoholism, *essential* being defined as alcoholism apparently unrelated to external events (as "endogenous" depression is often contrasted with "reactive" depression) as well as connoting severity and lack of other psychopathology. Amark [17] noted that periodic (severe) alcoholics more often had a family history of alcoholism than did less severe alcoholics.

In five recent studies (18–21; 12), familial alcoholics had a more severe illness than nonfamilial alcoholics. In three studies (16–18), they had a worse prognosis following treatment.

Absence of Other Conspicuous Psychopathology

This was found in both the Danish studies [5] and two subsequent adoption studies [9,10]. However, three groups [10,18,22] report that familial alcoholics more often have a childhood history of hyperactivity and conduct disorder; two groups [15,18] report more antisocial behavior; and two studies [13,14] found that multiple psychiatric syndromes characterize familial alcoholism. The issue of psychopathology associated with alcoholism is clearly unresolved.

Finally, a study by Begleiter [23] and colleagues compared familial and nonfamilial alcoholics (matched for age, education and drinking history) and found greater structural and functional abnormalities in the family-history-positive group as measured by computerized tomography and evoked brain potentials. Both groups had been abstinent for at least a month and off medication for at least three weeks. The study suggested the possibility of an anatomical substrate for the hyperactivity and conduct disorders associated with alcoholism in other studies.

The issue of general psychopathology associated with alcoholism remains unclear, but the early-onset and severity association is highly consistent across studies.

High-Risk Studies

Family and adoption studies suggest that between 20 and 25 percent of sons of alcoholics will themselves become alcoholic. Children of alcoholics therefore can be considered a "high-risk" group with regard to the future development of alcoholism. A number of high-risk studies of alcoholism are now in progress and have yielded the following results.

After drinking alcohol, college-age sons of alcoholics show greater tolerance for alcohol than do matched controls. The tolerance is reflected in superior performance on the pursuit rotor task and less subjective intoxication. At the same time, they show greater muscle relaxation. Schuckit et al., who reported these findings [24,25], also found that sons of alcoholics had higher blood levels of acetaldehyde after alcohol ingestion than did sons of nonalcoholics [26]. Attempts to replicate this finding have not always been successful. None of the subjects was alcoholic. They were all matched for drinking history.

In another study, Lipscomb [27] found that sons of alcoholics showed increased body sway after drinking when compared to controls.

High-risk studies conducted in Denmark found that sons of alcoholics generated more alpha rhythm on the EEG after drinking alcohol than did controls and also had lower scores on the categories test of the Halstead Battery (unpublished data.) Alcoholics fairly consistently have low scores on the categories test, usually attributed to the deleterious effects of alcohol. Since the Danish study suggests that their nonalcoholic sons also do poorly on the categories test, the interpretation of the previous studies may need revision.

Supporting a possible link between childhood hyperactivity and later alcoholism, one group [28] reported that sons of alcoholics more often give a history of hyperactivity than do controls. As noted earlier, hyperactivity and conduct disorders appear more common in familial alcoholics than in nonfamilial alcoholics.

Investigating the possibility that sons of alcoholics metabolize alcohol abnormally, Utne and co-workers [29] compared the disappearance rate of blood alcohol in two groups of adoptees, ten with an alcoholic parent and ten without. There was no difference.

High-risk studies are based on the assumption that one-fifth or one-quarter of the sons of alcoholics will become alcoholic. Long-term follow-up will be required to discover which of the sons become alcoholic. The rationale for high-risk studies ultimately depends on this follow-up information, permitting correlations with a broad range of premorbid variables.

In any case, group differences between children of alcoholics and nonalcoholics are consistently being found. This, together with twin and adoption data and variables correlated with familial alcoholism, tend to suggest that familial alcoholism represents a separate diagnostic entity.

References

1. Jellinek, E. M. and Jolliffe, N.: Effect of alcohol on the individual. *Q. J. Stud. Alcohol* 1:110, 1940.
2. Kaij, L.: Studies on the Etiology and Sequels of Abuse of Alcohol, thesis. Lund, Sweden: University of Lund, 1960.
3. Partanen, J., Bruun, K., and Markkanen, T.: *Inheritance of Drinking Behavior: A Study on Intelligence, Personality and Use of Alcohol of Adult Twins.* Helsinki: Finnish Foundation for Alcohol Studies, 1966, pp. 14–159.

4. Vesell, E. S., Page, J. F., Passananti, G. T.: Genetic and environmental factors affecting ethanol metabolism in man. *Clin. Pharmacol. Ther* 12:192, 1971.

5. Goodwin, D. W.: Alcoholism and heredity. *Arch. Gen. Psychiatry* 36:57, 1979.

6. Winokur, G. and Clayton, P. J.: Family history studies: IV Comparison of male and female alcoholics. *Q. J. Stud. Alcohol* 29:885, 1968.

7. Roe, A.: The adult adjustment of children of alcoholic parents raised in foster homes. *Q. J. Stud. Alcohol* 5:378, 1944.

8. Schuckit, M. A., Goodwin, D. W., and Winokur G.: A half-sibling study of alcoholism. *Am. J. Psychiatry* 128:1132, 1972.

9. Bohman, M.: Genetic aspects of alcoholism and criminality. *Arch. Gen. Psychiatry* 35:269, 1978.

10. Cadoret, R. and Gath, A.: Inheritance of alcoholism in adoptees. *Br. J. Psychiatry* 132:252, 1978.

11. Jones, R. W.: Alcoholism among relatives of alcoholic patients. *Q. J. Stud. Alcohol* 33:810, 1972.

12. McKenna, T. and Pickens, R.: Alcoholic children of alcoholics. *J. Stud. Alcohol* 42:1021, 1981.

13. Penick, E., Read, M., Crowley, P., and Powell, B.: Differentiation of alcoholics by family history. *J. Stud. Alcohol* 39:1944, 1978.

14. Powell, B., Penick, E., Othmer, E., et al.: Prevalence of additional psychiatric syndromes among male alcoholics. *J. Clin. Psychiatry*, in press.

15. Schuckit, M., Rimmer, J., Reich, T., and Winokur, G.: Alcoholism: Antisocial traits in male alcoholics. *Am. J. Psychiatry* 117:575, 1970.

16. Knight, R. P.: Dynamics and treatment of chronic alcoholism. *Bull. Menninger Clin.* 1:233, 1937.

17. Amark, C.: A study in alcoholism: Clinical, social-psychiatric and genetic investigations. *Acta. Psychiatr. Neurol. Scand. [Suppl.] 70:94*, 1953.

18. Frances, R., Timm, S., and Bucky, S.: Studies of familial and nonfamilial alcoholism. I. Demographic studies. *Arch. Gen. Psychiatry* 37:564, 1980.

19. Fitzgerald, J. and Mulford, H.: Alcoholics in the family? *Int. J. Addict.* 16:349, 1981.

20. Ohayon, J.: Familial and nonfamilial alcoholics. Ph.D. dissertation, University of Pittsburgh, 1981.

21. Templer, D., Ruff, C. and Ayres, J.: Essential alcoholism and family history of alcoholism. *Q. J. Stud. Alcohol* 35:655, 1974.

22. Tarter, R.: Minimal Brain Dysfunction as an Etiological Predisposition to Alcoholism. In Meyer, R. et al. (eds.), *Evaluation of the Alcoholic: Implications for Research, Theory and Practice.* Washington, D.C.: U.S. Government Printing Office, 1981, pp. 167–191.

23. Begleiter, H., Porjesz, B., Kissin, B.: Brain dysfunction in alcoholics with and without a family history of alcoholism. *Alcohol. Clin. Exp. Res.* 6:136, 1982.

24. Schuckit, M.: Biological markers: Metabolism and acute reactions to alcohol in sons of alcoholics. *Pharma. Biochem. Behavior* 13:9, 1980.

25. Schuckit, M.: Self-rating of alcohol intoxication by young men with and without family histories of alcoholism. *J. Stud. Alcohol* 41:242, 1980.

26. Schuckit, M. and Rayes, V.: Ethanol ingestion: differences in acetaldehyde concentrations in relatives of alcoholics and controls. *Science* 203:54, 1979.

27. Lipscomb, R., Carpenter, J., and Nathan, P.: Static ataxia: a predictor of alcoholism. *Br. J. Addict.* 74:289, 1979.

28. Lund, C. and Landesman-Dwyer, S.: Pre-delinquent and Disturbed Adolescents: The Role of Parental Alcoholism. In Galanter, M. (ed.), *Currents in Alcoholism.* New York: Grune and Stratton, 1979.

29. Utne, H. E., Hansen, F., Vallo, R., Winkler, K., and Schulsinger F.: Alcohol elimination rates in adoptees with and without alcoholic parents. *J. Stud. Alcohol* 38:1219, 1977.

8 A DANISH PROSPECTIVE STUDY OF YOUNG MALES AT HIGH RISK FOR ALCOHOLISM

Joachim Knop
Donald Goodwin
Thomas W. Teasdale
Ulla Mikkelsen
Fini Schulsinger

Alcoholism represents one of the most serious health problems in modern industrialized society. In spite of persistent research efforts and preventive initiatives the main problems concerning etiology remain unsolved, while the consumption of alcohol in a society such as Denmark still increases.

The study was supported from the National Institute of Alcohol Abuse and Addiction (Grant No. AA 03448) and the Danish Medical Research Council (Grant No. 512-10733).

A thanks to Professor B. Zachau-Christiansen and Dr. J. Merrick (Section for Prospective Pediatrics, State University Hospital, Copenhagen) for their cooperation in the utilization of the birth cohort used for the sampling.

A special thank to the Institute for Psychiatric Demography in Århus, Denmark (heads, E. Strömgren and A. Dupont, M.D.) for their help in screening the parents for alcoholism. For the same reason we are grateful to the Municipal Alcohol Clinic in Copenhagen (head, E. Jensen, M.D.).

The study of MAO activity was carried out in collaboration with Drs. R. J. Wyatt and Steven Potkin at St. Elisabeth's Hospital, Washington, D.C., where the analyses were performed.

The development of the acetaldehyde analysis was supported from Dumex, Copenhagen and performed at the Clinical Chemical Department of Bispebjerg Hospital, Copenhagen (heads, P. Lous and E. Magid, M.D.).

Alcohol-related disabilities and complications are well known and described. Most scientific experience originates from studies using subjects who have been alcohol-addicted for many years. In this way many interesting differences between alcoholics and nonalcoholics have been reported, but it is impossible to base etiological inferences on such results. Should the difference be regarded as a consequence of heavy drinking, or as a precursor/ antecedant to drinking problems?

The high-risk methodology involves a prospective follow-up of subjects, who are at empirically high risk for developing a disorder. The high-risk design was originally introduced in 1962 in a Danish study of children of chronic schizophrenic mothers [18] and has since been adopted in several studies all over the world. Recently an extensive review of the ongoing longitudinal studies of populations at risk in Europe has been published by WHO [17].

Sample

Our sample is selected from a total birth cohort of children born 1959–1961 at the maternity department of the State University Hospital in Copenhagen. A group of Danish obstetricians and pediatricians studied 9,006 consecutive pregnancies carefully and systematically. The primary purpose of this perinatal study was to determine the influence of pre- and perinatal factors in the development of cerebral dysfunction early in life [28]. A large number of follow-up studies have employed this sample, including the present alcohol study.

The extensive data from pregnancy, delivery, the neuropediatric examination on the fifth day after delivery and at the children's first birthday were stored on magnetic tape.

For other scientific purposes Psykologisk Institut undertook a systematic screening of all 18,012 parents in the Danish Psychiatric Register in Aarhus, where all admissions and discharge diagnoses in Danish psychiatric departments have been registered since 1916 [4].

All parents (mainly fathers) who have been admitted with a diagnosis of alcoholism were selected for the present study. In addition we screened the approximately 9,000 fathers in the Municipal Alcohol Treatment Clinic in Copenhagen.

In this manner we found a total of 250 sons and 226 daughters with at least one parent treated for alcoholism. We decided to exclude the daughters because the life expectancy rate for alcoholism in women still is 5–6 times less than for men. In a longitudinal, high-risk context, the "outcome" of alcoholic women would be too small.

Goodwin and associates have demonstrated a considerable genetic factor in the development of alcoholism in men [5,6]. Therefore we have chosen paternal alcoholism as the most solid risk criterion.

We initially aimed at getting all these 250 sons as high-risk probands (HR) in this longitudinal alcohol study. Twenty-six of them were, however, excluded from the outset primarily due to perinatal death and emigration during childhood and adolescence. So 224 sons were left for our study.

For the purpose of testing the adequacy of our instruments and to evaluate the validity of the specific hypotheses, we selected a control group from the same birth cohort: For two HR sons (matched for a variety of demographic characteristics), 106 sons, whose parents did not figure in the psychiatric register mentioned above, were selected as the low-risk group (LR).

Table 8-1 demonstrates the attrition in the sample. The social worker got in contact with 235 (156 HR and 79 LR) of the originally 330 subjects. Only 44 subjects actively refused to participate, but in addition 37 potential subjects never kept their appointment. Of the 235 subjects with an appointment at Psykologisk Institut, 204 (134 HR and 70 LR) subjects completed the assessment. From the table it can be deduced that there were 102 active and passive refusals, or 32.1 percent from the HR-group and 28.3 percent from the LR-group.

Table 8-1. Sample Attrition

	HR	LR	Total
Selected from birth cohort	224	106	330
Refusals	32	12	44
Never kept appointments	25	12	37
Unknown address, adopted, dead	7	3	10
Could not get permission from job	3	0	3
Emigrated	1	0	1
Total	68	27	95
Rest = social worker interview	156	79	235
Did not come to Psykologisk Institut	15	6	21
Could not get permission from job	5	2	7
Emigrated	1	1	2
Ill on date of assessment	1	0	1
Total	22	9	31
Rest = completed total assessment	134	70	204

Hypotheses and Variables

The etiological background for alcoholism is multifactorial with several pathways leading to drinking problems. The overview of the hypotheses and variables selected for the present study shown in figure 8-1 reflects this multidisciplinary approach.

Neurohypothesis

It is generally assumed that the majority of alcoholics develop a memory deficit or intellectual dysfunction after a certain number of years of alcohol abuse. Both neuropsychological tests and CAT scanning have demonstrated this deficit [8,19].

However, it has never been reliably demonstrated that this deficit should be regarded as a consequence of heavy drinking, or perhaps was present already before drinking accelerated, or possibly might have some etiological relation to alcoholism itself. Such "neuro" antecedants to alcoholism have been discussed in other contexts. Goodwin and co-workers demonstrated that the Hyperactive Childhood Syndrome (now named "attention deficit disorder") was found more in future alcoholics than in other comparable males [6].

Lennart Kaij located 174 male twin pairs where at least one twin was registered in the files of the temperance board as alcoholic [10]. He found that intellectual deterioration was more correlated with zygosity than with the extent of drinking. In no instance did the twin who drank more within each pair show more evidence of this CNS-dysfunction than his co-twin. Kaij interpreted this finding that cerebral dysfunction may be a genetically determinated contributor to alcoholism rather than a consequence.

Of course this hypothesis does not exclude other significant environmental contributions to this dysfunction, e.g., skull trauma or perinatal asphyxia.

Therefore we have selected an extensive neuropsychological test battery which appears in table 8-2.

The vast majority of the tests have been utilized in several alcohol studies as indicators of possible organic deficits in alcoholic subjects. The essential psychological functions focused on in this context are memory, attention, and categorizing ability.

The extensive pre-, peri-, and postnatal data contribute to the study as important variables to test the hypothesis concerning pregnancy and delivery complications as factors that may "trigger" the development of antisocial behavior and alcoholism later in life.

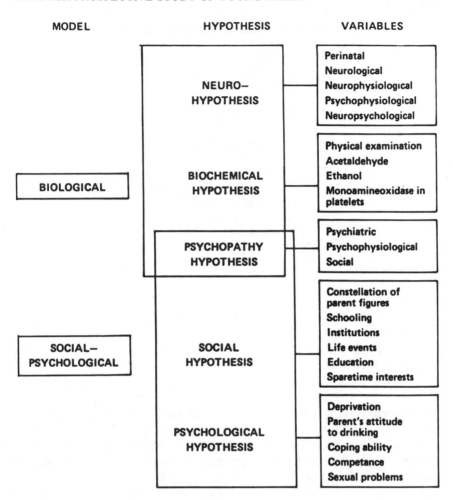

Figure 8-1. Review of Hypotheses and Variables in a Prospective High-Risk Study on Alcoholism

Concerning neurophysiological hypotheses: Propping [22] has shown that certain patterns of fast wave electroencephalogram (EEG) in alcoholics may be hereditarily determined. It has been demonstrated that alcoholics as a group are characterized by having a "poor alpha" EEG pattern. Ethanol has been shown to increase the amount of alpha activity [20].

Table 8-2. Neuropsychological
Test Battery

Vocabulary
Block Design
Digit Span
Subtraction Test
Word Fluency
Paired Associates
Picture Recognition
Visual Gestalt
Halstead Categorizing Test
Embedded Figure's Test
Porteus Maze Test
Association Test
Handedness

Visual evoked potentials (VEPs) are also affected by alcohol intake: Alcohol reduces the amplitude of the late component. Further, an inverse relation between the increase in tolerance to alcohol and the VEP amplitude has been demonstrated [21].

We have included an extensive neurophysiological program in our assessment (resting EEG and VEP).

Psychophysiological variables are of importance in this context; especially arousal and rate of recovery are of relevance, because they are known to correlate with antisocial behavior and psychopathy,, which, per se, correlate closely with alcoholism. Another important correlate is hyperactive behavior during childhood and adolescence as mentioned above.

Information concerning skull trauma, central nervous system (CNS) infections and epilepsy were obtained very carefully. A neurological examination is included in the program.

Biochemical Hypotheses

Several biochemical abnormalities have been proposed as biological markers of alcoholism. Until now the most promising hypotheses are those concerning monoamineoxidase and acetaldehyde.

An abnormally low activity of monoamineoxidase (MAO) in blood platelets have been found in subjects suffering from various mental disorders including alcoholism. In addition, it has been demonstrated that first degree relatives to "low MAO" subjects have more alcohol problems compared to "normal MAO" and "high MAO" relatives [13]. It is important to know whether this abnormality is a precursor or a consequence of heavy drinking. We included a MAO blood sample in the present study to answer this question.

Several studies have demonstrated an abnormally high acetaldehyde response in blood after a single alcohol dose in alcoholics [12]. Recently it has been suggested that this abnormality may be a valuable biochemical predictor of alcoholism [24].

A subset of the subjects (44 HR and 28 LR) participated in an alcohol session during the neurophysiological assessment and blood samples were drawn for determination of ethanol and acetaldehyde after a single dose of alcohol (solution of blackcurrant juice, club soda and 0.5 ml ethanol per kilogram body weight). Additionally a performance test and the Porteus Maze Test were performed during this session.

Psychopathy Hypothesis

It has been hypothesized for a long time that antisocial personality traits may be one of the most important "pathways" leading to development of alcoholism later in life [3,9,14,23]. The overlap in the population of antisocial individuals and alcoholics is well known.

But again, the causal chronology between antisocial personality and alcoholism is unknown. In the present high-risk context we wanted to test the hypothesis concerning antisocial behavior as an important predicting "pathway" toward alcoholism. Particularly such personality characteristics as impulsiveness, restless behavior, and impaired concentration ability are important in this connection.

Using the adoption method, Schulsinger demonstrated a considerable genetic component in the etiology of psychopathy [25]. In psychophysiological respects psychopaths and recidivistic criminals are characterized by a slow electrodermal recovery [16]. These more biological measures are a valuable supplement to the clinical diagnostic evaluation for character-deviant traits. A psychopathology interview (see below) covers these important items. Of course this does not exclude significant environmental factors in the development.

Social Hypotheses

The number of specific and testable hypotheses concerning social precursors to alcoholism is small. Most consistent are the hypotheses from learning theories and modeling theories. But it is generally believed that disruptive living conditions, poor housing conditions, parental loss or separation, experience of serious life events, etc. are correlated to a high prevalence of alcoholism later in life. The most relevant social variables in the development of alcoholism have recently been reviewed [27].

An extensive social history interview was conducted in the subject's home covering the following areas: household membership during childhood, parental constellation, institutionalization, schooling, vocational training, education, working situation, unemployment, military service, economic status, spare time interests, hobbies, significant life events, and exposure to alcohol.

Reliable information about schooling is being obtained by questionnaires sent out to the subjects' former teachers.

Psychological Variables

Many psychological theories have been applied to alcoholism, e.g. learning theories, labelling, addictive personality, anxiety reduction, psychiatric illness (primary affective disorder). Also, psychoanalytically oriented theories have been suggested as important "pathways" toward alcoholism later in life.

A trained clinical psychologist conducted a semistructured and precoded interview covering the following items: Early deprivation, character of the upbringing, the parents' drinking habits and attitude to alcohol, child abuse, coping in school, sexual development, signs of psychotic symptomatology, neurotic traits or symptoms, social and intellectual level, ability to cope, social exclusion etc. Further, a careful evaluation of the subject's character structure was performed, with special regard to impulsivity, restlessness, and similar traits. The information from the subject's school teacher will be a valuable supplement to these personality items.

Drinking History

The information about the subject's drinking pattern is an essential part of the study. Therefore the questions concerning this item were very specific and extensive. We asked about the consumption of alcoholic beverages every day during the preceding week. The quantitative questions include number of drinks, preferred days in the week, type of beverage, time during the day, place of drinking, circumstances, etc.

Further, each was asked about his first drink, the first time drunk, the physiologic and psychological effect of drinking, hangovers and other "side effects", tolerance, withdrawal symptoms. Also any social consequences of drinking were registered (traffic accidents, police records).

Finally, the subjects were asked about more "soft" issues such as attitudes, group mechanisms, anxiety reduction, contact ability, etc. in connection with alcohol consumption.

Assessment

The first step in the extensive assessment was the social worker's visit in the subject's home. He was informed in detail about the project, which was presented as a follow-up of the original perinatal study in 1959–1961. The primary purpose for the visit was to motivate the subjects to participate in the assessment in Psykologisk Institut and to get detailed information about the subject's social history.

The subjects arrived to Psykologisk Institut at 8.00 A.M. and during the following 8–9 hours the test program listed below was carried out:

Neuropsychological test program

Psychopathology interview

Physical health examination

Lunch

Neurophysiological test program

Psychophysiological test program

They were paid for loss of earnings, expenses for transportation, and a small honorarium. All subjects were informed about the follow-up aspect in the study and the vast majority promised to react positively next time we contacted them.

Results

Primarily this paper is a review of the extensive study and only a limited number of the main results will be reported here to demonstrate that at least some of the hypotheses and variables may be valid because some of the comparisons discriminate between the HR and LR groups.

Neurohypothesis

Regarding data from pregnancy, delivery, and postnatal period, no significant differences between the two risk groups were found.

Neither the neurological or physical health examination at the present assessment distinguished the HR and LR groups significantly. The same was the case with regard to: cranial trauma, CNS infections, and convulsions.

The neuro- and psychophysiologic data are not yet completely analyzed. They will be reported separately.

In the neuropsychological test battery some very interesting results emerged.

As shown in table 8-3, the HR subjects scored significantly poorer in the Halstead categorizing test compared to the LR subjects. Also in the Porteus Maze test the HR subjects made more errors compared to the LR subjects regarding one particular parameter: alteration of direction, i.e. entering blind alleys. The difference is significant ($p = 0.046$, Mann-Whitney's U-test).

Biochemical Hypotheses

The blood alcohol concentration showed no differences between the two risk groups with regard to peak level and elimination rate.

The study of blood-acetaldehyde gave us some unexpected difficulties concerning the methodology for determination. We had to develop a new gas-chromatographic assay with negligible artifactual formation of acetaldehyde [2,11]. This new method could not be implemented early enough to yield results from the present study.

The MAO activity in blood platelets were determined on all subjects. The

Table 8-3. Results of Halstead Categorizing Test in HR and LR Subjects.

	HR (N = 134)	LR (N = 70)	Mann-Whitney's U-test
Sum of errors	45.7	38.5	$p = 0.04$

Table 8-4. Personality Characteristics in HR and LR Subjects

	HR (N = 134)	LR (N = 70)	
Marked impulsivity	19.4%	8.6%	p = 0.045
Marked tendency of ruminating	8.2	21.4	p = 0.014
Marked antiaggressive personality	4.5	10.0	n.s.

processed blood samples were sent to St. Elizabeth's Hospital, Washington D.C., for analysis. The results are not yet available.

Psychopathy Hypothesis

The psychopathology interview was semistructured, lasted 1–2 hours, and covered traditional psychopathology, the subject's psycho-social development (parents, school, peers), and other psychological items.

The psychopathological diagnoses were distributed evenly over the HR and LR groups. Severe cases of psychosis, neurosis, and personality disorders were as infrequent as one would expect in an average sample of young males. Milder forms were more frequent, but showed the same prevalence in the two risk groups. Certain marked personality traits were distributed less evenly, as shown in table 8-4.

From ratings of three items: impulsiveness (hasty decisions, impulsive buying, spendthrift), ruminating (speculating, cannot stop worrying) and antiaggressiveness (submissiveness, others are always right, avoids conflicts) some interesting results emerged: the HR subjects were more frequently impulsive, whereas the LR subjects were more ruminative and antiaggressive. This distribution is also reflected in the subjects' information on their proneness to get into fights in school. This was significantly more frequent among the HR subjects ($p = 0.03$). Here it should be noted that the interviewer was blind regarding the risk status of the subjects.

These results on personality characteristics will be substantiated by the social history, from which preliminary analysis has shown a number of indirect indicators of impulsiveness in the HR group (school career and behavior). The behavior of the subjects during the psychopathology interview is illustrated in table 8-5.

Table 8-5. Behavior During Psychopathology Interview in HR and LR
Subjects

	HR (N = 134)	LR (N = 70)	
Calm, relaxed during whole interview	27.6%	21.4%	
Nervous at start, but calms down	35.0	57.1	$p = .0029$
Somewhat nervous during whole interview	39.1	17.1	$p = .0015$
Increasingly tense and nervous	0.0	4.3	
Suspicious, not cooperative, rejecting	0.7	0.0	

The LR group responded most adequately in the interview situation
namely with some initial nervousness. In the HR group there was, however,
frequently some nervousness during the whole interview.

Another important set of variables in connection with the "psychopathy"
hypotheses are the psychophysiologic measures, particularly a slow auto-
nomic recovery may possibly be a physiologic marker of antisocial behavior
and recidivistic criminality [16]. These data have not yet been analyzed.

Also the information from the subjects' teachers in school will be a
valuable supplement in this context.

Social Hypothesis

In spite of the criteria for selection, several from the HR group did not grow
up with their alcoholic father, and some from the LR group may have had an
alcoholic stepfather. The birth cohort was not completely representative of
the Danish population primarily because the maternity department of the
State University Hospital catered, to a certain extent, to unmarried mothers.
Table 8-6 illustrates these factors.

From the table it appears that there is an overall tendency toward more
stepfathers in the HR group (except for the 0–2 years age group). Until the
age of approximately 12 years, both risk groups lived equally frequently
together with both of their parents. Hereafter this began to be less frequent
for the HR group. There were, of course, other types of parental constellations, but they were much less frequent and did not differ between the two
risk groups.

The results are, to some extent, reflected in table 8-7, which illustrates
that, as reported by the subjects themselves, not all HR-fathers were
alcoholics and not all LR-fathers were abstainers. The differences are all in

Table 8-6. Parental Constellations in HR and LR Subjects

Age Years	Risk Group	Subjects with Both Parents	Subjects with Mother Alone	Subjects with Mother and Stepfather
0–2	HR	73.1%	14.9%	1.5%
	LR	70.0	15.7	2.9
3–5	HR	61.9	13.4	9.7
	LR	64.3	18.6	7.1
6–8	HR	53.0	15.7	17.9
	LR	55.7	22.	8.6
9–11	HR	46.3	16.4	22.4
	LR	48.6	20.0	14.3
12–14	HR	33.6	20.1	23.1
	LR	44.3	20.0	12.9
15–17	HR	23.1*	18.7	23.1*
	LR	41.4*	20.0	5.7*
18–20	HR	17.2*	16.4	18.7
	LR	37.1*	11.4	10.0

*$p < 0.01$.

the direction of higher alcohol consumption in the HR-parents. These results will gain in value, when they can be related to the outcome of alcoholism in the sample.

Concerning data from the school career, no significant differences came up in the two risk groups. But there was a tendency toward a more frequent completion of the highest grades among the LR-subjects. The frequency of repetition of a grade was significantly higher in the HR group ($p = 0.007$). This was also the case with regard to referral to a school psychologist ($p = 0.004$). Also, referral to the child welfare system was significantly more

Table 8-7. Parental Alcohol Problems in HR and LR Subjects

	HR (N = 134)	LR (N = 70)	
Father drank alcohol daily	30.6%	14.3%	$p = 0.0109$
Mother drank alcohol daily	14.2	10.0	
Father was drunk daily	8.2	1.4	
Father was drunk 2–3 times per week	7.5	0.0	$p = 0.0167$
Alcohol problems in family	53.0	25.7	$p = 0.0006$

frequent among the HR subjects. Self-reported delinquency was the same in the two groups.

In general the social history interview showed that the HR subjects experienced their home conditions during childhood as "disturbed" and that their childhood had been "bad" more frequently compared to the LR subjects (p values respectively 0.01 and 0.001).

Psychological Hypotheses

All data from the extensive psychopathology interview on the rearing type, on the parental attitudes, etc. have not yet been analyzed, and they will be reported separately in detail.

Drinking History

In table 8-8 the quantitative distribution of the drinking pattern is shown. It appears that no differences at all were found between the two risk groups. Nor was there any difference between the two groups regarding place of drinking (at home, at parties, at restaurants). The frequency of hangovers and tolerance to alcohol was also the same in the HR and LR groups.

None of the subjects, regardless of their consumption, met other criteria of alcoholism, as described by Cahalan [1]. Age at the first drink, the different motives for drinking alcohol, and attitudes toward drinking did not separate the two risk groups significantly. The prevailing motives reported were that

Table 8-8. Alcohol Consumption During Last Week in HR and LR Subjects

	HR (N = 134)	LR (N = 70)
Nothing	13.4	12.9
1–2 drinks	13.4	5.7
3–6 drinks	10.5	14.3
7–10 drinks	9.5	10.0
11–20 drinks	16.2	24.3
> 20 drinks	35.8	33.8
Mean consumption per week (no. of drinks)	16.8	17.9

alcohol made them feel glad or relaxed and that it had a good taste. In this connection the subjects were asked in detail about their possible drug experiences. Approximately 60 percent in both risk groups had experiences with cannabis. Use of other drugs was relatively infrequent and did not distinguish the two groups, apart from a tendency toward more frequent use of amphetamines in the HR group (9.2% vs. 3.5%). The difference is not significant.

Discussion and Conclusion

The results presented above form only a broad outline, primarily due to the fact that not all analyses are completed yet. We consider it worthwhile, however, to present the rationale and design together with some few variables which distinguished between the HR and LR groups. The interpretation of such differences must be cautious, in particular they have no direct etiological significance, but reflect some possible antecedants to disturbance, i.e. alcoholism [10,15]. In conclusion, we can describe the young male at high risk for alcoholism like this (when compared to his low-risk control):

1. He performs worse on the Halstead Categorizing test, WAIS vocabulary test, and Porteus' Maze test.
2. He does not show more signs of clinical personality disorder.
3. But he is more impulsive, gets more easily in fights, and behaves more nervously in the interview situation.
4. He is less "ruminative" and less antiaggressive.
5. He has had more problems in school (fails exams, referred to school psychologist).
6. His alcohol consumption, drinking pattern and attitude towards alcohol is exactly the same compared to his LR control.
7. His drug experiences are not remarkable, are dominated by cannabis, and he does not differ from the LR control.

The sample attrition was quite considerable, but the ages and social classes of the refusals did not differ significantly from the subjects who completed the assessment. From other population studies it is a general experience that young males in this age group are most difficult to motivate for participation. We intend to obtain external information about the schooling and criminality both on participants and refusals to evaluate the effect of the sample attrition.

The results concerning the same (sparse) amount of psychopathology in the two risk groups are in accordance with the results from the Danish adoption studies on alcoholism [5,6]. Our findings regarding marked impulsivity among the HR subjects are in accordance with earlier findings about the hyperactive childhood syndrome as a precursor of alcoholism [7].

The results about drinking pattern (no alcoholics, no differences between the HR and LR group) confirms that the sample was young enough for a prospective longitudinal study. The alcohol consumption seems high (see table 8-8). However, it is in full accordance with a recent study on the distribution of the alcohol consumption in the general Danish population [26].

In conclusion we feel that the "multi hypothesis" approach has already showed its validity in a high risk context.

Now we have to wait 5–10–15 years when the real index and control group will be created by nature's and society's experiment: the alcoholics and the nonalcoholics. At that time we will go back to the premorbid 1981 data to see which constellation of variables was most predictive. Then real etiologic correlations can be done, because it will be possible to distinguish sharply between antecedant factors and consequences of heavy drinking.

References

1. Cahalan, D., Cisin, I. H., and Crossby, H. M. *American Drinking Practices: A National Survey of Behavior and Attitudes*. New Brunswick, N.J.: Rutgers University Center of Alcohol Studies, 1969.
2. Christensen, J. M., Angelo, H., and Knop, J. A gaschromatographic method for determination of acetaldehyde in blood with negligable artefactual acetaldehyde formation. *Clin. Chem. Acta*. 116:389, 1981.
3. Curman, H. and Nylander, I. A 10-year prospective follow-up study of 2.268 Cases of the Child Guidance Clinics of Stockholm. *Acta Paediatr. Scand. [Suppl.]* 260:1976.
4. Dupont, A., Videbech, T., and Weeke, A. A cumulative national psychiatric register: Its structure and application. *Acta Psychiatr. Scand.* 50:161, 1974.
5. Goodwin, D. W., Schulsinger, F., Hermansen, L., et al. Alcohol problems in adoptees raised apart from alcoholic biological parents. *Arch. Gen. Psychiatry* 28:238, 1973.
6. Goodwin, D. W., Schulsinger, F., Hermansen, L., et al. Drinking problems in adopted and non-adopted sons of alcoholics. *Arch. Gen. Psychiatry* 31:164, 1975.
7. Goodwin, D. W., Schulsinger, F., Hermansen, L., Alcoholism and the hyperactive child syndrome. *J. Ment. Nerv. Dis.* 160:349, 1975.

8. Hill, S. Y. Comprehensive assessment of brain dysfunction in alcoholic individuals. In Ideström C.-M. (ed.), Alcohol and brain research. *Acta Psychiatr. Scand. [Suppl.]* 62:57, 1980.

9. Jones, M. C. Personality correlates and antecedents of drinking patterns in adult males. *J. Consult. and Clin. Psychology* 1:2, 1968.

10. Kaij, L. 1960. *Studies on the etiology and sequels of abuse of alcohol.* Ph.D. dissertation. University of Lund. Stockholm: Almquist & Wiksell.

11. Knop, J., Angelo, H., and Christensen, J. M. Is the role of acetaldehyde in alcoholism based on analytical artifact? *Lancet* 2:102, 1981.

12. Korsten, M. A., Matsuxakis, Feinman, L., and Lieber, C. S. High blood acetaldehyde levels after ethanol administration. *N. Engl. J. Med.* 292:386, 1975.

13. Major, L. F. and Murphy, D. L. Platelet plasma amine oxidase activity in alcoholic individuals. *Br. J. Psychiatry* 132:548, 1978.

14. McCord, W. and McCord, J. Origins of alcoholism. In Pitman D. J. and Snyder C. R. (eds.), *Society, Culture and Drinking Patterns.* New York: Wiley, 1962.

15. McNeil, T. F. and Kaij, L. Etiological relevance of comparisons of high-risk and low-risk groups. *Acta Psychiatr. Scand.* 59:545, 1979.

16. Mednick, S. A. A Biosocial Theory of Learning of Law Abiding Behaviour. In Mednick, S. A. and Christiansen, K. O. (eds.), *Biosocial Bases of Criminal Behaviour.* New York: Gardner Press, 1977.

17. Mednick, S. A. and Baert, A. E. *Prospective Longitudinal Research: An Empirical Basis for Primary Prevention of Psychosocial Disorders.* Oxford: Oxford University Press, 1981. (Published on behalf of the WHO Regional Office for Europe).

18. Mednick, S. A., Schulsinger, F., and Griffith, J. J. Children of Schizophrenic Mothers: The Danish High-risk Study. In Schulsinger, F., Mednick, S. A., and Knop, J. (eds.), *Longitudinal Research. Methods and Uses in Behavioral Sciences.* Boston: Martinus Nijhoff.

19. Miller, W. R. and Orr, J. Nature and Sequence of neurophysiological deficits in alcoholics. *J. Stud. Alcohol* 41:325, 1980.

20. Naitoh, P. The value of electroencephalography in alcoholism. *Ann. N.Y. Acad. Sci.* 215:303, 1980.

21. Pojesz, B. and Begleiter, H. Visual Evoked Potentials and brain Dysfunction in Chronic Alcoholics. In Begleiter, H. (ed.), *Evoked Brain Potentials and Behaviour.* New York, Plenum, 1978.

22. Propping, P. Alcoholism and alcohol. *Hum. Genet., [Suppl.]* 1:91–99.

23. Robins, L. R. *Deviant Children Grown Up: A Sociological and Psychiatric Study of Sociopathic Personality.* Baltimore: Williams & Wilkins, 1966.

24. Schukit, M. A. and Rayses, V. Ethanol ingestion differences in blood acetaldehyde concentration in relatives of alcoholics and controls. *Science* 203:54, 1979.

25. Schulsinger, F. Psychopathy: Heredity and Environment. *Int. J. Ment. Health* 1:190, 1972.

26. Vilstrup, H. and Nielsen, P. E. Distribution of the alcohol consumption in the
     Danish population in 1979. *Ugeskr. Laeger* 143:1047, 1981 (in Danish).
27. Whalley, L. J. Social and Biological Variables in Alcoholism: A Selective
     Review. In M. Sandler (ed.), *Psychopharmacology of Alcohol*. New York:
     Raven Press, 1980.
28. Zachau-Christiansen, B. and Ross, E. M. *Babies: Human Development
     During the First Year*. New York: Wiley, 1975.

9 A PROSPECTIVE STUDY OF ALCOHOLISM: ELECTROENCEPHALOGRAPHIC FINDINGS

Vicki E. Pollock,
Jan Volavka,
Sarnoff A. Mednick,
Donald W. Goodwin,
Joachim Knop, and
Fini Schulsinger

Research on biologic factors in the etiology of alcoholism was prompted by findings in family, twin and adoption studies that suggest genetic factors influence its development. These findings will be briefly reviewed, following which preliminary results from a prospective study of alcoholism are presented.

More men are alcoholic than women. The prevalence of chronic alcoholism among males is about 3–5 percent, but only 0.1–1 percent for females [22]. It is likely that these estimates reflect genuine differences in the population, and are not due to methodological or cultural biases against identifying female alcoholics [22]. As will become clear in the ensuing review, consideration of the sex of the alcoholic is important for interpreting family, twin, and adoption study findings on alcoholism.

Family Studies

Two important findings emerged from family studies on alcoholism. First, family studies revealed that the rates of alcoholism among the biologic relatives of alcoholics are higher than those observed in the general population. Cotton [13] reviewed 39 studies on familial alcoholism, providing information on 6,251 alcoholic and 4,083 nonalcoholic families. In two-thirds of those studies, 25 percent of the alcoholics had alcoholic fathers. The combined findings of these reports are impressive because in spite of numerous methodological inconsistencies, they permit the conclusion that biologic relatives of alcoholics constitute a high-risk group for alcoholism.

Interestingly, Cotton [13] detected a trend in the difference of alcoholism rates among male and female alcoholics' relatives. The biologic relatives of female alcoholics tended to have higher rates of alcoholism than those of male alcoholics. This underscores the importance of distinguishing the sexes for studying etiologic factors in alcoholism.

The second important finding to emerge from family studies of alcoholism concerns alcoholism as a specific psychiatric syndrome. Are the biologic relatives of alcoholics prone to develop alcoholism specifically, rather than other types of psychiatric syndromes? If alcoholics' relatives show higher rates of alcoholism than any other type of psychiatric disorder, this would provide tentative evidence that alcoholism constitutes a specific psychiatric syndrome. The evidence must be considered tentative inasmuch as the families share their environment as well as genetics.

The empirical evidence bearing on this issue is complex, but the answer to the question is straightforward. The evidence strongly suggests that alcoholics' families have higher rates of alcoholism rather than any other type of psychiatric disorder [13]. But here the complexities creep in. The biologic relatives of alcoholics also exhibit more psychopathologic symptoms, especially those indicative of affective disorders, than do relatives of nonalcoholics. The issue becomes especially murky if one examines family research literature on female alcoholics. The course of alcoholism in women is such that the diagnosis of alcoholism is often secondary to depression [22]. Furthermore, the daughters of male alcoholics often exhibit depressive symptomatology. Attempts to resolve these findings are hampered by the small numbers of female alcoholics that have been studied. Nonetheless, the most important point is that alcoholism is the most frequent disorder manifested by the alcoholics' relatives; other types of psychiatric disorders appear less frequently.

In summary, family studies of alcoholism provide evidence consistent with the hypothesis that alcoholism is biologically influenced. The findings are that (1) biological relatives of alcoholics have higher rates of alcoholism than those observed in the general population; and (2) that alcoholism constitutes a relatively specific psychiatric syndrome, (although the incidence of other psychiatric syndromes also appear to be elevated among alcoholics' biologic relatives).

The family study findings are consistent with the hypothesis that genetic factors influence the etiology of alcoholism. Twin and adoption studies of alcoholism were undertaken to evaluate this hypothesis.

Twin Studies

The first major twin study on alcoholism was conducted by Kaij [27] in Sweden. Kaij classified each member of 48 monozygotic (MZ) and 126 dizygotic (DZ) twins according to their severity of alcohol abuse. Each individual was classified into one of four categories of alcohol use, ranging from average to severe. Kaij found that 54.2 percent of MZs received the same classification, as compared to 31.2 percent of DZs. These results indicate that MZs exhibit more similar patterns of alcohol abuse than DZs.

It is possible that Kaij's results reflect conservative estimates for similarity of alcohol use among twins, because the sample did not include twins who abstained from alcohol, or those who consumed very little. This is important because in another twin study, the highest heritabilities were obtained for two features predisposing against alcohol use. Loehlin [30] reported the highest heritabilities for hangovers and not abusing alcohol, while heritability for excessive use of alcohol was lower.

Other twin study findings also emphasize the importance of studying alcohol abuse as well as abstinence. Partanen, Brunn, and Markkanen [37] studied 902 male twins' drinking practices. Factor analyses yielded three variables which described their drinking behaviors: (1) frequency of ethanol consumption, (2) amount of ethanol consumed per drinking session, and (3) loss of control over drinking. Heritabilities for the first two factors were 0.39 and 0.36 respectively. This result indicates that quantity and frequency of ethanol consumption is genetically influenced, a conclusion also warranted by Jonsson & Nilsson's [26] study of 750 male twin pairs. The strongest evidence of genetic influence was observed when drinkers and abstainers were compared.

The observation that MZ twins show more similarity in amount and frequency of ethanol consumption as compared to DZs may be related to ethanol metabolism rate. It is widely acknowledged that ethanol metabolism rates are genetically determined; it is therefore not too surprising to find that MZ twins show more similarities in terms of amount and frequency of ethanol consumption than DZ twins.

The twin study findings suggest two important considerations to be addressed in research on alcoholism. First, it is important to consider factors that mediate abstinence from alcohol as well as those that contribute to alcoholism. Second, the studies suggest that alcoholism (and abstinence from alcohol) may be mediated by genetically determined biological features.

Adoption Studies

Persuasive evidence for genetic factors in the etiology of alcoholism is derived from results of adoption studies on alcoholism. With one exception, adoption studies of alcoholism among females are based on such small samples that the results do not permit firm inferences.

Goodwin [23] conducted an adoption study of alcoholism in Denmark. He used material derived from interviews with adoptees, as well as information available on alcohol abuse among adoptees and both sets of their parents through information maintained by the Danish government. Goodwin found that the adopted-away sons of alcoholics were four times more likely to develop alcoholism than control adoptees. Since Goodwin's report, all subsequent adoption studies of alcoholism furnish results consistent with his. Cadoret and Gath [8] found higher rates of alcoholism among adoptees (N = 84) with a biological history of alcoholism as compared to controls. Bohman [6] used information on 2,000 adoptees available through Swedish governmental sources, and obtained a significant positive association between biologic parents' alcohol abuse and their adopted-away sons extent of alcohol use.

The distinction between alcoholism and heavy drinking is an important one. Roe [40] conducted an adoption study of alcoholism in the United States. Adopted children whose biologic parents were heavy drinkers (N = 27) were compared to foster control children (N = 22) on the basis of their adult drinking problems. No significant differences in adult drinking problems were found to distinguish the two groups of adoptees.

Although Roe's findings appear inconsistent with the bulk of adoption study results on alcoholism, Goodwin attempted to resolve the discrepancy. Goodwin [21] used the data he acquired in Denmark to compare rates of heavy drinking by adopted-away sons of alcoholics to control adoptees, and found no difference between the two groups. It was only when a strict definition of alcoholism was used that the adopted-away sons of alcoholics showed higher rates of alcoholism than controls; heavy drinking did not distinguish them.

An elegant adoption study of alcoholism was recently reported by Cloninger, Bohman, and Sigvardsson [10] that supports and refines previous findings of adoption studies on alcoholism. The study was conducted in Sweden, and its results relating severity of alcohol abuse among the adoptees to their biologic and adoptive parents' alcohol abuse led Cloninger and colleagues to postulate that there are two types of alcoholism, with differing extents of genetic and environmental influence.

Finally, the Swedish group has recently conducted the first adoption study of alcoholism among females with a large enough sample size to permit some tentative conclusions [6]. Using information derived from the Swedish Temperance Board register, the severity of alcohol abuse was assessed among 913 adopted women in relation to their biologic and adoptive parents extent of alcohol abuse. Among females, it appears that the biologic *mothers'* degree of alcohol abuse is a critical factor influencing alcohol use among their biological daughters.

A Prospective Study of Alcoholism

The evidence from family, twin, and adoption studies indicate that genetic factors influence the etiology of alcoholism. Therefore, research on genetically influenced biologic characteristics in prospective studies of alcoholism can prove useful in two ways. First, such research may furnish insights regarding specific biologic characteristics important to its etiology. Second, provided the indices used to assess biologic characteristics can be reliably measured from the intact, living human, it may be possible to *predict* which individuals are likely to become alcoholic *before* they develop it.

Biologic differences between alcoholics and controls have been reported in research findings spanning over four decades [31]. These studies share one common drawback: it is impossible to establish whether features associated with alcoholism constitute *antecedents* or consequences of alcohol dependence. Since deviant features observed among chronic alcoholics may represent consequences of alcohol abuse, it is not possible to draw definite conclusions regarding etiology on the basis of these research findings. For development of etiologic theory, we must determine whether such deviancies precede development of alcoholism. This important issue relating to theories of etiology can only be resolved within the context of a prospective, longitudinal study in which individuals are examined *before* they become alcoholic.

The biologic sons of alcoholics constitute one group at high risk (HR) for alcoholism [21] and are the subjects in this study. During 1979, we initiated a prospective study of alcoholism in Denmark. The HR (N = 134) and control (N = 70) subjects were then 19–21 years old and none were alcoholic. Sociological, psychological, and physiologic data were acquired. The electroencephalographic (EEG) findings are discussed in this report.

The remainder of this paper is divided into two sections. In the first, the EEG activity of subjects at HR for alcoholism is compared to controls. In the second, EEG changes that distinguish HR from control subjects after acute ethanol administration are presented.

EEG Activity in High-Risk Subjects

Estimates for the incidence of EEG abnormalities among chronic alcoholics range from 20 percent [29] to 79 percent [4]. The types of abnormalities exhibited by chronic alcoholics are excessive slow (e.g., delta, theta; [11]) and fast (e.g. beta; [11]; [45]) EEG activity. Alcoholics also exhibit deficient alpha activity while sober [18,29]. From studies on chronic alcoholics, it is impossible to know whether these EEG deviancies represent physiopathologic consequences of sustained alcohol abuse, or existed prior to the alcoholics' prolonged ethanol intake.

Studies utilizing electroencephalographic [4,16], computerized axial tomographic (CATs; [9]), and neuropsychologic indices [16,35] indicate abnormalities of brain function manifested by chronic alcoholics may revert to normal following abstinence from alcohol. These findings suggest that the EEG abnormalities observed among chronic alcoholics are likely to be consequences of prolonged ethanol intake.

Only one previous prospective study on alcoholism included EEG indices; its results suggest that EEGs of children at high risk for alcoholism differ from those of controls [19]. In that study, the EEGs of biologic sons of alcoholics contained higher amounts of relative beta than controls when they were 12 years old. There was no evidence that the 12-year old biologic sons of alcoholics showed elevations of relative delta or theta in their EEGs as compared to controls. This result suggests that higher amounts of relative beta activity could be an antecedent of alcoholism, and may function as a biological marker to identify persons with a genetic predisposition to alcoholism.

The hypothesis that elevations of beta characterize the EEGs of males at high risk for alcoholism receives evaluation in this section. Additional analyses performed are designed to evaluate the possibilities that delta, theta, and alpha activity distinguish the EEGs of subjects at high risk for alcoholism from controls.

Procedure

Subjects

The subjects were selected from a perinatal birth cohort [50]. Subjects deemed to be at high risk for alcoholism were those males of the birth cohort whose fathers had been admitted to a Danish hospital or clinic with a diagnosis of alcoholism. Control subjects were selected from among those members of the birth cohort whose fathers had not received a diagnosis of alcoholism, and were matched to pairs of HR subjects for sex, age, and social class.

All subjects were contacted by mail and invited to participate in a reassessment of the perinatal birth project [46]. Such reassessments have been conducted in the past. It is thus unlikely that subjects who participated in this project possessed direct knowledge that the purpose of this investigation was a prospective study of alcoholism. At the time of testing, the subjects ranged in age 19–21, and none had yet begun heavy drinking. All procedures were blind.

The sample identified consisted of 250 HR and 125 control subjects: of these, 134 HR and 70 controls participated in this study. The remaining subjects were unavailable for various reasons (death, emigration, refusal).

Drinking Practices.   All subjects were interviewed about their drinking practices. They were asked to report the age at which they first had an alcoholic beverage, and their age when first drunk; how much alcohol they had to drink before feeling "affected" by it, to be "tipsy" or to feel "drunk"; whether or not the quantities of alcohol to achieve these subjective states had altered during the past year; and how frequently they experienced hangovers. Multiple t-tests were used for analyses.

Alcohol Consumption.   All subjects were asked how much beer, wine, and hard liquor they had consumed during the previous week. This information was used as an estimate of subjects "typical" alcohol consumption. The quantities of beverages reported by subjects were converted to grams of ethanol for analysis. Multiple t-tests were used for analyses.

EEG. The montage for EEG recording included bilateral temporal (T3, T4) central (C3, C4), parietal (P3, P4) and occipital (01, 02) scalp derivations. All electrode scalp placements were performed according to the International 10/20 System [24] with scalp recordings referenced to linked ears.

Two minutes of EEG data were acquired as the subject sat, at rest, with his eyes closed. All EEG records were visually inspected by an experimenter unaware of the subjects' group membership to delete epochs contaminated by artifacts. For each 2-minute EEG recording a minimum of six, 2.5 second artifact free epochs were subjected to Fast Fourier Transformation (FFT) by computer. The A/D sampling rate was 256 cycles per second (c/sec) and bandpass was 0.3–40 cycles per second (c/sec).

Energy for each of the eight scalp derivations in the delta (0.78–3.12 c/sec), theta (3.51–7.03 c/sec), slow alpha (7.42–9.46 c/sec) fast alpha (9.75–12.10 c/sec) and beta (12.5–25.0 c/sec) frequency bands were obtained. The mean alpha frequency (for activity between 7.42–12.10 c/sec) was also obtained separately for each scalp derivation according to methods described previously [48]. Chi-squares and multivariate analyses of variance (MANOVAs) were used to compare HR and control subjects EEGs.

Results

Drinking Practices. The T-tests do not indicate that HR and control subjects differ significantly with regard to their self-reported drinking practices.

Alcohol Consumption. Estimates of subjects ethanol consumption during one week do not distinguish HR (MEAN = 202g) from control (MEAN = 221 g) subjects.

EEG. Inspection of the EEG data revealed that temporal scalp derivation recordings were frequently contaminated by muscle artifacts. Chi-squares to compare the number of HR and control subjects temporal scalp derivation recordings excluded due to muscle artifacts were performed separately for T3 and T4. The results suggest that more HR subjects data from the left temporal derivation (50.4%) were contaminated by muscle artifacts than controls (36.5%; chi-square, df = 1: 2.15, $p = 0.15$). For the right temporal derivation, deletions due to muscle artifacts do not tend to distinguish HR (36.1%) from controls (29.0%: chi-square, df = 1: 0.629, NS).

Due to the large number of subjects that showed muscle contamination in temporal scalp recordings, EEG energy and frequency measures derived from them were excluded from all subsequent analyses. MANOVAs were used to compared HR and control subjects EEGs using data from the bilateral central, parietal and occipital derivations with the restriction that subjects had no missing data. These procedures reduced the number of subjects for EEG comparisons to 107 HR and 57 controls.

Three independent variables were evaluated by MANOVAs: risk status for alcoholism (2 levels: HR vs. controls); scalp region (3 levels: central, parietal, or occipital scalp sites); and laterality (2 levels: left vs. right scalp regions). In total 7 such MANOVAs were performed: the dependent variables were energy in the delta, theta, slow alpha, fast alpha and beta bands; relative (or percentage) beta; and mean alpha frequency. All main effects and interactions were evaluated in each MANOVA, but only results that distinguish HR and control subjects EEGs are presented. None of the main effects for risk status were statistically significant.

Beta. A statistically significant risk $\times$ laterality interaction was obtained for analysis of beta energy ($F(1,162) = 4.72$, $p \leq 0.05$). Because the laterality $\times$ scalp region interaction was also significant ($F(2,161) = 26.33$, $p \leq 0.01$) simple interaction tests of the laterality $\times$ risk interaction were undertaken separately for central, parietal and occipital scalp regions.

The simple risk $\times$ laterality interaction was significant for the parietal ($F(1,162) = 5.65$, $p \leq 0.02$) but not for the central or occipital scalp regions. The means indicate that HR subjects show more bilateral symmetry of beta in the parietal region (MEANS: left parietal = 5.068, right parietal = 5.270) than controls (MEANS: left parietal = 4.851, right parietal = 5.297). Between group t-tests of these means were not statistically significant.

Relative beta is defined as the ratio of beta energy to total energy. A MANOVA was performed using relative beta as a dependent variable in an attempt to replicate the finding that 12-year old sons of alcoholics show more relative beta than controls. Although the laterality $\times$ scalp region interaction was statistically significant ($F(2,161) = 4.68$, $p \leq 0.02$), the laterality $\times$ risk interaction was not ($F(1,162) = 3.17$, $p \leq 0.08$) when relative, rather than energy measures were used as dependent variables for analysis of beta.

Alpha. Analyses for slow alpha energy, fast alpha energy and mean alpha frequency do not suggest that EEGs of the HR differ from those of control subjects.

Delta and Theta. MANOVAs for delta and theta energy revealed statistically significant interactions between risk, scalp region and laterality (delta: $F(2,161) = 4.42$, p ≤ 0.02; theta: $F(2,161) = 4.84$, p ≤ 0.01). Tests for simple interactions of risk and laterality were performed separately for delta and theta bands at the central, parietal and occipital scalp regions.

For delta, a significant laterality $\times$ risk interaction was obtained in the central, ($F(1,162) = 3.88$, p ≤ 0.05) but not for the parietal or occipital scalp regions. The HR subjects show more bilateral asymmetry of delta in the central scalp regions (MEANS: left central = 12.58, right central = 13.02) than controls (MEANS: left central = 12.58, right central = 12.60). Between group t-tests of these means were not statistically significant.

For theta, the lateratity $\times$ risk interaction was significant for the parietal ($F(1,162) = 6.53$, p ≤ 0.02) but not the central or occipital scalp regions. The means indicate that HR subjects show greater bilateral theta symmetry (MEANS: left parietal = 7.46, right parietal = 7.30) than controls (MEANS: left parietal = 7.21, right parietal = 7.44). Between group t-tests of these means were not statistically significant.

Comment

Lateral differences, based on quantitative measures of EEG delta, theta and beta activity distinguish subjects at high risk for alcoholism from controls. The HR subjects show higher delta energy in the right, as compared to left central scalp derivation; but they show *less* bilateral asymmetry of theta and beta energy in parietal scalp regions than do controls. The HR subjects do not exhibit elevations of slow (delta, theta) or fast (beta) EEG activity, nor do they exhibit deficient alpha as compared to controls. Only lateralized differences in slow and fast EEG activity distinguish the HR and control subjects.

The results of a previous prospective study on alcoholism [19] indicated that the EEGs of males at high risk for alcoholism contain higher amounts of relative beta than controls. We attempted to replicate this finding using both absolute and relative measures of EEG beta, but were unable to do so. There are at least two issues relevant to reconciling the different outcomes in these studies. In Gabrielli's et al.'s report [19], the HR subjects were 11–13 years old when EEG data were acquired; the subjects in this study were 19–21 years of age when tested. Although extensive data relating age to EEG changes exist for normal populations [25] comparable developmental EEG data among groups at risk for varied psychopathologies do not. Individuals at high risk for psychopathology may not exhibit the same developmental EEG trajectories shown by normal subjects. Prospective psychopathologic studies that include EEG recordings derived from the same individuals at different ages are required to evaluate this hypothesis.

The second issue relevant to reconciling our findings with those reported by Gabrielli et al. [19] concern the subject samples. In both studies, subjects at HR for alcoholism were defined as the biologic sons of alcoholics. These subjects, however, constitute a heterogenous group: not only are they at high risk for alcoholism, they are at high risk for other psychiatric disorders, too [13]. Directly comparing the outcome of Gabrielli et al.'s [19] study with the results reported here will not be possible until follow-up studies are conducted. At that time, the EEGs of pre-alcoholics can be evaluated.

The lateralized differences that distinguish subjects at HR for alcoholism from controls were based only on EEG measures in this study; their relationship to other laterality measures, such as handedness and neuropsychological indices awaits assessment. Both behavioral [47] and electrophysiologic studies of normal humans [39] indicate that acute ethanol administration selectively suppresses right hemisphere functioning. Neuropsychologic observations of alcoholics suggest they suffer right hemisphere dysfunction [7,36]. Such findings make it tempting to speculate that lateralized impairments exhibited by chronic alcoholics reflect consequences of long-term alcohol abuse. The EEG results of this study, however, suggest that lateralized hemispheric differences may characterize individuals at high risk for alcoholism *before* they begin drinking heavily.

Laterality differences in theta and beta that distinguish the EEGs of subjects at high risk for alcoholism from controls were localized to the parietal scalp region. Neurologic studies have shown that frontal and parietal lobe atrophy characterize alcoholics; therefore, cortical atrophy may be a consequence of long-term alcohol abuse. The results in this study, however, suggest that parietal lobe differences may distinguish persons with a biologic predisposition to alcoholism from controls *before* they begin drinking heavily.

Lateral differences in temporal muscle activity tended to distinguish subjects at high risk for alcoholism from controls. There was a tendency for more HR subjects to exhibit muscle activity in the left temporal scalp derivation. This finding suggests that the HR subjects may not have been as relaxed as controls during EEG recording sessions [20]. The subjects behavior during an interview was assessed by a psychologist's ratings know whether the subject was HR or control. The psychologist's ratings indicate that more HR subjects appeared tense throughout the entire interview, whereas control subjects exhibited initial nervousness that disappeared. This behavioral evidence provides independent support of the interpretation that HR subjects were not relaxed during EEG recordings.

Research on laterality in psychopathology is relevant to these findings. Schizophrenics are likely to exhibit dominant (left) hemisphere dysfunction [17] whereas patients with affective disorders are likely to show non-dominant hemisphere impairments [1,44]. The hypothesis that similar genetic mechanisms underly the etiology of alcoholism and affective disorder is puzzling in light of these temporal EEG findings. The tendency of males at HR for alcoholism to exhibit muscle activity in the left temporal scalp region might suggest the etiology of alcoholism is more closely related to schizophrenia rather than affective disorders.

EEG Changes After Ethanol Administration

Many chronic alcoholics exhibit deficient alpha activity while sober [18,29]. Alpha increases in normal subjects [2] and chronic alcoholics [14] can be elicited by administration of moderate alcohol doses. These observations suggest that prealcoholics may be characterized by reduced alpha activity, and that such persons are susceptible to alcoholism because drinking enables them to attain a subjective state associated with increased alpha [14]. The hypothesis evaluated in this section is that subjects at high risk for alcoholism will exhibit different alpha changes after alcohol than controls.

Procedure

Subjects. Only a subset of subjects (described above) participated in experimental alcohol session (N = 72, 44 HR and 28 controls). The subjects free at times corresponding to the laboratory schedule allotted for alcohol sessions were invited to participate. The procedure was blind, so that persons who had contact with the subjects at the time of the experiment did not know whether they were HR or controls. Information regarding these subjects drinking practices and ethanol consumption were acquired according to methods described above.

Subjects drank a solution containing 0.5 g/kg 95% ethanol dissolved in currant juice during a 15-minute period two hours after lunch. All were informed that the beverages contained a "small" amount of alcohol.

BACs. Blood samples were obtained 40 and 130 minutes after alcohol administration. Gas chromatography was used for blood alcohol concentration (BAC) assays. Due to technical difficulties, BACs are only available on a limited number of subjects.

EEG. Two-minute EEG recordings were obtained before and 30, 60, and 120 minutes after subjects finished the drink. The International 10/20 System for electrode placement was used [24]. Bilateral temporal (T3, T4) central (C3, C4) parietal (P3, P4) and occipital (01, 02) scalp derivations were inspected by an experimenter unaware of the subjects' group membership for artifact deletion. A minimum of six 2.5 second artifact free epochs were subjected to Fast Fourier Transformation (FFT). Bandpass was 0.3–40 c/sec. Energy in the slow (7.42–9.46 c/sec) and in the fast 9.75–12.10 c/sec) alpha frequency bands were obtained. The mean alpha frequency for EEG activity between 7.42 and 12.10 c/sec was also obtained.

Results

Drinking Practices. Eleven t-tests were performed in order to compare the 31 HR and 17 control subjects whose EEG data were statistically analyzed. Only one of the t-tests was statistically significant: HR subjects reported requiring more drinks (MEAN = 3.4 drinks) than controls (MEAN = 2.8 drinks) in order to feel "tipsy" ($t(28) = 2.43$, $p \leq 0.05$).

Ethanol Consumption. Estimates of the HR subjects' ethanol consumption during the course of one week (MEAN = 249 grams) were not significantly greater than estimates of control subjects' ethanol consumption for one week (MEAN = 248 grams).

BACs. Results of the t-tests do not indicate that HR and control subjects' BACs differ significantly 40 minutes (MEAN ± SEM: HR (N = 18), 36.16 mg/dl ± 1.54; controls (N = 14), 35.92 ± 2.64) or 130 minutes (HR (N = 19), 28.95 ± 1.89; controls (N = 15), 32.06 ± 1.61) after alcohol administration.

EEG. The data for temporal scalp derivations were often contaminated by muscle artifacts, and therefore were not statistically analyzed. Additionally, the analyses described require that each subject yield complete EEG data for six scalp derivations at each of four time periods. This requirement reduced the sample size for analyses of EEGs to 31 HR and 17 control subjects. The number of HR and control subjects EEG data excluded did not differ significantly (chi-square, df(1) = 1.07, NS).

Slow and Fast Alpha Energy. Alpha energy was evaluated by multivariate analysis of variance (MANOVA). The dependent variables were slow and fast alpha energy. The five independent variables were risk status for alcoholism (2 levels: HR vs. controls); time relative to alcohol administration (4 levels: before or 30, 60, or 120 minutes after alcohol); alpha band (2 levels: slow vs. fast alpha); scalp region (3 levels: central, parietal, or occipital scalp regions); and laterality (2 levels: left vs. right scalp sites). All main effects and interactions were examined, but only results relevant to risk status for alcoholism are presented here.

The risk main effect, which compares HR to control subjects, was not statistically significant. A significant interaction involving the factors risk, time and alpha band was obtained (F(3,44) = 5.82, p ≤ 0.01). The means for slow and fast alpha energy are depicted in the upper and lower panels of figure 9-1.

Univariate repeated measures ANOVAs were used to compare HR and control subjects pre-alcohol slow alpha energy to their slow alpha energy levels at each of the 3 postalcohol time periods. The HR subjects showed significantly greater increases of slow alpha energy than controls 30 minutes ($F(1,46) = 10.04$, p ≤ 0.01) and 120 minutes ($F(1,46) = 6.42$, p ≤ 0.02) after alcohol. Elevations of slow alpha energy 60 minutes after alcohol administration among HR subjects were not significantly greater than those shown by controls.

The lower panel of figure 9-1 shows that HR and control subjects' levels of fast alpha energy were similar prior to alcohol administration. The figure also shows that both HR and control subjects exhibit decreases in fast alpha energy 30 and 60 minutes after alcohol, but the HR subjects continue to exhibit low levels of fast alpha energy 120 minutes after alcohol, whereas controls do not. Univariate repeated measures analyses were used to compare prealcohol fast alpha energy levels of HR and control subjects to their fast alpha energy levels after drinking, separately for the 3 post alcohol time periods. Reductions of fast alpha energy 30 and 60 minutes after alcohol administration did not differentiate HR from control subjects. The reduction of fast alpha energy shown by HR subjects was statistically greater 120 minutes after alcohol as compared to controls ($F(1,46) = 6.85$, p ≤ 0.02).

Mean Alpha Frequency. A MANOVA was used to evaluate mean alpha frequency as a dependent variable. The four independent variables were risk status for alcoholism; time relative to alcohol administration; scalp region; and laterality.

The main effect for risk was not statistically significant. A statistically significant interaction involving the factors risk and time was obtained ($F(3,44) = 6.25$, p ≤ 0.01). Figure 9-2 depicts mean alpha frequencies for

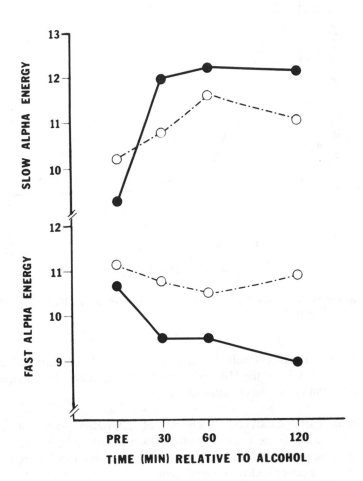

Figure 9-1. Slow and Fast Alpha Energy Before and After Alcohol Administration

Each point for the high risk sample represents the mean of 31 subjects; points for controls are based on 17 subjects. The values represent averages from six scalp sites.

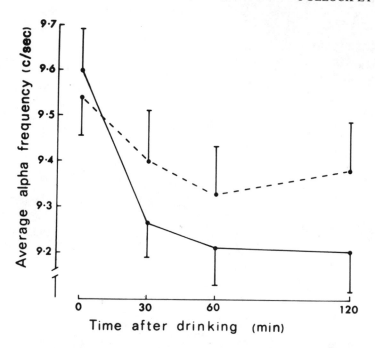

Figure 9-2. Mean Alpha Frequency Before and After Alcohol Administration

HR and control subjects before and after alcohol administration. Between group t-tests reveal that the HR and control subjects mean alpha frequencies differ significantly two hours after drinking.

Additional EEG Analyses. Inclusion of estimated grams of alcohol consumed as a covariate in analyses for slow and fast alpha energy, and for mean alpha frequency did not alter the statistical probability levels at which the interactions described were significant.

Comment

The principal finding is that subjects at high risk for alcoholism can be differentiated from controls after a single dose of alcohol using quantitative

Each point for the high risk sample represents the average of 31 subjects; points for controls are based on 17 subjects. The values represent averages from six scalp sites.

measures of EEG alpha. These findings are independent of subjects' alcohol consumption and appear to be unrelated to their current drinking practices.

Three speculations concerning intepretation of our results are proffered. First, the EEG changes that occur after alcohol administration may function as biological markers for CNS sensitivity to alcohol. There is some evidence to support this hypothesis. On the basis of their response to ethanol, different genetic strains of mice can be distinguished utilizing central nervous system indices, even though their ethanol metabolism rates do not differ [41, 45]. In humans, Propping [38] reported that identical twins show greater similarity in their EEG response to ethanol than do fraternal twins, even though the BAC curves of the identical twins are not more similar to one another than those of fraternal twins. Both findings imply that CNS sensitivity to ethanol is genetically determined.

Nongenetic interpretations of our results are also possible. We cannot exclude the possibility that mothers of some subjects drank during pregnancy, exposing the subjects to alcohol in utero. Nor can we convincingly exclude the possibility that some of the subjects tested in this study may have already developed tolerance to ethanol. The group mean ages at which HR and control subjects first reported consuming an alcoholic beverage were 11.26 years for HR and 11.57 years for controls. The mean age at which they first reported being drunk were 13.10 years for HR and 14.50 for controls. Since these subjects were 19 to 21 years old when tested, it is conceivable that some of them have been consuming large enough quantities of alcohol during long enough time periods to have developed tolerance. More critical to our findings, however, is whether more HR subjects may have developed tolerance to ethanol as compared to controls.

The evidence obtained in this study bearing on this issue is equivocal: even though the HR subjects did not report requiring more drinks in order to feel "high" or "drunk", the HR subjects did report requiring more drinks than controls in order to feel "tipsy." We have no other data to indicate whether such differences can be ascribed to longer durations of heavy ethanol intake among HR subjects, or whether it reflects differences in acute tolerance to ethanol effects among HR and control subjects.

A second speculation concerns periphereal metabolic processes as mediators of the differential EEG responses to ethanol exhibited by HR and control subjects. Evidence indicates that ethanol metabolism rates are genetically determined [49], but only weak associations between alcohol induced EEG changes and BACs have been obtained in previous research [2]. In this study, as well as others [42], BACs failed to distinguish HR from control subjects. On the other hand acetaldehyde mediates some of the EEG changes that occur after ethanol [32] and Schuckit's [43] findings (awaiting confirmation) suggest that HR males may exhibit higher levels of acetaldehyde than controls after alcohol administration. It is possible that the larger magnitudes of alpha changes shown by HR subjects are related to higher acetaldehyde concentrations after alcohol, but we have no adequate data to explore this hypothesis. We attempted to obtain measures of acetaldehyde in our subjects; our problems with the assay are reported elsewhere [28].

The third speculation relevant to interpretation to these results concerns the influence of subjects psychological expectations of alcohol effects [5] and their relation to the EEG. All subjects were informed that they would receive alcohol. It is possible that children who reside with an alcoholic parent have a realistic basis to formulate a different set of psychological expectancies about the potency of alcohol's effects than others. The procedures used in this study were blind, but the high-risk subjects were not.

References

1. Abrams, R. and Taylor, M. A. Differential EEG patterns in affective disorder and schizophrenia. *Arch. Gen. Psychiat* 36:1355, 1979.
2. Begleiter, H. and Platz, A. The Effects of Alcohol on the Central Nervous System in Humans. In Kissin, B. and Begleiter, H. (eds.), *The Biology of Alcoholism* Vol. 2: *Physiology and Behavior*. New York: Plenum Press, 1972.
3. Bennett, A. E. Diagnosis of intermediate state of alcoholic brain disease. *J.A.M.A.* 172:1143, 1960.
4. Bennett, A. E., Dot., L. T., and Mowrey, G. E. The value of electroencephalography in alcoholism. *J. Nev. Ment. Dis.* 124:27, 1956.
5. Berg C., Laberg, J. C., Skutle, A., and Ohman, A. Instructed versus pharmacological effects of alcohol in alcoholics and social drinkers. *Behav. Res. Ther.* 19:55, 1981.
6. Bohman, M. Some genetic aspects of alcoholism and criminality. *Arch. Gen. Psychiatry* 35:269, 1978.
7. Butters, N. and Cermak, L. S. *Alcoholic Korsakoff's Syndrome*. New York: Academic Press, 1980.
8. Cadoret, R. J. and Gath, A. Inheritance of alcoholism in adoptees. *Br. J. Psychiatry* 132:252, 1978.
9. Carlen, P. L., Wortzman, G., Holgath, R. C., et al. Reversible cerebral atrophy in recently abstinent chronic alcoholics measured by computed tomography scans. *Science* 200:1076, 1978.
10. Cloninger, C. R., Bohman, M., and Sigvardsson, S. Inheritance of alcohol abuse. *Arch. Gen. Psychiatry* 38:861, 1981.

11. Coger, R. W., Dymond, A. M., Serafetinides, E. A., et al. EEG signs of brain impairment in alcoholism. *Biol. Psychiatry* 13:729, 1978.

12. Coger, R. W., Dymond, A. M., and Serafetinides, E. A. Electroencephalographic similarities between chronic alcoholics and chronic non-paranoid schizophrenics. *Arch. Gen. Psychiatry* 36:91, 1979.

13. Cotton, N. S. The familial incidence of alcoholism. *J. Stud. Alcohol* 40:89, 1979.

14. Docter, R. F., Naitoh, P., and Smith, J. C. Electroencephalographic changes and vigilance behavior during experimentally induced intoxication with alcoholic subjects. *Psychosom. Med.* 28:605, 1966.

15. Epstein, P. E., Pisani, V. D., and Fawcett, J. A. Alcoholism and cerebral atrophy. *Alcohol Clin. Exp. Res.* 1:61, 1977.

16. Fleming, A. M. M. and Guthrie, A. The Electroencephalogram, Psychological Testing and Other Investigations in Abstinent Alcoholics: A Longitudinal Study. In Begleiter, H. (ed.), *Biological Effects of Alcohol*. New York: Plenum Press, 1980.

17. Flor-Henry, P. and Yeudall, L. T. Neuropsychological Investigation on Schizophrenia and Manic-depressive Psychoses. In Gruzelier, J. and Flor-Henry, P. (eds.), *Hemisphere Asymmetries of Function in Psychopathology*. Amsterdam: Elsevier, 1979.

18. Funkhauser, J. B., Nagler, B., and Walker, N. D. The electroencephalogram of chronic alcoholism. *South Med. J.* 46:423, 1953.

19. Gabrielli, W. F., Mednick, S. A., Volavka, J., et al. Electroencephalograms in children of alcoholic fathers. *Psychophysiol.* 19:404, 1982.

20. Goldstein, L. Some Relationships Between Quantified Hemispheric EEG and Behavioral States in Man. In Gruzelier, J. and Flor-Henry, P. (eds.), *Hemisphere Asymmetries of Function in Psychopathology*. Amsterdam: Elsevier, 1979.

21. Goodwin, D. W. Family and Adoption Studies of Alcoholism. In Mednick, S. A. and Christiansen, K. O. (eds.), *Biosocial Bases of Criminal Behavior*. New York: Gardner Press, 1977.

22. Goodwin, D. W. *Alcoholism: The Facts*. New York: Oxford University Press, 1981.

23. Goodwin, D. W., Schulsinger, F., Moller, et al. Drinking problems in adopted and non adopted sons of alcoholics. *Arch. Gen. Psychiatry* 31:164, 1974.

24. Jasper, H. H. The ten-twenty electrode system of the International Federation. *EEG. clin. Neurophysiol.* 10:371, 1958.

25. John, E. R., Ahn, H., Prichep, L., et al. Developmental equations for the electroencephalogram. *Science* 210:1255, 1980.

26. Jonsson, A. E. and Nilsson, T. Alkoholkonsumption hos monozygota och dizygota tvillingar. *Nord. Hyg. Tidsk.* 49:21, 1968.

27. Kaij, L. Studies on the etiology and sequela of abuse of alcohol. Department of Psychiatry, University of Lund, 1960.

28. Knop, J., Angelo, H., and Christensen, J. M. Is role of acetaldehyde in alcoholism based on analytical artifact? *Lancet 2*, 1981 (Jul) 102.

29. Little, S. C. and McAvoy, M. Electroencephalographic studies in alcoholism. *Q. J. Stud. Alcohol*, 13:9, 1952.
30. Loehlin, J. C. An analysis of alcohol related questionnaire items from the National Merit Twin study, in press.
31. Mendelson, J. H. and Mello, N. K. Biologic concomittants of alcoholism. *N. Engl. J. Med.* 301:912, 1979.
32. Mikeska, J. A. and Klemm, W. R. Evidence against a role of acetaldehyde in electroencephalographic signs of ethanol-induced intoxication. *Science* 203:27, 1979.
33. Naitoh, P. The value of electroencephalography in alcoholism. *Ann. N.Y. Acad. Sci.* 215:303, 1973.
34. Newman, S. E. The EEG manifestations of chronic ethanol abuse: relation to cerebral cortical atrophy. *Ann. Neurol.* 3:299, 1978.
35. Page, R. D. and Linden, J. D. Reversible organic brain syndromes in alcoholics: a psychometric evaluation. *Q. J. Stud. Alcohol* 35:98, 1974.
36. Parsons, O. A. Brain damage in alcoholics: altered states of unconsciousness. In Gross, M. (ed.), *Alcohol Intoxication and Withdrawal II*. New York: Plenum Press, 1975.
37. Partanen, J., Brunn, K., and Markkanen, T. *Inheritance of Drinking Behavior*. New Brunswick: Rutgers University Center of Alcohol Studies, 1966.
38. Propping, P. Alcohol and alcoholism. Human genetic variation in response to medical and environmental agents: pharmacogenetics and ecogenetics. *Hum. Genet. [Suppl. 1]*:91, 1978.
39. Rhodes, L. E., Obitz, F. W., and Creel, D. Effect of alcohol and task on hemispheric assymmetry of visually evoked potentials in man. *EEG clin. Neurophysiol.* 38:561, 1975.
40. Roe, A. The adult adjustment of children of alcoholic parents raised in foster homes *Q. J. Stud. Alcohol*, 5:378, 1944.
41. Ryan, L., Barr, J., and Sharpless, S. Electrophysiological responses to ethanol, pentobarbital and nicotine in mice genetically selected for differential sensitivity to ethanol, *J. Comp. Physiol. Psychol.* 93: 1035, 1979.
42. Schuckit, M. A. Peak blood alcohol concentrations in men at high risk for the future development of alcoholism. *Alcohol Clin. Exp. Res.* 5:64, 1981.
43. Schuckit, M. A. and Rayses, V.: Ethanol ingestion. Differences in blood acetaldehyde concentrations in relatives of alcoholics and controls. *Science* 203:54, 1979.
44. Taylor, M. A., Redfield, J., and Abrams, R. Neuropsychological dysfunction in schizophrenia and affective disease. *Biol. Psychiatry* 16:467, 1981.
45. Tabakoff, B., Ritzmann, R., Raju, T. and Deitrich, R. Characterization of acute and chronic tolerance in mice selected for inherent differences in sensitivity to ethanol. *Alc. Clin. Exp. Res.* 5:64, 1980.
46. Utne, H., Hansen, F., Winkler, K. & Schulsinger, F. Alcohol elimination rates in adoptees with and without alcoholic parents. *J. Stud. Alcohol* 38: 1219, 1977.

47. Valeriote, C., Tong, J. E., and Durding, B. Ethanol, tobacco, and laterality effects on simple and complex motor performance. *J. Stud. Alcohol* 40:823, 1979.
48. Volavka, J., James, B., Reker, D., et al. Electroencephalographic effects of naloxone in normal men. *Life Sci.* 25:1267, 1979.
49. Wallgren, H. & Barry, H. *Actions of Alcohol, Volume 1.* Amsterdam: Elsevier, 1970.
50. Zachau-Christiansen, B. and Ross, E. M. *Babies: Human Development during the First Year.* New York: Wiley, 1975.
51. Zilm, D. H., Huszar, L., Carlen, P. L., et al. EEG correlates of the alcohol induced organic brain syndrome in man. *Clin. Toxicol.* 16:345, 1980.

10 PROSPECTIVE MARKERS FOR ALCOHOLISM

Marc A. Schuckit

The importance of genetic factors in the development of alcoholism has been supported over the years by family, genetic marker, animal, twin, and adoption studies [15,38]. Numerous adoption-type investigations have shown that sons and daughters of alcoholics adopted out close to birth have four times or higher elevated risk for alcoholism themselves when compared to comparable offspring of nonalcoholic parents [5,16]. Controlling for the influence of the alcoholic biologic parent, being raised by an alcoholic parent figure, or going through a broken home or comparable childhood stressor appears to add little if anything to the final risk for the disorder itself.

However, as demonstrated by the lack of perfect concordance for alcoholism in identical twin pairs, genetics cannot explain the entire picture. Nor is it likely that any one single dominant or recessive gene is responsible. Rather the genetic pattern most closely fits a multifactorial, polygenic model of inheritance [7].

Supported by the Medical Research Service of the Veterans Administration NIAAA Grant No. 6-444960-24665 and by a grant from the Raleigh Hills Foundation. Parts of this chapter appeared in Hanin, I. and Usden, E. (eds.), *Biological Markers in Psychiatry and Neurology*. New York: Pergamon Press, 1982.

The work in our laboratory accepts the probable importance of genetic factors and attempts to go one step further. It is our aim to address possible biological mediators of a genetic propensity towards alcoholism. Thus, the studies noted below do not "prove" if alcoholism is genetically influenced but, following up on prior work, search out the mechanisms which might be involved if a genetic factor is present. After considering various alternatives, we have chosen to characterize nonalcoholic young men with close alcoholic relatives and compare them to similar men without alcoholic parents or siblings. Recognizing that the individuals with alcoholic families have a four times higher future risk for the disorder than controls, we explore factors which might help explain the differential risk. Our approach is to carefully match young men at elevated risk for the future development of alcoholism (as based on their family histories of this disorder) with controls and test possible differences at baseline and after ethanol challenge.

Possible Biologic Mechanisms
for a Genetic Influence in Alcoholism

To be of benefit, speculations about what might be inherited as part of a predisposition toward alcoholism must follow a number of guidelines. While almost anything is possible, it seems best to limit speculation to things that "make sense," those that have some tentative data supporting them, and those that are testable. As we have noted before [38] there are at least five possible mechanisms as indicated in table 10-1.

It is important to emphasize the possible complex interaction of factors involved in the elevated alcoholism risk. Even if a limited number of "final common pathways" of biologically mediated enhanced risk for alcoholism could be found, it is possible that the specific mechanisms might be different in different family groups. For instance, if future work were to prove the importance of an increased reinforcement from ethanol in the higher risk people (one example of a possible "final common pathway" of increased risk) this might relate to a greater reduction in muscle tension with ethanol in some families, an enhancement of brain alpha rhythm in others, etc. [50]. The sections below briefly review some specific *possible* biological mechanisms.

Absorption/Metabolism

It is possible that individuals at higher risk for alcoholism could differ from those at lower risk on their rate of absorption or metabolism of ethanol.

Table 10-1. Possible Biologic Mechanisms

1. Absorption/Metabolism
2. Acute Reaction
3. Subacute Reaction or Tolerance
4. Chronic Consequences
5. Personality

Genetic factors could influence the rate of disappearance of ethanol or the accumulation of the first major breakdown product, acetaldehyde.

For example, it is probable that the rate of absorption of ethanol may at least be in part under genetic control [31]. The overall rate of ethanol metabolism may also be genetically influenced as it has been demonstrated to be more similar in monozygotic (MZ) than in dizygotic (DZ) twin pairs [60]. While results are equivocal, it is possible that different ethnic groups may have different rates of ethanol metabolism, although such studies have rarely adequately controlled for habitual level of ethanol consumption or percent body fat [32,35]. The rate of metabolism is mediated by different patterns of the enzymes most closely involved in ethanol metabolism, alcohol and aldehyde dehydrogenase, and these are genetically controlled with divergent isoenzyme forms in different ethnic groups [14,22,53].

Not only might the rate of metabolism be important but the level of intermediary metabolites may have an effect. The accumulation of acetaldehyde appears to be higher in alcoholics than controls using a variety of methods in different populations, although some of the differential may relate to different drinking patterns [13,21,24,58,62]. An individual who consistently develops moderately elevated acetaldehyde levels after drinking could increase his risk for being identified as an alcoholic as this substance is associated with diverse organ damage to the pancreas, liver, heart, and brain. Two additional mechanisms could occur through the greater reinforcing effects of low levels of acetaldehyde as the stimulating properties of this substance could counteract the sedation produced by the ethanol itself and the possible condensation of acetaldehyde with brain monoamines could produce morphine-like substances that might alter brain functioning as false neurotransmitters [4,50]. If the levels of acetaldehyde surpass the moderate doses hypothesized above, then a state of physical discomfort characterized by flushing, palpitations, diarrhea, etc. could occur that might have the opposite affect and actually discourage drinking [47].

An additional factor could be the genetically-influenced accumulation of other biologically active abnormal metabolites. One possible example is 2-3-

butanediol that has been found in 90 percent of alcoholics coming off a binge [59].

In summary, one possible mediator of a genetic propensity in alcoholism could rest with genetic control of absorption and/or metabolism. This could relate to any single factor or the combination of the rate of absorption, absolute rate of metabolism of ethanol, rate of accumulation of acetaldehyde, rapidity of disappearance of this intermediary breakdown product, or accumulation of any of a variety of other metabolites.

Acute Reaction

A second possible biologic mediator of a genetic influence in alcoholism could relate to an individual's reaction to his first few drinks in any evening— i.e. his acute reaction to ethanol. It's possible to make a number of different cases here.

First, individuals at high risk for alcoholism could demonstrate a more pleasant or intense "high" that might encourage them to drink more. On the other hand, it is equally plausible that higher risk could be associated with a decreased sensitivity to lower ethanol doses with a resultant difficulty in determining when more severe impairment is developing and drinking should cease.

There are a variety of factors consistent with the possibility that the acute ethanol reaction (especially in the central nervous system [CNS]) could be under genetic control. Animal studies have demonstrated significant differences between mouse strains on the different impairment in righting reflex at equivalent rising or falling blood alcohol concentrations [56]. There are also genetic factors which determine CNS sensitivity to ethanol as measured by sleep time or impairment in peripheral reflexes [25,36]. It is plausible that these genetically mediated differences in sensitivity to acute ethanol effects could relate to ethanol intake. In one animal study, alcohol preferring (AA) rats showed less drug related motor impairment on a tilted plane than alcohol avoiding (ANA) strains—a finding noted for three aliphatic alcohols as well as barbital [27]. In human research there are some indications that drinking patterns may vary with the usual amount of sleep time required [46].

The acute ethanol reaction could relate to neurochemical mechanisms. Thus, there may be an association between platelet monoamine oxidase levels and the demonstration of alcoholism or a predisposition towards this disorder [26,55]. Some suggestive, but less impressive, evidence is also available regarding dopamine beta hydroxylase [51,54].

Functional Tolerance or Subacute Reactions

A possible biologic mediator for a genetic influence in alcoholism could rest with the development of differential levels of functional (as distinct from acute) tolerance. This, in turn, could influence the ability to tolerate higher and higher doses of ethanol over time and might indicate a differential susceptibility to physical dependence. There is some evidence to support the probability that mouse strains differing in their usual length of sleep in reaction to ethanol may also differ in their rate of development of functional tolerance and that this may be under genetic control [57]. Other strains demonstrating rapid acquisition of functional tolerance also showed a more brief and mild alcohol withdrawal syndrome. This raises the speculation that the genetically mediated ability to adapt rapidly in the presence of ethanol may relate to an ability to adjust rapidly to its removal [17]. It is conceivable that some similar factors might operate in humans with a resulting differential susceptibility to the development of tolerance or dependence.

Susceptibility to Chronic Consequences

A possible mechanism for genetic influence in alcoholism rests with the fact that studies are not carried out on all alcoholics, only those who are identified. Therefore, a factor that increases an individual's probability of developing an alcohol-related disorder more easily identified by health care deliverers could increase his probability of being studied. In this light, Bloom and Gibson [3] demonstrated that a genetically influenced susceptibility towards the development of a thiamine depletion syndrome, Wernicke-Korsadov's disorder, in some alcoholics is mediated by a genetically transmitted transketolase deficiency. Hrubec and Omenn [19] related a three-fold higher concordance rate for cirrhosis in MZ alcoholic twins than DZ and almost a four-fold higher MZ concordance rate for alcoholic psychosis. The various theories are not mutually exclusive as higher levels of acetaldehyde (in response to possible different modes of metabolism) could be a factor responsible for a higher risk for liver disease, while differential levels of genetically influenced enzymes such as superoxide dismutase could relate to vulnerabilities towards cirrhosis [9].

Personality

Another possible mechanism for increased susceptibility could rest with personality variables. It is very unlikely that there is a single alcoholic personality noted in the majority of alcoholics but rarely seen in non-alcoholics in the general population [28,48]. This, however, does not preclude the possibility that individual personality attributes could be associated with an elevated risk. Thus, it may be important that some studies report that alcoholics show higher levels of anxiety (not a consistent finding) and tend to score differently on the Minnesota Multiphasic Personality Inventory (MMPI) [34,41].

In summary, the number of possible biologic mediators of a genetic propensity to alcoholism is endless. Yet there is some preliminary evidence available to support the ideas behind the possible mechanisms discussed in this chapter. In looking at a genetic vulnerability, it should be recognized that it may be any one mechanism or, more likely, a combination of factors interacting with unknown environmental events which determine the final risk. The next section describes the approach we have chosen to preliminarily test some of these variables.

The Prospective Elevated Risk Studies

Some Options

There are a variety of options available for testing these hypotheses. Some investigators have chosen to compare alcoholics to controls, but any differences between the two groups could be the result of many years of heavy drinking and not reflect factors important in the original development of the alcoholism itself. To get around this, ideally we would like to study prealcoholics, but there is no foolproof way of choosing such individuals. Other scientists have opted to test both alcoholic and nonalcoholic family members of a limited number of established alcoholics. While this method has the advantage of being able to establish the pattern of inheritance, it has the disadvantage of only evaluating a small number of individuals and may yield limited results unless specific probable mechanisms have already been identified. We have taken another option, concentrating on the familial nature of alcoholism as a way of selecting groups at elevated risk for the future development of the problem. Our studies therefore focus on sons of alcoholics who, by virtue of their family status, are about four times more likely to develop alcoholism than the general population [38].

In selecting such a group, we have chosen to concentrate on males because their actual risk for development of alcoholism is higher than females [18]. In addition, studies of acute reaction to ethanol and its metabolites can be carried out without the necessity of controlling for the phase of the menstrual cycle or the presence versus absence of birth control pills [20]. To select people at high risk for the future development of alcoholism who are old enough to drink (which makes such studies easier), but not yet likely to have developed their alcoholism, we have centered in on men aged 21–25. If our results are replicated, testing will be expanded to women as well.

Comparisons of higher risk men with suitable controls can yield important results, even if later follow-ups do not show that all of the individuals carrying the factor actually develop alcoholism. The trait, even if not expressed, might lead to identification of other genetic factors or environmental events which mediate the actual final development of alcoholism. However, the groups presently under study will be follow-up in the future to determine the correlation between the trait and the eventual development of alcoholism.

Within such individuals we simultaneously study multiple possible biological mediators of a genetic influence of alcoholism. This is because it is impossible to be sure which (if any) of the hypothesized elements might be important and because of the probability that multiple genetic factors could interact to determine the final risk [7,33,38].

Any studies of higher risk individuals must, to be optimally effective, compare results with lower risk controls. We have chosen to use family history positive (FHP) and family history negative (FHN) pairs of men matched on demography, height/weight ratio (as these may affect absorption or metabolism) and drinking history. Regarding this last variable, there is no way to be absolutely certain than an accurate drinking history was given but the self-reported drinking history is probably more valid than the information from relatives or friends and appears to generate higher estimated levels of consumption than those ancillary sources [1,52]. While no perfect validity check for drinking history is available, FHP/FHN pairs are also matched on the Michigan Alcohol Screening Test and on a variety of blood markers known to increase with excessive drinking including gamma glutamyl transferase (GGT), uric acid, and mean corpustular volume [42,61].

The Study Methods

Our investigations are carried out in two phases. The first step is to identify groups of individuals who are FHP and FHN and establish matched pairs. The second phase is to carry out actual testing of the two groups.

In Phase I, a short (20 minute) structured questionnaire is distributed to all men aged 21 to 25 who are either students or nonacademic staff at the University of California, San Diego. In order to improve homogeneity of studied samples, we have limited our investigations to white males, as there may be metabolic differences between ethnic groups [35,38].

The questionnaire gathers information on demography, height/weight ratio, drinking history as established by Cahalan's Quantity/Frequency/ Variability Index [6], personal history of drug abuse as defined in the DSM III [2], and alcoholism. Alcoholism, for both subjects and family members, is defined in a manner similar to that used in most of the major adoption studies and rests with the occurrence of any of a series of major life problems related to heavy drinking [37]. After excluding all potential subjects who demonstrate either alcoholism or drug abuse or evidence of other psychiatric or major medical disorders themselves (usually less than 10% of the population), all men with a family history of alcoholism in a close relative (parents or siblings) are included in the FHP group. Similar individuals with no family history of alcoholism are matched on the relevant variables and selected as the FHN controls.

In Phase II of the study, members of matched pairs are individually invited to the laboratory for testing by personnel blind to their family history status. Upon arrival at 7:00 A.M. after an overnight fast, relevant drinking and medical history data are reviewed, the individual is weighed and the height measured, subcutaneous skinfold thickness established, and an 18 gauge scalp vein needle is inserted in an antecubital vein in the nondominant arm and attached to a heparin-lock to allow for ease of blood drawing repeatedly throughout the experiment. The individual then fills out questionnaires measuring personality characteristics and feeling state, performs baseline psychomotor and cognitive tests and, after a minimum of 30 minutes to ensure that physiologic functioning has returned to baseline after needle insertion, baseline blood is drawn.

At this point the ethanol is administered in a manner that attempts to standardize, as best one can, for factors relevant to absorption. Ninety-five percent USP laboratory grade ethanol mixed as a 20% solution in sugar-free beverage administered at room temperature is then consumed over a 5-minute period [40]. Relevant tests from baseline are then repeated at 15 minutes (time of maximal increase in blood alcohol concentration (BAC)), 30 minutes, 60 minutes (the time of usual blood alcohol peak) and every 30 minutes thereafter. While BAC measurements are carried out using a gas chromograph on blood samples, throughout the experiment they are roughly monitored using an Alko-Analyzer (Luckey Laboratories, Irvine, Calif.), for breath. The results reported below come from one testing session for each individual but will be supplemented in the near future as data from our new paradigm becomes available. In this expanded approach, each individual is tested on three occasions when he is given in random order 0.75 ml/kg ethanol, 1.1 ml/kg ethanol, or placebo—the latter being important to control for expectancy.

Over the last 3 years our laboratory has generated results on selected aspects of personality, absorption/metabolism of ethanol, and acetaldehyde levels, and a number of aspects of the acute reaction to ethanol. The major metabolic and acute reaction results have been replicated in our laboratory, but the final determination of their relevance will depend upon results from similar studies carried out in other laboratories to ensure that no systematic biases in sample selection or study methodology explain the data.

Results from Our Present Series of Investigations

The data presented here are given as a rapid overview to demonstrate the type of data that can accrue from this methodology. Almost all results have been reported in other journals and the reader is referred to those publications where materials are presented in greater detail.

Absorption/Metabolism

We have monitored BACs in all investigations with resulting inferential data on alcohol absorption and metabolism. While large individual differences were noted within FHP and FHN groups, the average and standard deviation for the groups of matched pairs have been almost identical for the time elapsed between drinking ethanol and the peak BAC, the magnitude of the peak BAC, and the rate of disappearance of ethanol [40]. While these are not true elimination rate studies (which would require intravenous ethanol), they indicate that it is unlikely that differences on these factors between higher and lower risk pairs could explain the relative risk for alcoholism in the two study groups.

A second aspect of metabolism was our observation of blood acetaldehyde levels after the ethanol load. As has been discussed in greater depth elsewhere [43] the methodology for determining acetaldehyde in blood is fraught with difficulties resulting in the spurious elevation of acetaldehyde when blood is deproteinized as part of preparation for analysis, apparent spurious loss of acetaldehyde to the atmosphere, and potential loss of acetaldehyde through binding to blood proteins. Breath acetaldehyde determinations are also difficult to evaluate because of the possibility that even end-expiratory acetaldehyde may reflect production of the substance by lung microsomes and microbes in the respiratory tract rather than the actual concentration of the substance in the lungs [23]. Therefore, it is most difficult to compare absolute acetaldehyde values between two laboratories or, even, to compare results from two methods in the same laboratory. Nonetheless, there may be some relevance to studies of relative acetaldehyde values in matched pairs when the exact same methodology is used for both groups.

With these caveats in mind, we have followed up on the observation that alcoholics may demonstrate higher levels of acetaldehyde than controls [43]. Looking at acetaldehyde over 3–5 hours in FHP/FHN matched pairs, we have twice demonstrated an apparent two-fold higher acetaldehyde level in the FHP group compared to the FHN. Even though this was done by two different methods and subsequently corroborated in breath by Zeiner [62], the absolute acetaldehyde levels are quite low and it is not possible to determine whether they accurately reflect differences between the two groups in liver acetaldehyde levels or if there are some differences in blood binding or processing of ethanol and/or acetaldehyde which could explain the findings [43,49]. We are presently attempting to replicate these findings using blood and breath acetaldehyde along with blood aldehyde oxidizing capacity determined simultaneously.

A twofold increase in the level of acetaldehyde is much less than the possible tenfold increase expected with a disulfiram or Antabuse reaction [37]. As discussed above, it is possible that these acetaldehyde levels could enhance the quantity of intoxication or might increase the risk for alcoholism through other means. For instance, individuals with higher acetaldehyde levels might carry an increased risk for organ damage with ethanol due to higher levels of this toxic substance [38] or produce morphine-like alkaloids (tetrahydroisoquinolines or beta-carbolines) that might serve as false neurotransmitters and induce a stronger drive to drink or mediate a heightened predisposition towards addiction [8,11,30]. Recent preliminary data from our laboratory has demonstrated an increase in some of these alkaloids in the urine of FHP men after drinking [45].

Acute Ethanol Reaction

We have also utilized a variety of methods to observe different aspects of the acute reaction to ethanol. First, using two forms of a standardized measure of intoxication, the Subjective High Assessment Scale or SHAS, we have twice demonstrated a statistically significant trend for FHP men to report less intense intoxication throughout the experiment, despite almost identical BACs when compared to FHN matched pairs [10,39]. These results were reflected in similar trends for less significant change from baseline for ten

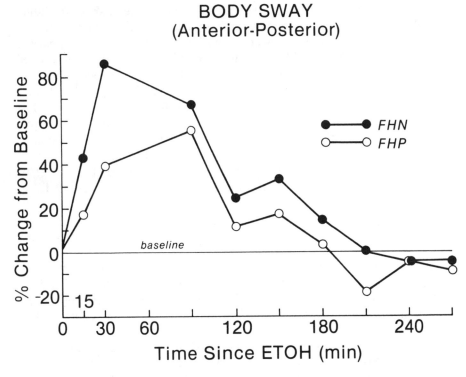

Figure 10-1. Body Sway Seen After an Ethanol Load

FHP when compared to FHN matched pairs on the increase in body sway seen after an ethanol load (fig. 10-1) using the methodology for sample selection and ethanol administration described above.

Of equal importance are the differences between FHP and FHN matched pairs on ethanol induced changes in auditory brainstem event related potentials (ERPs). Between the N1 and P2 time points following ethanol, the FHP demonstrated a trend for less attenuation in peak height and less increase in the latency of the peak than the FHN. An intriguing related finding is the significant difference between the two groups on the changes in height of the P3 after drinking, although in this instance, the FHP demonstrated more change than the FHN [12]. The decreased P300 could reflect FHP men paying less attention to their surroundings during the experiment.

These findings may indicate that young men at elevated risk for the future development of alcoholism may differ from matched FHN controls on their subjective intoxication with ethanol as well as their physiologic response to an ethanol load. When differences were found, they almost demonstrated *less* reactivity to ethanol in men at high risk for the future development of alcoholism, despite matching on drinking history. It may be that such individuals receive less intoxication at 3–4 drinks with consequent less warning when they are beginning to become intoxicated. This may lead to a greater desire to drink more in their attempt to feel the same effects of ethanol as noted by their peers. The end result could be subsequent high levels of intoxication with all the attendant problems. These speculations must be considered quite tentative until studied in greater depth and replicated.

Personality

Finally, we were able to compare the matched pairs on their scores on a limited number of personality tests which have been hypothesized to differ between alcoholics and controls. There were no significant differences between the two groups on their trait of anxiety nor on their level of assertiveness.

Both FHP and FHN individuals scored within the "normal" range on all relevant MMPI subtests although there was a small (but statistically significant) higher score for the FHP on the MacAndrew "alcoholism scale," indicating the possibility that the MMPI might tap some critical personality attribute associated with higher alcoholism risk [34]. However, the small numerical difference between the two groups and the scores within the "normal" range indicate this finding may be of limited practical significance. Similar negative findings have noted on their "locus of control" as well as the Eysenck Personality Inventory scores on extraversion and neurotocism [29,41,44].

Summary

A variety of studies using different methodologies are consistent with the probability that alcoholism is a genetically-influenced disorder. This in turn has led to speculation about possible biologic mediators of a genetic propensity. In order to carry out some preliminary tests of the hypotheses, we have chosen to study men who, by virtue of their family histories, are at elevated risk for the future development of alcoholism and compared them to controls matched on demography, height/weight ratio, and drinking history. Our research has been carried out in two phases, the first of which surveyed groups of young men who, after excluding those who already demonstrate disorders, were then separated into matched pairs of FHP and FHN individuals. The second phase then observed differences between the two groups at baseline and after an ethanol load.

Studies to date indicate no significant differences between the family history groups on the apparent rate of absorption or disappearance of ethanol. Our laboratory has twice demonstrated small but statistically significant differences between the two groups on their levels of acetaldehyde which may indicate possible differences on their mode of ethanol and/or acetaldehyde metabolism. This in turn may relate to the acute effects of intoxication, may increase the risk for alcohol related organ damage from higher acetaldehyde levels, or might tie in with possible development of morphine-like false neurotransmitters in the brain, the tetrahydroisoquinolines and the beta carbolines. The two groups have also demonstrated probable differences in their subjective level of intoxication and some more objective correlates of the acute effects of ethanol, consistent with a possible decreased reactivity to ethanol in nonalcoholic young men at higher risk for future alcoholism.

These data do not address possible differences between the groups on the development of functional tolerance nor do they directly test potential differences in susceptibility to the chronic consequences of heavy drinking. It is not possible to state from the present data whether the genetic mechanisms, if important, relate to a specific vulnerability to alcoholism or to CNS depressants in general—a possibility raised by the crossover between alcohol preference and levels of CNS impairment to aliphatic alcohols and a barbiturate reported in at least one animal study [27].

At the very least this series of studies has heuristic value. It has been our goal to raise the level of consciousness of relevant clinicians and researchers to the possibility of genetic influences in alcoholism and to present one possibly important methodology for learning more about such possible mechanisms. The present results, while tentative, can serve as a starting point for additional research in this area.

References

1. Adams, K. M., Grant, I., Carlin, A. S., Reed, R. Cross-study comparisons of self-reported alcohol consumption in four clinical groups. *Am. J. Psychiatry* 138:445, 1981.

2. American Psychiatric Association. *Diagnostic and Statistical Manual of Mental Disorders* (3rd ed.). Washington, D.C., American Psychiatric Association, 1980.

3. Bloom, J. P., Gibson, G. E. Abnormality of a thiamine-requiring enzyme in patients with Wernicke-Korsakoff syndrome. *N. Engl. J. Med.* 297:1367, 1977.

4. Bloom, F. E. and Barchas, J. *Workshop on beta carbolines and tetrahydroisoquinolines: proceedings of a workshop.* Back, N. Brewer, G. J., Eijsvoogel, V. P., et al. (eds.). New York: Alan R. Liss, 1982.

5. Bohman, M., Sigvardsson, S., and Cloninger, R. Maternal inheritance of alcohol abuse. *Arch. Gen. Psychiatry 38*:965, 1981.

6. Cahalan, D. *Problem Drinkers* San Francisco: Jossey-Boss, 1970.

7. Cloninger, C. R., Christiansen, K. O., Reich, T., and Gottesman, I. I. 1970. Implications of sex differences in the prevalences of antisocial personality, alcoholism, and criminality for familial transmission. *Arch. Gen. Psychiatry*, 35:941, 1970.

8. Davis, V. E. and Walsh, M. J. Alcohol, amines, and alkaloids: A possible biochemical basis for alcohol addiction. *Science* 167:1005, 1970.

9. Del Villano, B. C., Miller, S. I., Schacter, L. P., and Tischfield, J. A. Elevated superoxide dismutase in black alcoholics. *Science* 207:991, 1980.

10. Duby, J. and Schuckit, M. A. Subjective effects of alcohol intoxication in young men with alcoholic relatives. Presented at National Council on Alcoholism Annual Scientific Meeting, New Orleans, La., 1981.

11. Duncan, C., and Deitrich, R. A. A critical evaluation of tetrahydroisoquinoline induced ethanol preference in rats. *Pharmac. Biochem. Behav.* 13:1, 1980.

12. Elmasian, R., Neville, H., Woods, D., et al. P3 Amplitude differentiates subjects with and without a family history of alcoholism. Presented in part in *Society for Neuroscience Abstracts, 7*, 1981.

13. Freund, G. and O'Hollaren, P. Acetaldehyde concentrations in alveolar air following a standard dose of ethanol in man. *J. Lipid Res.* 6:471, 1965.

14. Goedde, H. W., Harada, S., and Agarwal, D. P. Racial differences in alcohol sensitivity; A new hypothesis. *Hum. Genet. 51*:331, 1979.

15. Goodwin, D. W. *Is Alcoholism Hereditary.* New York: Oxford University Press, 1976, pp. 51–84.

16. Goodwin, D. W., Schulsinger, F., Moller, N., et al. Drinking problems in adopted and nonadopted sons of alcoholics. *Arch. Gen. Psychiatry* 31:164, 1974.

17. Grieve, J., Griffiths, P. J., and Littleton, J. M. Genetic influences on the rate of development of ethanol tolerance and the ethanol physical withdrawal syndrome in mice. *Drug Alcohol Depend.* 4:77, 1979.

18. Haglund, R. M. J. and Schuckit, M. A. The Epidemiology of Alcoholism. In Estes N. and Heinemann E. (eds.), *Alcoholism: Development, Consequences and intervention.* St. Louis: C. V. Mosby, 1977, pp. 28–43

19. Hrubec, A. and Omenn, G. S. Evidence of genetic predisposition to alcoholic cirrhosis and psychosis: twin concordances for alcoholism and its biologic end

points by zygosity among male veterans. *Alcoholism: Clin. Exp. Res. 5:*207, 1981.

20. Jones B. M., Jones, M. K. and Paredes A. Oral contraceptives and ethanol metabolism. *Alcohol Tech. Rep.* 5:28, 1976.

21. Korsten, M. A., Matsuzaki, S., Feinman, L., and Lieber, C. S. High blood acetaldehyde levels after ethanol administration. *N. Engl. J. Med. 292:*386, 1975.

22. Li, T., Bosron, W. F., Dafeldecker, W. P., Lange, L. G., and Vallee, B. L. Isolation of II-alcohol dehydrogenase of human liver: is it a determinant of alcoholism? *Proc. Natl. Acad. Sci. 74:*4378, 1977.

23. Lieber, C. Discussion of Breath acetaldehyde: Highly sensitive evaluation of endogenous and exogenous ethanol metabolism. Presented at the American College of Neuropsychopharmacology meeting in San Juan, Puerto Rico, 1980.

24. Lindros, K. O., Stowell, A., Pikkarainen, P., and Salaspuro, M. Elevated blood acetaldehyde in alcoholics with accelerated ethanol elimination *Pharmac. Biochem. Behav.* 13:119, 1980.

25. McClearn, G. E. The genetic aspects of alcoholism. In Bourne, P. G., and Fox, R. (eds.), *Alcoholism: Progress in Research and Treatment*, New York: Academic Press, 1973, pp. 337–358.

26. Major, L. F. and Murphy, D. L. Platelet and plasma amine oxidase activity in alcoholic individuals. *Br. J. Psychiatry 132:*548, 1978.

27. Malila, A. Intoxicating effects of three aliphatic alcoholics and barbital on two rat strains genetically selected for their ethanol intake. *Pharmac. Biochem. Behav.* 8:197, 1978.

28. Miller, W. R. Alcoholism scales and objective assessment methods: a review. *Psychol. Bull.* 83:649, 1976.

29. Morrison, C. and Schuckit, M. A. Locus of control in young men with alcoholic relatives and controls. *J. Stud. Alcohol.* In press.

30. Myers, R. D. Tetrahydroisoquinolines in the brain: The basis of an animal model of alcoholism. *Alcoholism: Clin. Exp. Res.* 2:145, 1978.

31. Radlow, R. and Conway, T. L. Consistency of alcohol absorption in human subjects. Presented at the American Psychological Association Convention in Toronto, Canada, 1978.

32. Reed, T. E. Racial comparisons of alcohol metabolism: Background, problems, and results. *Alcoholism: Clin. Exp. Res., 2:*83, 1978.

33. Reich, T., Winokur, G., and Mullaney, J. The transmission of alcoholism. In Rieve, Rosenthal, Brill (eds.), *Genetic Research in Psychiatry*. Baltimore: Johns Hopkins University Press, 1975, pp. 17–31.

34. Saunders, G. R. and Schuckit, M. A. MMPI scores in young men with alcoholic relatives and controls. *J. Nerv. Ment. Dis.:* in press.

35. Schaefer, J. M. Alcohol metabolism and sensitivity reactions among the Reddis of South India. *Alcoholism: Clin. Exp. Res.* 2:61, 1978.

36. Schneider, C. W., Trzil, P., and D'Andrea, R. Neural tolerance in high and low ethanol selecting mouse strains. *Pharmac. Biochem. Behav.* 2:549, 1974.

37. Schuckit, M. D. *Drug and Alcohol Abuse: A Clinical Guide to Diagnosis and Treatment* New York: Plenum Press, 1979.
38. Schuckit, M. A. Alcoholism and genetics: possible biological mediators. *Biol. Psychiatry* 15:437, 1980.
39. Schuckit, M. A. Self-rating of alcohol intoxication by young men with and without family histories of alcoholism. *J. Stud. Alcohol* 41:242, 1980.
40. Schuckit, M. A. Peak blood alcohol levels in men at high risk for the future development of alcoholism. *Alcoholism: Clin. Exp. Res.* 5:64, 1981.
41. Schuckit, M. A. A comparison of anxiety and assertiveness in sons of alcoholics and controls. *J. Clin. Psychiat.*, in press.
42. Schuckit, M. A. Gamma glutamyl transferase and the diagnosis of alcoholism. *Advances in Alcoholism*, in press.
43. Schuckit, M. A. Acetaldehyde and alcoholism: Methodology. Presented at the American College of Neuropsychopharmacology meeting in San Juan, Puerto Rico, 1981.
44. Schuckit, M. A. Extroversion and neuroticism in young men at higher and lower risk for alcoholism. *Am. J. Psychiatry*, in press.
45. Schuckit, M. A. and Beck, O. Acetaldehyde in alcoholism. *Lancet* 28:502, 1982.
46. Schuckit, M. A. and Bernstein, L. I. Sleep time and drinking history: A hypothesis. *Am. J. Psychiatry* 138:528, 1981.
47. Schuckit, M. A. and Duby, J. Alcohol-related flushing and the risk for alcoholism in sons of alcoholics. *J. Clin. Psychiatry1, 43*:415, 1982.
48. Schuckit, M. A. and Haglund, M. J. In Estes, N. J. and Heinemann, M. E. (eds.), *Alcoholism: Development, Consequences and Intervention.* St. Louis: C. V. Mosby, 1977.
49. Schuckit, M. A. and Rayses, Y. Ethanol ingestion: Differences in blood acetaldehyde concentrations in relatives of alcoholics and controls. *Science* 203:54, 1979.
50. Schuckit, M. A. and von Wartburg, J. P. Hypothesis: developing a model for causation for alcoholism. In press.
51. Schuckit, M. A., O'Connor, D., Duby, J., Vega, R., and Moss, M. DBH activity levels in men at high risk for alcoholism and controls. *Biol. Psychiatry* 16:1067, 1981.
52. Sobell, M. B. Sobell, L. C., and Samuels, F. H. Validity of self-reports of alcohol-related arrests by alcoholics. *Q. J. Stud. Alcohol 35:* 276, 1974.
53. Stamatoyannopoulos, G. Chen, S., and Fukui, M. Liver alcohol dehydrogenase in Japanese: High population frequency of atypical form and its possible role in alcohol sensitivity. *Am. J. Hum. Genet.* 27:789, 1975.
54. Sullivan, J. L., Cavenar, Jr. J. O., Maltbie, A. A. et al. Familial biochemical and clinical correlates of alcoholics with low platelet monoamine oxidase activity. *Biol. Psychiatry* 14:385, 1979.
55. Sullivan, J. L., Stanfield, C. N., Schanberg, S., and Cavenar, J. Platelet monoamine oxidase and serum dopamine-β-Hydroxylase activity in chronic alcoholics. *Arch. Gen. Psychiatry* 35:1209, 1978.

56. Tabakoff, B. and Ritzmann, R. F. Acute tolerance in inbred and selected lines of mices. *Drug Alcohol Depend.* 4:87, 1979.

57. Tabakoff, B., Ritzmann, R. F., Raju, T. S., and Deitrich, R. A. Characterization of acute and chronic tolerance in mice selected for inherent differences in sensitivity to ethanol. *Alcoholism: Clin. Exp. Res.* 4:70, 1980.

58. Truitt, E. B. Blood acetaldehyde levels after alcohol consumption by alcoholic and nonalcoholic subjects. *Biol. Aspects Alcohol* 3:212, 1971.

59. Veech, R. L., Felver, M. E., Lakschmanan, M. R., Wolf, S., et al. Abnormal metabolite in alcoholic subjects. Personal Communications, 1981.

60. Vesell, E. S. Ethanol metabolism: Regulation by genetic factors in normal volunteers under a controlled environment and the effect of chronic ethanol administration. *Ann. N.Y. Acad. Sci.* 197:79, 1975.

61. Whitehead, T. O., Clarke, C. A., and Whitfield, A. G. W. Biochemical and haematological markers of alcohol intake. *Lancet* 1:978, 1978.

62. Zeiner, R. Acetaldehyde and the risk for alcoholism. Presented at the 20th International Congress on Applied Psychology in Edinburg, Scottland, July 25–31, 1982.

III TYPOLOGICAL STUDIES

11 SUBTYPING ALCOHOLICS BY COEXISTING PSYCHIATRIC SYNDROMES: COURSE, FAMILY HISTORY, OUTCOME

Elizabeth C. Penick
Barbara J. Powell
Ekkehard Othmer
Stephen F. Bingham
Audrey S. Rice
Bruce S. Liese

This chapter will describe two studies designed to examine the clinical validity of a relatively *new method* of classifying alcoholics that was derived from a descriptive, syndromatic approach to psychiatric diagnosis. The rationale for the validation studies was based upon an *old model* of clinical

This research was supported, in part, by the Cooperative Studies Program (CSP #183) and the Medical Research Service, Veterans Administration, Washington, D.C.

The authors wish to thank Alcoholism Treatment Unit Chiefs from the following Veterans Administration Medical Centers for their cooperation: Ilse Lowenstam, M.D., Los Angeles, Calif.; John Pucel, Ph.D., St. Cloud, Minn.; Pamela Parish, M.D., Oklahoma City, Okla.; Sidney Ogden, M.S.W., Little Rock, Ark.; and Richard Sword, M.D., Leavenworth, Kan. The assistance of C. James Klett, Ph.D., Chief, Perry Point VACSPCC is also greatly appreciated. The *Journal of Clinical Psychiatry* generously gave its permission to reproduce table 11-1.

research that has been successfully used in the past to evaluate the diagnostic significance of major syndromes in both medicine and psychiatry. It is suggested that the proposed approach to subtyping alcoholics may be potentially useful to both the practitioner desirous of finding more effective methods of treatment as well as the clinical researcher interested in exploring etiological factors associated with alcoholism.

The Method and the Model

It is generally acknowledged that the diagnosis of alcoholism includes a relatively broad, heterogenous group of individuals whose family history, natural course and prognosis can differ substantially [34]. Efforts to reduce this clinical diversity have focused upon the development of methods by which large numbers of unselected alcoholics can be identified and reliably classified or subtyped. The earliest attempts to subtype alcoholics were typically based upon an experiential-intuitive approach such as those suggested by Knight [26] and Jellinek [23]. Later, empirical methods were constructed and tested. The most common empirical approaches to sub-typing alcoholics are those derived from the statistical associations found among a number of measures. Typically, measures obtained from large groups of alcoholics are subjected to some kind of multi-variant analysis in order to create clusters or factors from which alcoholic subtypes are then extracted. Measures used to subtype alcoholics have included: (1) results of personality tests, most prominently the MMPI [19]; (2) sociodemographic variables such as sex, education, marital status; (3) indices of cognitive-motor functioning such as IQ or neuropsychological status; and (4) items which describe the pattern of drinking or the effects of abusive drinking [5,6,11,12,22,27,29,32,33,42]. Other, less well-studied empirical methods have subdivided alcoholics according to age of onset, response to treatment and family history [9,15,35,40].

Although most of the empirical approaches to subtyping alcoholics have been shown to possess adequate reliability, none have become widely accepted or used in practice [41]. We suggest that there are two reasons for this. First, the diagnostic significance or clinical validity of the empirical methods of subtyping alcoholics has not been addressed until quite recently. Second, in spite of the extremely large number of measures and procedures that have been studied, no conceptual framework has emerged from this work that is capable of providing some sort of unifying rationale for the alcoholic subtypes.

The failure of investigators to adequately consider the clinical validity of alcoholic subtypes has been noted by Finney and Moos [8] who state: "Rather than merely identify homogenous subtypes. . . . Researchers need to use typologies to explore differential etiologies and prognoses and to search for differentially effective treatment strategies. . . . [p. 36].

Within the descriptive syndromatic approach to psychiatric diagnosis, a model derived from general medicine has been used to evaluate the clinical validity of the major diagnostic classes in psychiatry [14,17]. Acknowledging that the pathophysiology and etiology of most psychiatric disorders are unknown, inclusion and exclusion criteria derived from an interplay between clinical experience and research are used to define the different diagnostic entities. Indirect methods are then employed to establish their diagnostic significance or clinical validity. These methods have traditionally included: (1) symptom comparison studies, (2) follow-up and follow-back studies, (3) family history studies, and (4) treatment response studies. Confidence in the usefulness of diagnostic criteria is strengthened when it can be shown that the clinical features, natural course, response to treatment and family history differ for individuals assigned to different diagnostic classes. We suggest that the model used to establish the clinical significance of relatively broad diagnostic categories in psychiatry and medicine can *also* be used to examine the clinical validity of subtypes derived from these broader diagnostic groups. That is, in order to fully demonstrate the usefulness of any method of subtyping, it should be possible to show that:

1.   The method is reliable (i.e., short-term consistency).
2.   The subtypes are stable over time (i.e., long-term consistency).
3.   The developmental course varies as a function of subtype (i.e., age of onset, medical and social sequelae, spontaneous remission and morbidity differ across subtypes).
4.   The prognosis of the subtypes differ over time (i.e., the subtypes are associated with different outcomes).
5.   The subtypes are distinguished by the family history of psychiatric disorder (i.e., the prevalence of psychiatric syndromes among relatives differs by subtype).
6.   Certain interventions are more effective for individual representatives of the different subtypes (i.e., differential responsiveness to treatment).

At present, none of the existing methods of subtyping alcoholics have been evaluated in this manner. The two studies presented in this chapter represent the first in a series designed to apply this model of validation to a new method of classifying abusive drinkers that utilizes certain *combinations* of psychiatric syndromes for the purpose of subtyping alcoholics.

Alcoholism and Other Psychiatric Syndromes

Although alcoholism is considered a major psychiatric disorder in its own right, a number of investigators have shown that individuals who carry the diagnosis of alcoholism also suffer from symptoms common to other psychiatric syndromes such as depression, mania, and antisocial personality. Recently, increasing interest has become focused upon the alcoholic presenting with another psychiatric disorder. Gottheil, McLellan, and Druley, in their preface to *Substance Abuse and Psychiatric Illness*, have recently stated:

> Many psychiatric patients use and abuse alcohol and other drugs, and many addicted patients also have psychiatric problems . . . there has been a growing awareness of the existence of these patients and of the difficult research and treatment problems presented by them . . . few theoretical, research or clinical studies have been reported concerning how one might determine which disorder should take precedence in given cases, where such patients should be treated and by whom, and what types of therapy would be most appropriate . . . [16, p. ix].

As noted by several authors, the diagnostic significance of multiple psychiatric syndromes is not well understood for alcoholics in particular, or for psychiatric patients in general [7,37,38]. This lack of understanding is partly due to the somewhat bewildering variety of instruments and procedures that have been used to assess psychopathology in patients presenting with diverse and complex clinical pictures. The growing acceptance of the descriptive syndromatic approach to psychiatric diagnosis, reflected in the recent publication of the *Diagnostic and Statistical Manual of Mental Disorders*, third edition (DSM-III) (1980), has stimulated the development of several criterion-based instruments (Hedlund and Vieweg, 1981). These structured diagnostic interviews use specific questions to operationalize criteria which correspond to various clinical phenomena; explicit scoring procedures are used to operationalize criteria that correspond to formal requirements associated with syndrome identification and diagnosis. Typically, inclusion criteria are first used to "rule in" or "rule out" syndromes reviewed by the instrument. Later, exclusion criteria are applied to generate one or more final diagnoses. When applied in this manner, a number of studies have shown that a substantial proportion of patients with quite different chief complaints will fulfill *inclusive* criteria for more than one psychiatric syndrome [see 21]. This is also true of alcoholics [36].

In our view, the identification of multiple syndromes in a significant number of psychiatric patients provides the unique opportunity to develop reliable and clinically relevant methods of subtyping individuals who represent the more broadly defined, major diagnostic classes such as alcoholism. It appeared reasonable to hypothesize that the age of onset, natural course, family history and clinical picture of individuals positive for a single syndrome would differ from that of individuals positive for two or more syndromes. Furthermore, we suggest that certain syndromes (e.g., schizophrenia), acting in concert with other syndromes (e.g., alcoholism), would exert a greater influence on the patients' course and treatment requirements than other more benign syndrome combinations (e.g., simple phobia and alcoholism). We propose that a *reduction in symptom heterogeneity* among the major diagnostic classes by subtyping individuals according to the presence or absence of other coexisting syndromes may increase predictive power and facilitate the search for more effective methods of treatment. The clinical advances associated with the delineation of manic-depressive illness from other affective disorders and schizophrenia is a case in point for this syndrome-combination approach to subtyping.

The work presented in this chapter utilized a relatively new criterion-based, structured diagnostic interview for the purpose of defining and subtyping alcoholics: the *Psychiatric Diagnostic Interview* or PDI [30]. A considerable body of research has indicated that many alcoholics report symptoms similar to those found among antisocial individuals or those diagnosed suffering from an affective disorder [2,5,28,29,31]. Based upon these findings, three syndromes were selected a priori for the purpose of assigning alcoholics into four mutually exclusive groups. They were: Antisocial Personality, Depression, and Mania or Manic-Depressive disorder. The fourth subtype consisted of alcoholics positive for no other major psychiatric syndrome (the Primary or Uncomplicated alcoholic subtype).

Study I

Purposes

The purposes of this study were to (1) determine the prevalence and onset of 15 psychiatric syndromes among a large group of male alcoholics, and (2) retrospectively examine the course, clinical picture, family history and medical/social sequelae associated with various alcoholic subtypes.

Subjects

The patients who served as subjects for this study have been described in an earlier publication [36]. Briefly, 594 patients from five VA inpatient alcoholism treatment programs were invited to participate in the study once detoxification was completed. Twenty-nine were eliminated for the following reasons: Refused initially: 9; confused/disoriented: 6; female: 5; refused to complete the evaluation: 4; negative for alcoholism on the PDI: 5. This left a total of 565 patients who successfully completed the two research protocols and fulfilled formal diagnostic criteria for alcoholism. Their mean age was 47 (SD = 10.9); 81 percent were white; over two-thirds (68%) had completed high school or beyond; and, the socioeconomic status of the majority (59%) approximated the lower middle to lower class. Twenty-six percent were married; 58 percent divorced or separated; 16 percent were single or widowed. Approximately one-half (49%) were employed or successfully retired during the month prior to entry into the study; the remainder were unemployed or medically disabled.

Method

Information was obtained from two, precoded structured interviews administered to each patient during a two-hour session by specially trained technicians once informed consent was obtained. The *Psychosocial Interview* contained questions about the patients' (1) sociodemographic background; (2) family history of psychiatric disorder; (3) treatment for alcoholism and/or other psychiatric disorder; and (4) drinking history, including social/personal and medical sequelae common to alcohol abuse. The *Psychiatric Diagnostic Interview* (PDI) is a criterion-based, structured diagnostic interview that was constructed to systematically review 15 basic and three derived psychiatric syndromes [30]. Developed from research diagnostic criteria proposed by Feighner et al. [7] and modified to ensure symptom compatibility with DSM-III, the PDI was designed to determine whether an individual is suffering or has ever suffered from any of the syndromes covered by the instrument. Simply worded questions are used to elicit information about symptomatic experiences and other characteristics of diagnostic interest. Questions are arranged by syndromes that are independently reviewed. Age of onset and age of termination are determined for all syndromes that are scored positive. Explicit procedures for scoring the syndromes are indicated in the reusable administration booklet and on the recording form in order to insure accuracy and allow scoring during the course of an interview. Hierarchical principles of differential diagnosis are used to produce a Current and Lifetime diagnosis for each patient. Results from a series of studies conducted over the last eight years have shown that the PDI is both reliable and diagnostically accurate, even when administered by the nonclinician.

Alcoholic Subtypes

In creating the four alcoholic subtypes, principles used to obtain a differential diagnosis on the PDI were waived. That is, when a patient fulfills inclusive diagnostic criteria for two or more psychiatric syndromes on the PDI, a series of hierarchial rules are utilized to generate a Current and Lifetime diagnosis. Within this conceptual framework, "masking" disorders such as Alcoholism, Drug Abuse, and Organic Brain Syndrome (OBS) are given precedence over all other positive syndromes during the period in which a masking disorder was active [30]. These principles were not employed in the present studies. Furthermore, the reported onset of problem drinking and the three syndromes used to subtype patients were not a consideration in forming the four groups [36].

Two methods were used to generate the alcoholic subtypes. Initially, very stringent criteria were used to define the four groups. Thus, the Primary subtype contained patients positive for alcoholism only. The Depressed subtype contained patients positive only for alcoholism and major depression (exclusive of heavy binge drinking). The Manic-Depressive subtype contained individuals positive for alcoholism and mania or mania and depression only. The Antisocial subtype contained individuals positive only for alcoholism and antisocial personality. Using these highly rigorous selection criteria, patients were often excluded because of relatively minor syndromes such as simple phobia, homosexuality, obsessive ruminations, mild drug abuse and the like. The entire data set was used to contrast the four subtypes. In reviewing the results, it was clear that the four groups differed on a majority of the measures. It also became evident that many of the comparisons approached significance ($p < .15 > .05$) but failed to achieve the statistical level established for this study ($p < .05$) because of the very small Ns in some subgroups. This was especially true for the Antisocial group ($N = 26$) that generally differed most from the other three groups. Proportionally more of the alcoholics positive for antisocial personality were excluded from this initial analysis (i.e., 89 out of 115) because they were most likely to fulfill diagnostic criteria for additional syndromes, especially depression.

In order to increase the size of the subgroups, a second analysis was undertaken that employed less stringent selection criteria. In this approach, all patients positive for either OBS or schizophrenia were excluded; however, no patients were excluded if they were positive for relatively minor syndromes. Patients positive for an affective disorder and antisocial personality were assigned to the Antisocial subtype. The subtypes were then reformed. Thus the Primary subtype contained alcoholics who were negative for OBS, schizophrenia, depression, mania or antisocial personality but could be positive for any of the remaining syndromes: Somatization disorder, Anorexia Nervosa, Panic Attacks, Phobia, Obsessive-Compulsive disorder, Mental Retardation, Homosexuality, Transsexualism, and Drug Abuse. (The five programs involved in this study were established to treat alcoholism, not other kinds of substance abuse. As a consequence, for most of the patients who were positive for Drug Abuse on the PDI, drugs placed a relatively minor role in their disorder.) Similarly, the Depressed subtype contained alcoholics positive for depression (and possibly other relatively minor syndromes) but negative for mania, antisocial personality, OBS, or schizophrenia. Alcoholics assigned to the Manic-Depressive subtype fulfilled criteria for mania or mania and depression but not antisocial personality or the other major exclusionary syndromes. Finally, the revised antisocial subtype contained individuals positive for antisocial personality (and possibly for an affective disorder and other minor syndromes) but negative for the major exclusionary syndromes (48% of the antisocial alcoholics were positive for depression and/or mania). The data were reanalyzed using the more broadly defined selection criteria for subtyping. The findings showed no basic changes in the pattern of measures that had previously distinguished the four groups when the more restrictive criteria were used to subtype alcoholics. As a result, the revised criteria were selected to subtype the alcoholic subjects in this study.

Results

In this section, we shall first examine data obtained from the entire sample of patients who fulfilled diagnostic criteria for alcoholism on the PDI. Next, we shall present the results of a series of analyses that were used to contrast patients assigned to four alcoholic subtypes.

Prevalence of Psychiatric Syndromes. Table 11-1 shows the prevalence of the 15 basic syndromes reviewed by the PDI and their mean age of onset for the 565 patients who met the criteria for alcoholism [36]. The mean

Table 11-1. Prevalence of Psychiatric Syndromes and Age of Onset Among 565 Male Alcoholics in Five VA Treatment Programs

Syndromes*	N	%	Age of Onset	
			Mean	SD
Alcoholism only	210	37	32.8	12.4
Alcoholism and ≥ 1 other syndrome	355	63	25.6	10.5
OBS	11	2	—	—
Drug Abuse	68	12	23.9	8.5
Mania	125	22	21.2	10.6
Depression	238	42	26.3	13.3
Schizophrenia	23	4	21.0	11.8
Antisocial	115	20	13.7	3.5
Somatization	5	<1	17.4	5.5
Anorexia nervosa	1	<1	23.0	—
Obsessive-compulsive	68	12	25.0	8.8
Phobic disorder	54	10	16.2	7.5
Panic attacks	71	13	23.7	9.5
Mental retardation	8	1	8.0	1.4
Homosexuality	6	1	16.2	6.9
Transsexuality	0	0	—	—

*Because a patient could be positive for more than one syndrome, the percentages for the 15 basic syndromes sum to more than 100%. (Courtesy of the *Journal of Clinical Psychiatry*, slightly modified).

number of positive syndromes was 2.4 (SD = 1.07). Slightly over one third (37%) of the patients fulfilled diagnostic criteria for alcoholism only; 63% were positive for at least two syndromes. Twenty-nine percent fulfilled criteria for one syndrome in addition to alcoholism; 14 percent were positive for two additional syndromes; 14 percent were positive for three to four additional syndromes; while, 6 percent were positive for five or more additional syndromes. Depression occurred most frequently (42%) followed by Mania (22%) and Antisocial Personality (20%). Between 10 and 15 percent of the sample were positive for Drug Abuse, Panic Attacks, Phobia, and Obsessive-Compulsive disorder. The remaining syndromes occurred in less than 5 percent. (The absolute, not relative, prevalence of the syndromes varied somewhat by treatment center because of different admission policies. For example, all but seven of the 23 schizophrenics came from one rural center that received poorly screened patients directly from the Emergency

Room of another nearby urban VA center which did not have an identified alcoholism treatment program at the time of this study.)

For the *total* sample, the reported age of onset of problem drinking was 28 years. On the average, patients positive for alcoholism only reported a significantly later onset of problem drinking ($\bar{X} = 32.8$ years) than patients positive for at least one other syndrome in addition to alcoholism ($\bar{X} = 25.6$ years). This difference was highly significant ($p < .001$). The mean ages of onset for the other 14 syndromes corresponded reasonably well to those reported in the literature for nonalcoholic individuals diagnosed as suffering from the various disorders. Thus, the average age of onset for Depression (26 years) was later than that reported for either Mania (21 years) or Antisocial Personality (14 years). When the family history of alcohol abuse was examined among this sample, we found that 56 percent of the patients positive for alcoholism only ($N = 210$) reported one or more first degree relatives who abused alcohol. In contrast, 74 percent of the patients positive for an additional psychiatric syndrome ($N = 355$) reported that one or more of their first degree relatives abused alcohol ($p < .001$). The number of first degree relatives did not differ among these two groups.

These findings indicate that a large number of male alcoholics experience other kinds of psychiatric disorders that cause suffering to themselves or others. They also suggest that the presence of another psychiatric syndrome is associated with an earlier onset of problem drinking and a *greater* likelihood of having a first degree relative who has abused alcohol.

Characteristics of the Four Alcoholic Subtypes. Table 11-2 presents information about the socio-demographic characteristics of patients assigned to the four subtypes ($N = 530$). It will be noted that approximately 48 percent of those eligible were assigned to the Primary or Uncomplicated subtype: 18 percent were assigned to the Depressed subtype; 13 percent to the Manic subtype; and 20 percent met the selection criteria for the Antisocial subtype. As can be seen, the mean age of patients assigned to the four subtypes differed significantly. The primary patients were older than the affective disorder or antisocial alcoholics: the antisocials were younger than the affective disorder subtypes. However, the two affective disorder subtypes did not differ with respect to age. Neither education or months worked in the past year significantly distinguished the four groups although there was a trend toward less education among the antisocial subtype. Proportionally more of the antisocials had never married or were separated or divorced. The earned income and occupational status tended to be lower among antisocial alcoholics while few differences were found among the other three subtypes for these variables. Antisocials reported more recent job turnovers

Table 11-2. Social-Demographic Characteristics of Four Alcoholic Subgroups

Characteristics	Primary (N = 237)	Depressed (N = 98)	Manic (N = 71)	Antisocial (N = 104)	Total Sample (N = 530)	p*
Age: $\overline{X}$	49.7[a]	47.2[b]	45.4[b]	40.3[c]	46.8	.0001
					±10.70	
Education						NS
0–11	28.4%	32.6%	32.4%	35.6%	31.1%	
HS or GED	28.4	26.5	22.5	34.6	28.5	
>12	43.2	40.8	45.0	29.8	40.4	
Occupation						.005
Unskilled or semiskilled	24.2%	23.4%	25.4%	30.8%	25.5%	
Skilled	30.7	25.5	33.8	47.1	33.4	
Clerical	18.7	20.4	21.1	12.5	18.1	
Professional	26.5	30.6	19.7	9.6	23.0	
Income Last Year						.03
None	3.5%	2.0%	2.8%	2.9%	3.0%	
To 5,000	35.8	39.8	33.8	53.8	39.8	
5001–10,000	26.1	29.6	32.4	25.0	27.4	
10,000–15,000	18.3	14.3	16.9	7.7	15.3	
>15,000	16.3	14.3	14.1	10.6	14.5	
Months Worked Last Year: $\overline{X}$	5.8[a]	6.0[a]	6.0[a]	5.7[a]	5.8	NS
					±4.80	
Longest Job (years): $\overline{X}$	13.5[a]	11.5[b]	8.5[c]	6.1[c]	11.0	.0001
					±8.03	
Number Jobs Last 5 Years: $\overline{X}$	2.4[a]	2.7[a]	3.4[a]	7.8[b]	3.6	.0001
					±5.09	
Times Fired: $\overline{X}$	2.4[a]	2.2[a]	1.4[a]	5.5[b]	2.8	.0001
					±6.26	

(continued next page)

Table 11-2 (continued)

Characteristics	Primary (N = 237)	Depressed (N = 98)	Manic (N = 71)	Antisocial (N = 104)	Total Sample (N = 530)	p*
Work Status Last Month						
Wage earner	41.3%	33.7%	36.6%	31.7%	37.4%	.003
Retired	17.5	13.3	9.9	2.9	12.8	
Unemployed	37.0	49.0	46.5	61.5	45.3	
Other	4.3	4.1	7.0	3.9	4.5	
Marital Status:						
Never	10.5%	8.2%	21.1%	18.3%	13.0%	.01
Married	32.7	26.5	22.5	15.4	26.8	
Div or Sep	55.2	59.2	52.1	64.4	57.4	
Widowed	1.6	6.1	4.2	1.9	2.8	

*Based on χ^2 for categorical data and ANOVA with quantitative data. The Duncan Multiple Range Test was used to contrast subgroups; subscripts indicate statistical similarities or differences among subgroup means (*p* established at .05).

and more times fired from a job than the primary, depressed or manic subtypes. All four subtypes differed with respect to longevity on one job. Longest time spent on one job was greatest for the primary alcoholics followed by the depressed, manic, and antisocial alcoholics in that order.

These findings indicate that the antisocial alcoholics were younger, less well educated, and had experienced greater work instability at lower paying jobs than the primary and affective disordered patients. They were less likely to be married or living with a spouse. The primary alcoholics showed the greatest occupational and marital stability with the affective disordered patients assuming an intermediate position.

Development of Alcohol-Related Symptoms Among the Four Subtypes.
Table 11-3 presents a summary overview of the reported onset and duration of problem drinking as well as the occurrence of some of the more serious sociomedical sequelae that are associated with alcoholism. The reported onset of problem drinking for the primary alcoholics was significantly later than that reported for the manic and antisocial subtypes. There was a trend ($p < .09$) for depressed alcoholics to experience drinking problems before the primary alcoholics. Antisocial alcoholics reported the earliest onset of problem drinking. The duration of problem drinking did not distinguish the four subtypes. Antisocials reported the greatest number of alcohol-related hospitalizations, arrests, lost jobs, and separations from loved ones. The primary and affective disorder subtypes did not differ from each other on these measures. Fewer medical complaints were reported by the primary alcoholics in comparison to the other three subtypes.

Table 11-4 shows the percent of patients in each subtype who acknowledged symptoms common to abusive drinking. Nine of the 17 symptoms significantly distinguished the four subtypes. For all comparisons that achieved statistical significance, fewer of the primary alcoholics had experienced the symptom relative to the antisocials. The depressed and manic subtypes tended to swing between these two extremes. For some symptoms, the depressed and manic alcoholics most resembled the primary alcoholics while for other symptoms they more closely resembled the antisocial alcoholics. For example, blackouts were equally common among the depressed, manic and antisocial alcoholics but occurred more frequently in these groups than in the primary group. In contrast, drinking arrests occurred more often among the antisocials than among the primary, depressed or manic alcoholics which did not differ in this respect. In general, the affective disorder alcoholics tended to most closely resemble the antisocial alcoholics on symptoms associated with the physical concommitants of alcoholism (except severe withdrawal). They tended to least

Table 11-3. Onset, Duration, and Serious Sequelae of Abusive Drinking Amount Four Alcoholic Subtypes

Characteristic	Primary (N = 257)	Depressed (N = 98)	Manic (N = 71)	Antisocial (N = 104)	Total Sample (N = 530)	p*
Onset Problem Drinking (age)	32.1[a]	30.4[a]	25.9[b]	20.3[c]	28.6 ±10.83	.001
Duration Problem Drinking (years)	17.6[a]	16.8[a]	19.5[a]	20.0[a]	18.2 ±11.17	NS
ETOH-Related Hospitalizations: $\bar{X}$	3.4[a]	3.4[a]	4.1[a]	7.5[b]	4.3 ±6.97	.001
ETOH-Related Arrests: $\bar{X}$	6.1[a]	7.0[a]	7.4[a]	17.9[b]	8.8 ±16.94	.001
ETOH-Related Loss of Jobs: $\bar{X}$	2.2[a]	2.0[a]	1.3[a]	5.1[b]	2.6 ±6.25	.001
ETOH-Related Separation from Loved One:	49%	57%	51%	81%	57%	.001
$\bar{X}$ Medical Complaints (out of 26)	5.9[a]	7.5[b]	7.8[b]	8.5[b]	6.9 ±3.93	.001

*Based on χ^2 for categorical data and the ANOVA for quantative data. Subscripts are based upon results of the Duncan Multiple Range Test used to determine differences among subtypes; subtypes with the same subscript are not significantly different (p established at .05).

Table 11-4. Symptoms Reported by Four Alcoholic Subtypes

Alcoholism Symptoms*	Primary (N = 257)	Depressed (N = 98)	Manic (N = 71)	Antisocial (N = 104)	Total Sample (N = 530)	$p^†$
Two-day binges	94%	97%	97%	98%	96%	NS
Family Complained	89	92	84	89	89	NS
Guilt and Shame	89	94	90	95	91	NS
Blackouts	87	94	94	95	91	.02
Drinking Arrests	87	80	80	96	86	.002
Loss of Control	87	96	93	97	91	.003
DWI	84	83	86	93	86	NS
Unable to Stop	80	89	83	80	82	NS
Limit to Certain Times	80	82	87	82	82	NS
Morning drink	79	88	77	86	82	NS
Shakes when stopped ETOH	74	85	66	76	75	.04
Trouble at work	68	70	76	91	74	.001
Friends Complained	66	75	73	79	71	NS
Medical Problems	63	70	73	72	69	.01
Fighting	47	59	59	88	59	.001
Visions, convulsions, DTs when stopped ETOH	37	34	30	49	37	.008
Alcohol Substitutes	12	17	17	36	18	.001
X̄ Number Symptoms	12.2[a]	13.1[b]	12.7[a,b]	14.1[c]	12.8 ±2.77	.001

*Symptoms reviewed under the Auxiliary Section of the Alcoholism Syndrome on the Psychiatric Diagnostic Interview.
†Based on χ^2 for the categorical symptomatic data and the ANOVA for total number of PDI Auxiliary symptoms. Superscripts are based upon results of the Duncan Multiple Range Test used to determine differences among subtypes; subtypes with the same superscript are not significantly different (p established at .05).

resemble the antisocial alcoholics on symptoms associated with social manifestations of the disorder.

Medical Complaints Among the Four Subtypes. In Table 11-5, the reported occurrence of 26 medical complaints commonly associated with alcoholism are shown across the four subtypes. For those complaints which represent a definite medical disorder (e.g., cirrhosis of the liver, heart disease), the item was not scored unless diagnosed by a physician. For other complaints, the patients' subjective experiences were accepted (e.g., diarrhea, nightmares, vomiting blood, muscle weakness). During the interview, every effort was made to assure that the problems were related, in part, to heavy drinking (e.g., a physician told the patient drinking contributed to his heart disease).

Fourteen of the complaints differed across the four groups (two were included although the significance levels did not quite reach $p < .05$). In all instances, the primary patients experienced fewer of the alcohol-related medical complaints than the antisocial patients. This is especially striking since many of these complaints increase with age, yet the primary alcoholics were nine years older than the antisocial alcoholics on the average. Although the frequency of complaints among the depressed and manic alcoholics generally fell between that reported by primary and antisocial alcoholics, there were some exceptions. Serious sleep problems occurred most often among the depressed alcoholics while diarrhea and ulcer/gastric pain occurred most often among the manic alcoholics.

Treatment of Patients Assigned to the Four Subtypes. Table 11-6 presents different kinds of psychiatric or psychosocial treatment received by patients assigned to the four alcoholic subtypes. Primary alcoholics were less likely to have received mental health treatment for problems not specifically due to excessive drinking: they were less likely to have been hospitalized on a psychiatric unit for problems not exclusively related to abusive drinking. Primary alcoholics were also less likely to have utilized the services of Alcoholics Anonymous (AA) or to have received some type of somatic treatment. In contrast to results presented earlier, the antisocial alcoholics *did not* generally represent the extreme group among the four subtypes. Depressed and manic alcoholics were more likely to have received treatment for mental health problems not specifically due to drinking. However, inpatient psychiatric care or AA attendance did not differ among the antisocial and affective disorder subtypes. The nonprimary alcoholics were more likely to have received minor and major tranquilizers. Sedatives and pain medication were somewhat more often used by antisocial alcoholics in

Table 11-5. Medical Complaints Reported by Four Alcoholic Subtypes

Medical Complaint	Primary (N=257)	Depressed (N=98)	Manic (N=71)	Antisocial (N=104)	Total Sample (N=530)	p*
Numbness hands/feet	49%	61%	61%	58%	54%	.09
Serious sleep problem	47	72	56	64	56	.001
Impotency with ETOH	42	59	55	61	50	.001
High blood pressure	41	38	37	34	38	NS
Diarrhea	40	46	68	63	49	.001
Unsteady gait without ETOH	38	45	42	44	41	NS
Hallucinations withdrawal	37	40	46	57	43	.006
Ulcer/gastric pain	37	55	69	57	48	.001
Significant memory problem w/out ETOH	33	41	52	56	42	.001
Muscle weakness	35	41	55	51	42	.004
Other lung disorder	26	23	21	24	24	NS
Severe Nightmares	24	41	44	55	36	.001
Other liver problem	24	26	24	36	27	.08
Vomiting blood	21	36	24	36	27	.007
Bronchitis	16	20	30	28	21	.02
Seizure with ETOH	12	13	14	26	15	.007
Kidney Problem	12	10	11	18	13	NS
Seizure without ETOH	11	16	13	19	14	NS
Cirrhosis of Liver	10	9	5	11	9	NS
Heart disease	10	15	7	13	11	NS
Bladder problem	7	10	14	10	9	NS
Gall Bladder problem	7	5	3	2	5	NS
Prostate problem	7	10	13	11	9	NS
Diabetes	5	4	3	7	5	NS
Pancreatitis	3	8	10	11	7	.03
Thyroid disorder	1	1	1	4	2	NS

*Based on χ^2.

Table 11-6. Treatments Received for Psychiatric Complaints Reported by Four Alcoholic Subtypes

Treatments	Primary (N = 257)	Depressed (N = 98)	Manic (N = 71)	Antisocial (N = 104)	Total Sample (N = 530)	p*
Mental health treatment not specifically due to drinking:	20%	43%	44%	36%	31%	.001
Psychiatric hospitalization not exclusively related to alcohol abuse:	8	21	22	20	15	.001
AA (6 meetings):	39	46	51	53	44	.06
Drugs/Ect						
Minor Tranquilizer	56	70	76	71	64	.002
Antabuse	54	63	56	59	57	NS
Pain Medication	28	40	30	48	34	.001
Sedative	11	28	28	39	22	.001
Other Sleeping Meds	7	10	13	16	10	.09
Major tranquilizers	10	16	21	24	15	.004
Anti-Histamines	4	5	10	14	7	.005
Tricyclic Anti-depressant	4	19	20	16	11	.001
Electroshock	2	4	4	5	3	NS
Lithium	1	1	4	2	2	NS
MAO	0	0	1	0	0	NS
Number of above treatments: $\bar{X}$	2.7[a]	3.5[b]	3.6[b]	4.0[b]	3.2 ±1.83	.001

*Based on χ^2 for categorical data and the ANOVA for total number of Drug/Ect Treatments. Subscripts are based upon results of the Duncan Multiple Range Test used to determine differences among subtypes; subtypes with the same subscript are not significantly different (p established at .05).

comparison to depressed and manic alcoholics. Tricyclic antidepressants were more often prescribed to the affective disorder subtypes.

Family History of Alcoholism and Other Psychiatric Disorders by Subtype. Table 11-7 shows the prevalence of probable psychiatric disorder among the first degree relatives of patients assigned to the four alcoholic subtypes. After determining the number and sex of all siblings and offspring, patients were asked to indicate those relatives whom they knew little or nothing about. (Because of time constraints, the ages of first degree relatives were not obtained. The number of first degree relatives did not differ significantly across the four groups [Primary $\bar{X} = 7.6$; Depressed $\bar{X} = 8.2$; Manic $\bar{X} = 7.8$; Anti-Social $\bar{X} = 7.1$]. Very few of these relatives (less than 2%) were unknown to the patients. Psychiatric disorder among relatives was determined for nine conditions (see table 11-7) by a series of questions designed to focus on the cardinal features of the various disorders (these may be had upon request). When given an affirmative answer, the interviewer followed with probe questions in order to make certain that the cardinal symptoms interfered with the relative's ability to function, required treatment or caused significant concern to others. As can be seen, the prevalence of five conditions among first degree relatives significantly distinguished the four subtypes. Primary alcoholics, in contrast to antisocial alcoholics, were *less* likely to report a relative showing symptoms associated with Alcoholism, Depression, Mania, Antisocial Personality, and Panic Attacks. Hysteria/ Somatization disorder tended to be reported more often in the nonprimary subtypes, especially the manics and antisocials. Except for alcoholism, the prevalence of probable psychiatric disorder among relatives of the depressed and manic subtypes tended to fall between these two extremes. A family history of alcohol abuse was equally high among the three nonprimary subtypes. Differences between the primary and antisocial alcoholics are especially noteworthy because patients in the primary subgroup were older and thus presumably had more first degree relatives at risk for the various psychiatric conditions.

Table 11-8 provides more detailed information about specific relatives reported to have abused alcohol by subtypes. Not surprising, male relatives were more likely to have abused alcohol than female relatives. Brothers and fathers accounted for most of the relatives said to have experienced problems with alcohol. Primary and depressed alcoholics reported lower rates of alcohol abuse among their mothers than manic and antisocial alcoholics. On the other hand, equally high rates of excessive drinking were reported for the fathers of the three nonprimary subtypes. Sisters of the manic alcoholics

Table 11-7. Psychiatric Disorder in First-Degree Relatives of Four Alcoholic Subtypes

Probable Disorders in Family*	Primary (N = 257)	Depressed (N = 98)	Mania (N = 71)	Antisocial (N = 104)	Total Sample (N = 530)	χ^2 p
Alcoholism	58%	74%	68%	74%	65%	.003
Depression	24	30	45	45	32	.001
Mania	7	15	20	28	14	.001
Antisocial	23	32	38	45	31	.001
Panic Attack	5	8	8	15	8	.05
Somatization	8	14	18	13	12	.07
Psychosis	3	7	8	6	5	NS
Suicide Attempt	7	10	8	13	9	NS
Completed Suicide	3	5	3	2	3	NS

*The figures refer to the percent of patients within each subtype who reported *one or more* relative with the various psychiatric disturbances. A given relative may have been positive for more than one disturbance.

Table 11-8. First-Degree Relatives Positive for Probable Alcoholism Across the Four Alcoholic Subtypes

Affected Relative Category*	Primary (N = 257)	Depressed (N = 98)	Mania (N = 71)	Antisocial (N = 104)	Total Sample (N = 530)	X^2 p
Mothers	5%	6%	14%	15%	8%	.002
Fathers	30	43	45	46	38	.008
Sisters	10	16	1	16	11	.006
Brothers	29	39	31	27	31	NS
Daughters	1	1	1	2	1	NS
Sons	5	7	1	7	5	NS
Males	51	67	63	67	59	.006
Females	15	20	17	32	20	.004

*For categories reflecting siblings or offspring, the figures refer to the percent of patients within each subtype who reported *one or more* relative who experienced problems because of drinking.

were less likely to abuse alcohol than sisters of the other subtypes (the manic alcoholics had proportionally fewer sisters).

Because the relatives of patients were not examined directly, these findings must be regarded as tentative. Nevertheless, previous research has indicated that family histories obtained from psychiatric patients are reasonably accurate [1]. The results of the present study suggest that differential rates of psychiatric disorder among the four alcoholic subtypes are likely. Primary alcoholics appeared to have fewer affected first degree relatives than antisocial alcoholics. Once again, the rates of psychiatric disorder among relatives of the depressed and manic subtypes generally assumed an intermediate position. Although the family history data provide some support for the diagnostic validity of the four subtypes, familial disorders did not strickly "breed true." That is, relatives of the depressed subtype did not show the greatest tendency to suffer from depression; relatives of the manic subtype did not show the greatest tendency to suffer from mania or manic depressive disorder. Instead, first degree relatives of anti-social alcoholics appeared at greater risk for a broad spectrum of psychiatric conditions. (This was not due to the relatively large number of anti-social alcoholics who were also positive for an affective disorder. The proportion of relatives likely to suffer from a psychiatric disorder among anti-socials negative for mania and depression was similar to that of anti-socials who were positive for an affective disorder.)

Study II

Purpose

To provide preliminary information about the one-year outcome of alcoholics subtyped according to the presence or absence of another major psychiatric disorder in addition to alcoholism. Two subtypes were studied: Primary and Combined.

Subjects

Patients who served as subjects (N = 117) were drawn from two prospective studies currently in progress at the Kansas City VA Medical Center. Eighty (68%) were obtained from a study designed to evaluate the efficacy of lithium carbonate in reducing abusive drinking among primary, antisocial, depressed, and manic or manic-depressed alcoholics (Librium was given as an active placebo to one-half). Only eight of these subjects continued their medication during the entire 12-month followup period; most had discontinued taking lithium or Librium by the third month. In order to participate in this study, subjects had to be 21–60 years of age. Thirty-seven of the subjects (32%) were obtained from a second study that was conducted to examine the one-year outcome of alcoholics subtyped according to the presence of certain other co-existing psychiatric syndromes. Age was not a criterion for the second study. All were males hospitalized for treatment of alcoholism; 9 percent were black. All fulfilled diagnostic criteria for alcoholism on the PDI. Because of the relatively small N, the subjects were divided into two subtypes: Primary = negative for OBS, Drug Abuse, Schizophrenia, Mania, Depression and Antisocial Personality (as above, they could be positive for one or more of the lesser syndromes); Combined = negative for OBS, Drug Abuse, or Schizophrenia; positive for Mania, Depression, or Antisocial Personality (as before, the lesser syndromes could also be positive). Sixty-four percent of this sample (N = 71) were assigned to the primary subtype; thirty-six percent (N = 42) were assigned to the combined subtype. This division of subjects into primary and combined subtypes was based upon the findings presented in Study I, which indicated that primary alcoholics typically differed most from patients assigned to the depressed, manic or anti-social subtypes. Within this sample, only 20 patients (17%) fulfilled criteria for Anti-social Personality.

Method

While hospitalized, all patients received the *Psychiatric Diagnostic Interview* (PDI), which was used to assign patients to the Primary and Combined subtypes. In addition, they were given a structured *Psychosocial Interview* resembling that described in Study I as well as other psychological tests. A 33-item Alcoholism Severity Scale was also administered to the subjects. It contained questions about medical, social, interpersonal, and legal problems that often accompany excessive drinking. Patients drawn from the lithium outcome study were scheduled to be seen monthly in a special followup clinic; patients drawn from the PDI subtype outcome study were seen during their hospitalization and 12 months later. At follow-up one year later, many of the measures administered at entry into the two studies were repeated.

Results

As was true in the previous study, the primary alcoholics were significantly older than patients assigned to the combined subtype ($\overline{X} = 45.2$ vs. 39.0 years; $p < .05$). More of the combined alcoholics (58%) were single, separated, or divorced than the primary alcoholics (43%). Proportionally more of the combined alcoholic group (69%) had been fired from a job (compared to 57% for the primary alcoholics). The reported mean onset of problem drinking was 28.3 years (SD = 10.2) for the primary subtype and 24.8 years (SD = 10.1) for the combined subtype ($p < .05$). (The slight differences in current age and onset of problem drinking for this sample compared to those in Study I, are due to the age restriction for patients admitted to the lithium outcome study.) More of the patients in the combined subtype (62%) had been hospitalized one or more times for drinking before entry into the study (vs. 52% for the primary alcoholics).

Table 11-9 presents a summary of measures selected to examine change in excessive drinking and its complications during the one-year followup. During the one-year period *before* entering the two studies, fewer of the primary alcoholics: (1) had been hospitalized for excessive drinking, (2) had reported episodes of fighting associated with drinking, or (3) had been unable to work because of drinking ($p < .05$). Separation from a loved one because of drinking did not differ among the primary and combined alcoholic subtypes; there was a trend for more of the combined alcoholic group to experience problems with the police. Although days drinking during the six-month period before entering the studies did not distinguish the two groups, the total number of symptoms on the Alcohol Severity Scale for the combined alcoholic group was greater ($p < .05$) than that of the primary alcoholics. The findings presented thus far generally replicate those reported in Study I. The course of alcoholism among patients assigned to the primary subtype began later and was typically more benign than found for the combined subtype.

As noted in table 11-9, *both* the primary and combined subtypes reported substantial improvement after one year on all measures ($p < .05$). With one exception (i.e., separation from a loved one), the *magnitude* of the improvement did *not* differ among the two groups. Although the improvement was roughly parallel for the primary and combined alcoholic subtypes, the primary alcoholics continued to experience fewer difficulties because of drinking at the end of the one-year followup. These findings indicate that patients assigned to the combined subtype were more impaired because of drinking at the start of the studies and continued to manifest greater impairment at the end of one year in spite of their overall reduction in symptoms during that time.

Table 11-9. Complications of Drinking During the 12-Month Period Before Entry in the Study and During the One-Year Follow-up For Two Alcoholic Subtypes (N = 117)

Drinking Complications During the Previous Year	*Entry Into Study*		*One Year Later*		*Change*	
	Primary	*Combined*	*Primary*	*Combined*	*Primary*	*Combined*
ETOH Hospitalization	25%	40%	20%	36%	−5%	−4%
Fighting	53	74	23	40	−30	−34
Unable to Work	32	52	11	28	−21	−24
Trouble with Police	60	68	16	21	−44	−47
Separated from Loved One	45	43	14	28	−31	−15
Days Drinking (Last 6 months)						
$\bar{X}$	124.5	126.0	51.1	56.7	−73	−69
SD	57.2	45.1	58.0	58.3		
Alcoholism Severity Score						
$\bar{X}$	16.4	18.5	8.2	11.6	−8.2	−6.9
SD	4.8	4.6	6.9	8.1		

Discussion

The results of two studies indicate that male alcoholics often experience symptoms associated with other psychiatric syndromes. Roughly one- to two-thirds of the patients were found to fulfill inclusive diagnostic criteria for one or more syndromes in addition to alcoholism. It was hypothesized that subtyping alcoholics according to certain syndrome combinations might serve to account for some of the diversity in course and outcome often observed among large, unselected groups of alcoholics.

In the first study, the onset of problem drinking and complications associated with abusive drinking were found to differ significantly among four subtypes (Primary, Depressed, Manic or Manic-Depressed, and Antisocial). Family history of probable psychiatric disorder among first degree relatives also distinguished patients assigned to the four subtypes. Primary alcoholics, positive for no other major psychiatric syndrome, generally showed a later onset of problem drinking, fewer and less severe complications as well as fewer relatives with a psychiatric disturbance than the antisocial alcoholics. The onset, course, and family history of the depressed and manic subtypes typically fell between these two extremes. The second study examined the 12-month outcome of primary alcoholics and a combined group containing alcoholics positive for depression, mania or antisocial personality. The results indicated that the primary alcoholics suffered less impairment from drinking than the combined group when first examined and one year later although both groups showed significant improvement during the followup period.

The findings of these studies offer support for the clinical validity of using syndrome combinations to classify or subtype alcoholics. This empirical approach to subtyping alcoholics appears to produce groups which are more homogenous with regard to family history, development and severity of excessive drinking, complications associated with alcohol abuse and outcome following treatment for alcoholism. We are not aware of any method of classifying alcoholics that has achieved this degree of empirical support.

Although the use of syndrome combinations to subtype alcoholics has not been studied as such, several investigators have reported multiple psychiatric syndromes among alcoholics. For example, Fowler et al. [10] reported that 67% of their alcoholic patients fulfilled diagnostic criteria for at least one other syndrome. Weissman et al. [43], in a nonclinical community study which included females, reported a similar rate of 70 percent. Although Winokur et al. [44] originally stated that only 27% of their male alcoholics were positive for an additional syndrome, a subsequent report of the same data [2] showed that approximately 50 percent of the patients were positive for another syndrome when depression secondary to alcoholism is included. In all of these studies but one [10], depression was most often identified, followed by anti-social personality, drug abuse and mania. Recently, Lee Robins [38] also reported that additional psychiatric syndromes among patients treated for alcoholism are relatively common. She found that 69 percent of the in-patient alcoholics (which apparently included females) were positive for Depression, 32 percent were positive for Panic Attacks, 13 percent were positive for Somatization Disorder and 20 percent were positive for Antisocial Personality.

As we stated earlier, the diagnostic significance of multiple psychiatric syndromes has not been systematically studied among alcoholics (or psychiatric patients in general for that matter). Nevertheless, the literature contains some instances in which research has focused on alcoholic patients who are positive for one or more additional psychiatric syndromes. Unfortunately, the subject samples have been typically quite small and mostly drawn from psychiatric inpatient units. For example, Woodruff et al. [46] and Keeler [24] have attempted to summarize studies that have examined the relationship between alcoholism and affective disorder. It is noted that depression among alcoholics seems to result in an increased risk for suicidal manifestations. Other differences observed between alcoholics with and without depression have included clinical features, sex ratio, onset of the disorder and family history although the findings are not always consistent. Keeler [24] tentatively concludes that the clinical pictures of alcoholics with depression more closely resemble those of alcoholics without depression than depressed patients who are not alcoholic. Similarly, studies of alcoholism among prisoners, most of whom were positive for antisocial personality, have indicated that the family history and social/personal adjustment of alcoholic sociopaths differ from those of depressed alcoholics. Results of these studies also suggested that the long-term outcome of antisocial alcoholics differs from that of antisocial individuals who were not positive for alcoholism [13,18]. Though tentative from the perspective of classification, these findings in addition to our own, support the view that subtyping alcoholics by the presence or absence of co-existing psychiatric syndromes may result in a topology of considerable predictive value that would be useful to the practitioner and researcher [44,45]. Historically, advances in the understanding, control, treatment and clinical management of medical disorders have often followed refinements in diagnostic procedures [25]. The recent availability of several criterion-based, structured diagnostic interviews (such as the PDI) provides both a rationale and method for separating the broadly defined class of alcoholism into clinically meaningful subtypes.

References

1. Andreasen, N. C., Endicott, J., Spitzer, R. L., and Winokur, G. The family history using diagnostic criteria: Reliability and Validity. *Arch. Gen. Psychiatry*, 34:1229, 1977.
2. Cadoret, R., Winokur, G. Depression in alcoholism. *Ann. NY Acad. Sci.* 233:34, 1972.
3. Crane, D. L. Manic Depressive Disease and Alcoholism. In Seixas, F. A. (ed.), *Currents in Alcoholism*, Vol. 2. New York: Grune and Stratton, 1977.
4. *Diagnostic and Statistical Manual of Mental Disorders*, (3rd ed.). Washington, D.C.: American Psychiatric Association, 1980.
5. Donovan, D. M., Chaney, E. F., and O'Leary, M. R. Alcoholic MMPI subtypes. *J. Nerv. Ment. Dis.* 166:553, 1978.
6. Evenson, R., and Altman, H., Sletten, V. W., and Knowles, R. Factors in the description and grouping of alcoholics. *Am. J. Psychiatry* 30:49, 1973.
7. Feighner, J. P., Robins, E., Guze, S. B., et al. Diagnostic criteria for use in psychiatric research. *Arch. Gen. Psychiatry* 26:57, 1972.
8. Finney, J. W. and Moos, R. H. Treatment and outcome for empirical subtypes of alcoholic patients. *J. Consult. Clin. Psychol.* 47:25, 1979.
9. Foulds, G. A. and Hassall, C. The significance of age of onset of excessive drinking in male alcoholics. *Br. J. Psychiatry* 115:1027, 1969.
10. Fowler, R. C., Liskow, B. I., and Tanna, V. L. Psychiatric illness and alcoholism. *Alcoholism* 1:125, 1977.
11. Gibbs, L. E. A classification of alcoholics relevant to type-specific treatment. *Int. J. Addict.* 15:461, 1980.
12. Goldstein, S. G. and Linden, J. D. Multivariate classification of alcoholics by means of the MMPI. *J. Abnorm. Psychol.* 74:661, 1969.
13. Goodwin, D. W., Crane, J. B., and Guze, S. B. Felons who drink: An 8-year follow-up. *Q. J. Stud. Alcohol* 32:136, 1971.
14. Goodwin, D. W. and Guze, S. B. *Psychiatric Diagnosis.* New York: Oxford University Press, 1979.
15. Goodwin, D. W. Familial alcoholism: a separate entity? Paper presented to the World Congress of Psychiatry, Los Angeles, California, January, 1983.
16. Gottheil, E., McLellan, T. A., and Druley, K. A. *Substance Abuse and Psychiatric Illness.* New York: Pergamon Press, 1980.
17. Guze, S. B. The need for tough-mindedness in psychiatric thinking. *South. Med. J.* 63:662, 1970.
18. Guze, S. B. *Criminality and Psychiatric Disorders.* New York: Oxford University Press, 1976.
19. Hathaway, S. R. and McKinley, F. C. *Minnesota Multiphasic Personality Inventory.* New York: Psychological Corporation, 1967.
20. Hedlund, J. L. and Vieweg, B. W. Structured psychiatric interviews: A comparative review. *J. Oper. Psychiatry* 12:39, 1981.
21. Helzer, J. E., Robins, L. N., Croughan, J. L., and Welner, A. Renard

diagnostic interview: its reliability and procedural validity with physicians and lay interviewers. *Arch. Gen. Psychiatry* 38:393, 1981.

22. Horn, J. L. and Wanberg, K. W. Symptom patterns related to excessive use of alcohol. *Q. J. Stud. Alcohol* 30:35, 1969.

23. Jellinek, E. M. *The Disease Concept of Alcoholism.* New Brunswick, N.J.: Hillhouse Press, 1960.

24. Keeler, M. H. Alcoholism and Affective Disorder. In Pattison, E. M. and Kaufman, E. (eds.), *Encyclopedic Handbook of Alcoholism.* New York: Gardner Press, 1982, pp. 618.

25. Klein, D. F. A Proposed Definition of Mental Illness. In Spitzer, R. L. and Klein, D. F., (eds.) *Critical Issues in Psychiatric Treatment.* New York: Raven Press, 1978.

26. Knight, R. P. The dynamic and treatment of chronic alcohol addiction. *Bull. Menninger Clinic* 1:233, 1937.

27. Morey, L. C. and Blashfield, R. K. A empirical classification of alcoholism. *J. Stud. Alcohol* 42:925, 1981.

28. Morrison, J. R. Bipolar affective disorder and alcoholism. *Am. J. Psychiatry* 131:1130, 1974.

29. Nerviano, V. J. Common personality patterns among alcoholic males: a multivariate study. *J. Consult. Clin. Psychol.* 44:104, 1976.

30. Othmer, E., Penick, E. C. and Powell, B. J. *Psychiatric Diagnostic Interview.* Los Angeles: Western Psychological Services, 1981.

31. Owen, P. L. and Butcher, J. N. Personality Factors in Problem Drinking: A Review of the Evidence and Some Suggested Directions. In Pickens, R. W. and Heston, L. L. (eds.), *Psychiatric Factors in Drug Abuse.* New York: Grune and Stratton, 1979.

32. Parsons, O. A., and Leber, W. R. The relationship between cognitive dysfunction and brain damage in alcoholics: Causal, interactive or epiphenomenal? *Alcoholism* 5:326, 1981.

33. Partington, J. T. and Johnson, F. G. Personality types among alcoholics. *Q. J. Stud. Alcohol* 30:21, 1969.

34. Pattison, E. M. The Selection of Treatment Modalities for the Alcoholic Patient. In Mendelson, J. H. and Mello, N. K. (eds.), *The Diagnosis and Treatment of Alcoholism.* New York: McGraw-Hill, 1979.

35. Penick, E. C., Read, M. R., Crawley, P. A., and Powell, B. J. Differentiation of alcoholics by family history. *J. Stud. Alcohol* 39:1944, 1978.

36. Powell, B. J., Penick, E. C., Othmer, E., et al. Prevalence of additional psychiatric syndromes among male alcoholics. *J. Clin. Psychiatry* 43:404, 1982.

37. Robins, E., Gentry, K. A., Munoz, R. A., and Marten, S. A contrast of the three more common illnesses with the ten less common in a study and 18-month follow-up of 314 psychiatric emergency room patients. *Arch. Gen. Psychiatry* 34:259, 1977.

38. Robins, L. N. The Diagnosis of Alcoholism after DSM-III. In Pattison, E. M.

and Kaufman, E. (eds.), *Encyclopedic Handbook of Alcoholism*. New York: Gardner Press, 1982.

39. Schuckit, M., Rimmer, J., Reich, T., and Winokur, G. Alcoholism: anti-social traits in male alcoholics. *Br. J. Psychiatry* 117:575, 1970.

40. Schuckit, M. A., Gunderson, E. K. E., Heckman, N. A., and Kolb, D. Family history as a predictor of alcoholism in U.S. Navy personnel. *J. Stud. Alcohol* 37:1678, 1976.

41. Skinner, H. A. and Blashfield, R. K. Increasing the impact of cluster analysis research: the case of psychiatric classification. *J. Consult. Clin. Psychol.* 50:727, 1982.

42. Wanberg, K. W., Horn, J. L., and Foster, F. M. A differential assessment model for alcoholism. *J. Stud. Alcohol* 38:512, 1977.

43. Weissman, M. M., Meyers, J. K., and Harding, P. S. Prevalence and psychiatric heterogeneity of alcoholism in a United States urban community. *J. Stud. Alcohol* 41:672, 1980.

44. Winokur, G., Reich, T., Rimmer, T. and Pitts, F. Alcoholism III. Diagnosis and familial psychiatric illness in 259 alcoholic probands. *Arch. Gen. Psychiatry* 23:104, 1970.

45. Winokur, G., Rimmer, J. and Reich, T. Alcoholism: IV. Is there more than one type of alcoholism? *Br. J. Psychiatry* 118:525, 1971.

46. Woodruff, R. A., Guze, S. B., Clayton, P. J. and Carr, D. Alcoholism and Depression. In Goodwin, D. W. and Erickson, C. K. (eds.), *Alcoholism and Affective Disorder*. New York: SP Medical and Scientific Books, 1979.

12 ANTISOCIAL BEHAVIOR, PSYCHOPATHOLOGY AND PROBLEM DRINKING IN THE NATURAL HISTORY OF ALCOHOLISM

Michie N. Hesselbrock
Victor M. Hesselbrock,
Thomas F. Babor
James R. Stabenau
Roger E. Meyer
Meredith Weidenman

It is well known that alcoholism often occurs in persons having an antisocial personality. Conversely, the behavior of persons with alcoholism often appears to be antisocial in nature. Thus, the differentiation of alcoholism from antisocial personality can be quite difficult and lead to diagnostic confusion [27]. While these two disorders are similar in some respects, and may sometimes occur together, their natural histories probably differ.

The chronologic ordering of events leading to alcohol dependence may be useful in distinguishing alcoholic persons with antisocial personality from

Supported by NIAAA grant #AA 03510-04, Center for the Study of Alcoholism, and by Research Scientist Development Grant K01 AA 00025-04 (Dr. Babor)

those alcoholics without antisocial personality. According to formalized diagnostic criteria (e.g. Diagnostic Statistical Manual of Mental Disorders, 3rd ed. [DSM-III], [RDC]), persons with antisocial personality are likely to engage in unusually early regular alcohol use and frequent intoxication. As a result, their precocious use of alcohol may precipitate the usual consequences (social, psychological, physical) earlier than in alcoholic persons without antisocial personality. While the severity of the psychological and physical consequences experienced by alcoholics with antisocial personality may be moderated by their youth and better physical condition, the severity of the social consequences experienced should be similar to those experienced by alcoholics without antisocial personality.

The following study will examine whether family history of alcoholism, childhood behavior problems, psychopathology, and drinking history can be used to distinguish the development of two potentially different types of alcoholism, one type associated with antisocial personality and the other type not associated with antisocial personality.

Family history research suggests that alcoholism and antisocial personality are different entities. While both alcoholic probands and antisocial probands tend to have more alcoholic relatives than the general population, the prevalence of antisocial personality found among relatives of alcoholic probands is similar to that of the general population. Additionally, Reich et al. [18] have found that the risk for alcoholism among the relatives of probands with both alcoholism and antisocial personality is higher than the risk for alcoholism among relatives of probands with alcoholism only or probands with antisocial personality only. On the other hand, a high rate of antisocial personality was found only among the relatives of probands with antisocial personality, while the prevalence of antisocial personality among the relatives of alcoholic probands did not differ from general population figures. The implication of these findings is that alcoholism and antisocial personality are separate disorders and are not necessarily transmitted in the same families.

Problem behavior in childhood is often cited as an etiologic factor for a variety of adult psychiatric disorders. The most consistent finding is that childhood conduct disorder is associated with adult antisocial behavior. Robins has examined this association in depth [19–21,24]. While adult antisocial behavior by definition virtually requires childhood antisocial behavior, Robins' studies indicate that most children with antisocial behavior do not become antisocial adults. Further, she has found that it is the variety of problem behaviors in childhood that is most predictive of adult behavior, not any single behavior.

The development of alcoholism has also been associated with conduct problems in childhood. In a longitudinal follow-up study of delinquent boys,

McCord and McCord [13] found that those boys who later became alcoholic tended to be more active, aggressive, and sadistic in childhood. Robins [22] found that antisocial behavior by clients at a child guidance clinic was a distinguishing characteristic of males who later became alcoholic. In addition to studies of atypical samples, a similar personality pattern has also been identified in general population surveys of problem drinking and in follow-up studies of nonclinic samples. The Oakland Growth Study [11] found that boys who later became problem drinkers tended to be more assertive, extroverted, rebellious, and impulsive in childhood. Using retrospective methods to study problem drinkers drawn from a general population survey, Cahalan and Room [2] identified youthful rashness, "hell-raising," and unhappiness as early predictors of adult drinking problems.

The literature linking antisocial personality and alcoholism in adulthood with childhood conduct disorder suggests that alcoholics with antisocial personality may have an early onset of alcohol-related problems. Several studies of adolescent problem drinkers have identified tolerance of deviance [10,17,33] and related personality traits (e.g., waywardness, distrust, aggressive sociability, cynicism) as correlates, as well as predictors, of acute alcohol problems in adolescence.

A particular class of childhood problem behaviors indicating "hyperactivity" (HK) or "minimal brain dysfunction " (MBD) has received considerable attention as a putative risk factor for the development of psychopathology in adult life. Tarter [28,29] has found that many persons diagnosed as having primary alcoholism report having had more of HK/MBD behaviors in childhood than persons with secondary alcoholism. He suggests that HK/MBD may be a necessary (but not sufficient) condition for primary alcoholism. Other investigators, including Morrison and Stewart [14] and Hale et al. [5], have found a relationship between childhood MBD and the later development of alcoholism and adult antisocial personality. It should be noted, however, that HK/MBD is a rather loosely defined concept that is not clearly distinguished from childhood antisocial behavior. Operational definitions of the two disorders often overlap in terms of the behaviors cited. If the HK/MBD syndrome were more clearly separated from childhood antisocial behavior, its predictive value might be increased. For example, it might be hypothesized that adults with alcoholism had a higher frequency of HK/MBD behaviors during childhood, while adults with antisocial personality and alcoholism would report more childhood antisocial behavior. It is possible, however, that HK/MBD and childhood antisocial behavior may occur simultaneously.

The presence of other psychopathology in adulthood may also serve to distinguish the two groups. Substance abuse is often found with both alcoholism and antisocial personality [3,4]. However, one would expect to find a higher prevalence and an earlier age of onset of substance abuse in persons with antisocial personality than in persons with alcoholism. Depression, on the other hand, is commonly found among alcoholics [4,30] but is less frequently associated with antisocial personality. Other types of psychopathology, particularly those of a subclinical nature, may also distinguish persons with alcoholism and antisocial personality from other persons with alcoholism.

Method

The study sample was drawn from three inpatient alcoholism treatment facilities in the greater Hartford, Connecticut area. At the end of the admission day randomly selected patients were asked to participate in a multidisciplinary research project on alcoholism. The following day subjects who volunteered began spending several afternoons in research activities. Informed consent was obtained from each subject. Between January 1979 and June 1981, 250 subjects were evaluated.

A variety of data were collected from each subject, including demographic information, indications of childhood adjustment, personality characteristics, neuropsychological functioning, biomedical status, and drinking history. A psychiatric screening interview was conducted by a trained research assistant using the NIMH-DIS [1981]. The reliability of this interview method has been reported [8,23]. Diagnoses were made using DSM-III. The psychiatric status of first and second degree biological relatives was assessed using methods developed by Andreasen et al. [1]. Family history-RDC criteria were used to diagnose family members [1]. Using information obtained from the NIMH-DIS, all subjects in this sample met DSM-III criteria for alcohol dependence. Eighty-nine men (49%) and 12 women (19%) also met DSM-III criteria for the diagnosis of antisocial personality (ASP).

Results

Demographic Characteristics

Table 12-1 provides a demographic description of the subjects with and without antisocial personality (ASP) by sex. The men and women with ASP

Table 12-1. Demographic Characteristics of the Sample

	Males		Females	
	ASP (N = 89)	NonASP (N = 91)	ASP (N = 12)	NonASP (N = 52)
Age (years)	34.2 (±9.7)	43.7 (±11.2)*	29.1 (±5.8)	39.2 (±11.7)*
Education				
<H.S.	33.0%	33.0%	50.0%	15.4%
H.S.	39.0	27.7	16.7	48.1
H.S.+	21.8	21.1	33.0	26.9
College Degree & Graduate Degree	5.7	17.8	0.0	9.6
Marital Status				
Single	40.2%	22.2%	25.0%	25.0%
Married	21.8	36.7	41.7	36.5
Sep/Div	37.9	41.1	33.3	38.5
Occupation				
I-II Professional	1.2%	9.0%	0.0%	3.9%
III-IV Sales, Clerical	16.7	31.8	33.3	52.9
V Skilled	27.4	23.9	0.0	5.9
VI+ Semi-Skilled, Unskilled	54.8	35.2	66.7	37.3

*$p < .05$

were significantly younger than those without the diagnosis of ASP at the time of admission to the hospital (34.2 vs. 43.7 years for males, and 29.1 vs. 39.2 years for females respectively). Subjects without ASP had also achieved a higher level of education. While the majority of all males had completed a high school education, only half of the ASP females as compared to a majority of the nonASP females completed high school (50% vs. 85%). The rate of separation and divorce were similar for the ASP and non-ASP males, while the non-ASP women had a higher rate of separation and divorce than ASP women. The proportion of nonASP men and women who held a professional occupation was higher than for the ASP subjects. More than half of ASP men and women held semi-skilled or unskilled jobs.

Family History

An examination of the drinking style of the relatives of our sample revealed a much higher lifetime prevalence of alcoholism than would be expected from general population data ($\approx$8% males; $\approx$3% females). In table 12-2 the sample was divided according to the diagnosis of the proband. The frequency of alcoholism was generally higher among both first and second degree relatives of probands with ASP than relatives of probands without ASP. The frequency of alcoholism found among the fathers of ASP probands was particularly high. While alcoholism was about equally distributed among the first and second degree relatives of ASP probands, alcoholism was noticeably higher among the first degree relatives as compared to the second degree relatives of probands without ASP.

It is also of interest to note the extent of assortative mating found in this sample. While probands with ASP were more likely to have an alcoholic spouse than probands without ASP, female probands (regardless of whether

Table 12-2. Alcoholism Among the Relatives of Alcoholic Probands With and Without ASP

	Males			
	ASP Probands		NonASP Probands	
Relative	f/n	%	f/n	%
Father	37/89	41.6	26/79	32.9
Mother	12/89	13.5	8/79	10.1
Siblings	45/300	15.0	42/265	15.8
All 1°	94/478	19.7	76/423	18.0
All 2°	124/731	16.9	65/521	12.5*
Spouse	9/100	9.0	7/92	7.6
	Females			
Father	7/12	58.3	16/48	33.3
Mother	1/12	8.3	11/51	21.6
Siblings	10/38	26.3	15/120	12.5
All 1°	18/62	29.0	42/219	19.2
All 2°	30/109	27.5	15/381	13.4†
Spouse	8/17	47.1	16/61	26.2

$*\chi^2 = 3.55 \; p \leq .10$
$†\chi^2 = 42.29 \; p \leq .01$

Table 12-3. Indicators of Childhood Adjustment Problems

HK/MBD	Childhood Antisocial Behavior
Impulsive	Daydreamed a lot
Talked too much	Tended to anger friends
Didn't work up to ability	Easily frustrated
Preferred to stay alone	Hard to get to bed at night
Overactive	Trouble accepting corrections
Fidgety	Demanded attention
Unable to sit still	Unpredictable
Poor Handwriting	Unresponsive to discipline
Did not complete projects	Lied a lot
Short attention span	Fought a lot
Couldn't tolerate delay	Problems with stealing
Got into things	Overly aggressive
Accident prone	Temper tantrums
Felt left out	Truant
Difficulty learning to read	Preferred to stay alone
Poor coordination	Wore out toys, clothes

they have ASP or not) were three to five times more likely to have an alcoholic spouse than male probands.

Childhood Behaviors

Retrospective information on indicators of childhood adjustment was collected using items from Tarter's [29] and Wender's [31] behavior checklists. Each subject reported on the occurrence of these behaviors prior to the age of 12. Although Tarter and Wender use these items to assess childhood HK and MBD, a number of the items are indicative of childhood antisocial behavior. Of the 32 items used, 17 were identified as indicators of HK/MBD, while 16 items were identified as childhood antisocial behaviors. One item, "preferred to stay alone," appeared in both groups (see table 12-3). Positively endorsed items were summed to create a HK/MBD scale and a childhood ASP scale. Because of the large differences in current age between the ASP and nonASP groups, age at the current admission was used as a covariate. Table 12-4 shows the differences in childhood HK/MBD and childhood ASP behaviors between ASP and nonASP alcoholic subjects.

Male and female alcoholics with ASP reported significantly more adjustment problems prior to age 12 than nonASP alcoholics. Surprisingly,

Table 12-4. Comparison of the Occurrence of Childhood Problem Behaviors

	Raw Score		Males* Age Adjusted			
	ASP $\bar{X}$	NonASP $\bar{X}$	ASP $\bar{X}$	NonASP $\bar{X}$	F	Significance Level
HK/MBD	7.63	5.61	7.39	5.84	6.7	.010
ASP	7.35	4.38	7.07	4.66	18.7	.000
Total	14.98	10.0	14.46	10.5	13.2	.000
			Females[†]			
HK/MBD	9.75	5.86	9.43	5.93	10.2	.002
ASP	9.34	3.93	8.65	4.08	20.2	.000
Total	19.08	9.79	18.08	10.2	17.6	.000

*Male ASP (N = 89) NonASP (N = 91)
[†] Female ASP (N = 12) NonASP (N = 52)

both HK/MBD and childhood antisocial behaviors were more frequently found among ASP alcoholics than nonASP alcoholics.

Psychopathology

The extent of other psychopathology was also assessed from the NIMH-DIS using DSM-III criteria. No differences were found between ASP and nonASP subjects (67% ASP females, 65% nonASP females: 38% ASP males, 32% nonASP males). However, it was found that the occurrence of major depressive disorder (lifetime) was higher among female than male subjects (66% vs. 35%; $\chi^2 = 22.4$, df = 1, $p \leq .01$).

Other types of substance abuse/dependence were also found to be quite common in this sample. In order to summarize the wide variety of other substances used by these subjects, a single category of "drug abuse problem" was created. As expected, the occurrence of a drug abuse problem was found to be significantly higher for both men and women with ASP than for those without ASP. Drug abuse (lifetime) was found among 65 percent of ASP men as compared to 26 percent of the non-ASP men ($\chi^2 = 27.3$, df = 1, $p \leq$

.01). Among the females, drug abuse (lifetime) was found in 75 percent of those with ASP versus 29 percent of those without ASP ($\chi^2 = 8.9$, df $= 1$, $p \leq .01$).

Each subject also completed a Minnesota Multiphasic Personality Inventory (MMPI) (550 items) as part of their evaluation. The mean MMPI profiles, adjusted for age, for the males with and without ASP were similar in configuration and in elevation. No differences in elevation were found on any subscale, including the Pd scale. The average profile for both male groups was a 2-4-8 configuration, which is rather typical among persons with alcoholism. The age-adjusted MMPI profiles for women with or without ASP were also examined. All subscale scores were higher for the ASP women than the nonASP women. Differences in elevation were significant for the Sc, Ma, and Si scales. The average configuration for the ASP women was 4-6-8, which suggests schizophrenia. The profile configuration of the non-ASP women was very similar to that found for the men, i.e. 2-4-8. While the profile of ASP women differed from that of the nonASP women and that of men, it could be due to the small sample of ASP women.

Course of Alcoholism

A historical description of the course of alcoholism for both ASP and nonASP alcoholics is shown in table 12-5. Both men and women with ASP were found to begin drinking at a much earlier age and to progress from regular drinking to alcoholism much faster than nonASP subjects. Even though the sample of ASP women was small, this trend was consistent for both men and women with ASP.

Since the average age of ASP alcoholics at admission was significantly younger than that of nonASP alcoholics, the chronicity of alcohol problems was examined by analysis of covariance, treating age at admission as a covariate (see table 12-6). Without correcting for age, no differences between ASP and nonASP subjects were found in terms of the number of years spent in problem drinking, regular drunkenness, drinking for relief and number of previous treatment experiences. However, once an age correction was used, ASP men were found to be more chronically involved with alcohol and to have experienced more alcohol-related problems than nonASP men. Although a similar trend was found for women, the only significant difference found between ASP and nonASP subjects was in the number of years of regular drunkenness.

Table 12-5. Course of Alcoholism of Probands With or Without ASP

	Males		Females	
	ASP (N = 89)	NonASP (N = 91)	ASP (N = 12)	NonASP (N = 52)
Current age	34.2 (±10)	43.7 (±11)	29.1 (±6)	39.2 (±12)
Age first				
Drink	12.1 (±4)	15.6 (±5)‡	14.2 (±3)	16.3 (±4)
Got drunk	14.7 (±3)	19.6 (±6)‡	15.3 (±3)	21.0 (±7)†
Age				
Began regular drinking	16.3 (±3)	20.3 (±6)‡	16.0 (±2)	23.3 (±8)†
Drunk regularly	18.7 (±4)	26.3 (±9)‡	16.7 (±3)	29.9 (±10)‡
Realized alcohol gave relief	17.8 (±5)	26.1 (±9)‡	17.6 (±4)	27.0 (±9)‡
Realized drinking was problem	26.0 (±7)	35.7 (±10)‡	23.1 (±6)	33.5 (±10)‡
Others said drinking was problem	23.0 (±7)	34.2 (±11)‡	19.8 (±3)	32.6 (±10)‡
First tried to stop	27.7 (±8)	37.9 (±10)‡	21.4 (±4)	34.7 (±10)‡
First AA contact*	29.5 (±9)	39.0 (±11)‡	26.1 (±7)	37.3 (±11)‡

For those who have contacted AA.
†$p \leq .01$
‡$p \leq .001$

Consequences of Drinking

Various consequences of drinking were derived from two self-report assessments. One instrument, a survey of the past six months of drinking experiences, was designed to provide a comprehensive description of recent drinking practices, motivation for drinking, quantity and frequency of consumption, and consequences of drinking. Items were selected primarily from the National Council on Alcoholism criteria [15]. The scales discussed in the present report were derived conceptually to investigate various aspects of the consequences of heavy drinking.

A second instrument concentrated on withdrawal symptoms and drinking behavior during the thirty days just prior to hospital admission [6]. Subclinical withdrawal symptomatology, particularly somatic discomfort and psychological disturbance, were assessed in addition to the quantity and frequency of consumption. Scales describing the consequences of drinking were derived from a factor analysis, and then validated by external criteria [7].

Scales reflecting consequences of alcohol abuse and dependence were examined using age as a covariate. The results are displayed in table 12-7. Not only was the course of alcoholism more chronic among ASP men, but they also reported significantly more physical and withdrawal symptoms during the month prior to admission. The greater intensity of alcohol involvement among ASP men was also reflected in their having consumed greater amounts of alcohol. While ASP females tended to report more withdrawal symptoms and affective disturbance in the month prior to hospital admission, they also reported significantly more physical disturbances. In the six-month period prior to admission, however, ASP and nonASP subjects (both men and women) reported similar consequences of drinking except for social problems. ASP men experienced a higher degree of social consequences (i.e. involved in accident, picked up by police, became violent, etc.) than nonASP men. While no differences were found between ASP and nonASP subjects in terms of family problems, this could be due to the fact that many ASP men were either single, divorced or separated.

Table 12-6. Chronicity of Alcohol Problems Among ASP and NonASP Alcoholics

	Males					
	Raw Score		Age Adjusted Score			
	ASP (N = 89) $\bar{X}$	NonASP (N = 91) $\bar{X}$	ASP (N = 89) $\bar{X}$	NonASP (N = 91) $\bar{X}$	F	p
Number of Years						
Problem drinking	7.49	7.61	9.31	5.79	10.3	.002
Got drunk regularly	15.48	15.38	18.90	12.00	28.7	.000
Drink for relief	15.75	16.34	19.18	12.96	22.9	.000
Number of previous treatments	3.9	3.2	4.2	2.9	5.7	.019
	Females					
Problem drinking	5.84	5.18	7.65	4.70	2.7	N.S.
Got drunk regularly	12.42	7.29	14.10	6.90	12.3	.001
Drink for relief	11.50	11.51	14.53	10.80	2.9	N.S.
Number of previous treatments	3.9	3.0	4.4	2.9	1.2	N.S.

Table 12-7. Consequences of Drinking Experienced by Alcoholics With and Without ASP: Age Adjusted

	Males				Females			
	ASP (N=89) $\bar{X}$	NonASP (N=91) $\bar{X}$	F	p	ASP (N=12) $\bar{X}$	NonASP (N=52) $\bar{X}$	F	p
In last month								
Average daily consumption*	10.4	7.7	6.9	.01	10.1	6.3	1.9	n.s.
Physical symptoms	20.0	17.8	6.0	.02	24.0	17.7	13.9	.01
Withdrawal symptoms	21.7	18.8	10.6	.01	20.7	19.5	0.5	n.s.
Affective symptoms	29.3	27.4	2.8	n.s.	33.1	30.0	2.5	n.s.
In past 6 months:								
Social problems	7.1	5.6	16.8	.01	6.0	5.5	1.6	n.s.
Physical symptoms	12.1	11.4	0.7	n.s.	15.5	12.3	2.0	n.s.
Alcohol dependency	12.1	11.2	1.3	n.s.	12.3	11.0	0.6	n.s.
Loss of control	27.7	26.1	1.5	n.s.	27.9	26.6	14.7	n.s.
Preoccupation with alcohol	15.5	14.4	1.8	n.s.	14.8	15.0	0.1	n.s.
Psychological problems	13.0	11.9	2.3	n.s.	16.1	13.8	2.8	n.s.
Family problems	8.8	8.6	0.1	n.s.	9.9	8.3	1.2	n.s.
Cognitive functioning (at admission)	(N=57)	(N=66)	t	p	(N=10)	(N=42)	t	p
WAIS (VIQ)	103.2 (±13.5)	107.5 (±15.4)	1.6	n.s.	102.0 (±13.0)	107.4 (±13.7)	1.1	n.s.
WAIS (PIQ)	100.7 (±11.5)	101.7 (±14.0)	0.4	n.s.	102.9 (±15.2)	107.3 (±12.1)	0.8	n.s.
WAIS (FSIQ)	102.3 (±12.1)	106.0 (±12.9)	1.6	n.s.	102.7 (±14.2)	107.7 (±12.8)	1.0	n.s.
BAQ	82.7 (±14.9)	85.2 (±13.6)	0.9	n.s.	83.1 (±21.3)	88.3 (±15.5)	0.9	n.s.

*Not age adjusted; ounces of absolute alcohol.

A screening battery of neuropsychological and intelligence tests was completed by each subject. This battery provides an objective measure of cognitive functioning. The results of the Halstead Neuropsychological test and Wechsler Adult Intelligence Tests (WAIS) are shown in table 12-7. No significant differences were found in terms of the WAIS subtests or IQ between ASP and nonASP subjects.

Subtests of the WAIS and of the Halsteady battery known to be sensitive to cognitive functioning were used to compute the Brain Age Quotient (BAQ). The BAQ is an age adjusted score [26] that permits comparison of cognitive functioning across different age groups. Although the overall level of cognitive functioning measured by the BAQ is slightly higher for the nonASP subjects as compared to the ASP subjects, this difference was not significant. Thus, the younger ASP subjects appeared to be as impaired in their cognitive functioning as the older (by almost ten years on average) nonASP subjects.

Discriminant Analysis

As a means of summarizing the data analysis and as a way of determining the predictive value of the variables studied, a discriminant function analysis was performed. The mathematical objective of discriminant function analysis is to form a linear combination of variables that will maximally distinguish groups of individuals. Since relatively few ASP females were studied, the entire sample was used to predict the presence/absence of ASP. The order of entry of the predictor variables into the discriminant equation was controlled in the following step-down manner. Current age was entered first in order to correct for group differences in average age. Next, the presence of a family history for alcoholism, followed by the sum of childhood HK/MBD behaviors and sum of childhood antisocial behaviors were evaluated for their discriminating power. Variables related to the subject's drinking career (e.g. age at first drink, age first drunk) were then allowed to enter in the stepwise manner. Last, variables reflecting possible consequences of drinking (e.g. affective symptoms, withdrawal symptoms) were allowed to enter in a stepwise manner. This particular ordering of variables entering into the predictive equation was chosen as an approximation to the chronology of events in the natural history of alcoholism. The minimization of Wilk's Lambda was used as the discriminant criterion. In general, the greater the disparity among the group (ASP vs. nonASP) centroids relative to the within-group's generalized variance, the smaller the value of Lambda. The analysis was conducted using the SPSS update (1979). The resulting

Table 12-8. Summary of Discriminant Function Analysis Using Life History Factors to Predict ASP

Summary Table

Step	Variable	Wilks' Lambda	p
1	Age	.919	.001
2	Family History-Alcoholism	.870	.001
3	HK/MBD	.802	.001
4	Childhood ASP	.728	.001
5	Age Began Regular Drunk	.629	.001
6	Age First Drink	.621	.001
7	Withdrawal Symptoms	.600	.001

Classification Table

Actual Group	Predicted Group Membership	
	NonASP	ASP
NonASP	81.8%	18.2%
ASP	22.8%	77.2%

$(\chi^2 = 84.39;\ df = 1;\ p \leq .001)$

discriminant function presented in table 12-8 includes current age (which was used as a covariate), the presence of both HK/MBD and childhood ASP, the age at which the first nonreligious drink was taken, the age at which the subject began getting drunk regularly, and the experiencing of withdrawal symptoms following cessation of drinking. No other life history factors met criteria for entry into the equation. When this function was used to classify the sample according to the presence or absence of ASP, 81.8 percent of the nonASP subjects and 77.2 percent of the ASP subjects were correctly classified.

Discussion

Examination of the history and the consequences of abusive drinking experienced by alcoholics with ASP would suggest that they do indeed, have an early onset of alcoholism, followed by a more chronic and severe course. In general, alcoholics with ASP were found to have taken their first drink and to have begun regular drinking and drunkenness much earlier than their non-ASP counterparts. Although almost ten years younger, the alcoholics with ASP in this sample have had a drinking problem as long as the older subjects without ASP. In addition, their disorder was more likely to be complicated by other substance abuse. Depression was quite prevalent in both groups. While many of these features are consistent with established diagnostic criteria for antisocial personality only, the severity of alcohol-related consequences serves as an indicator of the extent to which alcoholism is a problem for these ASP individuals. Alcohol consumption and alcohol-related withdrawal symptomatology experienced within the month prior to admission were greater in ASP as compared to nonASP subjects. In the six months prior to admission, ASP subjects experienced social, physical, and psychological consequences at a level similar to nonASP subjects. While it is often thought that many physical consequences of alcoholism are the result of a combination of excessive drinking and the aging process, our data suggests that this may not necessarily be true. The younger ASP subjects report as many physical consequences of their drinking as the older nonASP subjects. The findings of the objective neuropsychological testing support the self-report data. Most chronic alcoholics manifest rather profound cognitive deficits in abstracting abilities, memory, learning [12,16,32]. These deficits have been particularly noted in older alcoholics. In this study younger subjects with alcoholism and ASP were found to perform as poorly on the neuropsychological test battery as the older nonASP alcoholic subjects. A "premature aging" hypothesis [25] might be suggested to account for this finding, i.e., heavy alcohol consumption produces changes in cognitive functioning similar to those resulting from aging. An alternative explanation can also be offered. Ryan and Butters suggest that chronic heavy alcohol consumption may produce physical symptomatology and cognitive deficits that are additive to, but independent of, the aging process. Because of the early onset of drinking and heavy rates of consumption the ASP alcoholics suffer the same level of consequences as older nonASP alcoholics.

The data from this study clearly demonstrate significant differences in the course and chronicity of alcoholism in two types of alcoholic individuals, those affected wth ASP and those individuals without ASP. The differences found were consistent in both male and female samples. A high prevalence of alcoholism among biologic relatives and behavioral problems in childhood antedate the onset of excessive drinking for persons with ASP. However, since heavy drinking begins at such an early age for these individuals, the causal sequence of events during the adolescent years becomes difficult to study. In adolescents, problem drinking may exacerbate a person's deviant lifestyle and initiate a labeling process that may further determine the course of alcohol problems. The initially acute problems associated with adolescent intoxication may become more related to the development of antisocial personality than to a more incipient form of alcoholism often characterized by a biologic or psychological vulnerability. For individuals with ASP, early drinking may serve a functional purpose by either providing an escape from an intolerable family life or by providing a means of adapting to a deviant subculture. As heavy drinking and the associated acute problems continue to interact with personality and environmental factors, the person's drinking pattern may become autonomous from the earlier factors and become more dominated by alcohol dependence. Thus, etiology becomes transformed from a stage of acute problems to a stage of chronic alcoholism. Individuals without ASP, on the other hand, have fewer biologic relatives with alcoholism, fewer behavioral problems in childhood, are less likely to abuse other substances, and begin drinking later. However, the type and severity of consequences resulting from excessive alcohol consumption are similar for both groups. What remains to be seen is whether the prognosis following treatment differs for these two subtypes of alcoholism.

References

1. Andreasen, N. C., Endicott, J., Spitzer, R. L., and Winokur, G. The family history method using diagnostic criteria. *Arch. Gen. Psychiatry* 34:1229, 1977.
2. Cahalan, D., and Room, R. *Problem Drinking Among American Men*. New Brunswick: Rutgers University Center of Alcoholic Studies, 1974.
3. *Diagnostic and Statistical Manual* (3rd ed.). American Psychiatric Association 1981.
4. Goodwin, D. W., and Guze, S. B. *Psychiatric Diagnosis* (2nd ed.). New York: Oxford University Press, 1979.
5. Hale, M., Hesselbrock, M., and Hesselbrock, V. Childhood deviance and sociopathy in alcoholism. *Psychiatric Treatment and Evaluation*, 4:33, 1982.
6. Hershon, H. Alcohol withdrawal symptoms and drinking behavior. *J. Stud. Alcohol* 38:953, 1977.
7. Hesselbrock, M., Babor, T., Hesselbrock, V., et al. "Never believe an alcoholic?" On the validity of self-report measure of alcohol dependence and related constructs. *Int. J. Addict.*, 18:678, 1983.
8. Hesselbrock, V., Stabenau, J., Mirkin, P. et al. A comparison of two interview schedules: The NIMH-DIS and SADS-L. *Arch. Gen. Psychiatry*, 39:674, 1982.
9. Hull, C. H., and Nie, N. H. *SPSS Update: New Procedures and Facilities for Releases 7 and 8*. New York: McGraw-Hill, 1979.

10. Jessor, R., and Jessor, S. L. Adolescent drinking and the onset of drinking: A longitudinal study. *J. Stud. Alcohol* 36:27, 1975.
11. Jones, M. C. Personality correlates and antecedents of drinking patterns in adult males. *J. Consult. Clin. Psychol.* 32:2, 1968.
12. Løberg, T. Alcohol misuse and neuropsychological deficits in men. *J. Stud. Alcohol* 41:119, 1980.
13. McCord, W., and McCord, J. *Origins of Alcoholism.* Palo Alto, California: Stanford University Press, 1960.
14. Morrison, J. R., and Stewart, M. A family study of the hyperactive child syndrome. *Biol. Psychiatry* 3:189, 1971.
15. National Council on Alcoholism, Criteria Committee, Criteria for the diagnosis of alcoholism. *Am. J. Psychiatry* 129:127, 1972.
16. Parsons, O. Cognitive dysfunction in alcoholics and social drinkers. *J. Stud. Alcohol,* 41:105, 1980.
17. Rachal, J. V., Hubbard, R. I., Williams, J. R., and Tuchfeld, B. S. Drinking levels and problem drinking among junior and senior high school students. *J. Stud. Alcohol* 37:1751, 1976.
18. Reich, T., Cloninger, C. R., Lewis, C., and Rice, J. Some recent findings in the study of genotype-environment interaction in alcoholism. In R. E. Meyer et al. (eds.), *Evaluation of the Alcoholic* (NIAAA Research Monograph No. 5). Washington, D.C.: 1981.
19. Robins, L. N. Etiological implications in studies of childhood histories of antisocial personality. In Hare, R. D. and Schalling, D. (eds.), *Psychopathic Behavior: Approaches to research.* Chichester, England: Wiley, 1978.
20. Robins, L. N. Antisocial behavior disturbance of childhood: Prevalence, prognosis and prospects. In Anthony, E. J. and Koupernick, C. (eds.), *The Child in His Family: Children at psychiatric risk* (Yearbook of the International Association for Child Psychiatry and Allied Professions, Vol. 3). New York: Wiley, 1974.
21. Robins, L. N. *Deviant Children Grown Up: A sociological and psychiatric study of sociopathic personality.* Baltimore: Williams & Wilkins, 1966.
22. Robins, L., Bates, W. M., and O'Neil, P. Adult drinking patterns of former problem children. In: Pittman, D. J. and Snyder, C. R. (eds.), *Society, Culture and Drinking Patterns.* New York: Wiley, 1962.
23. Robins, L. N., Helzer, J., Croughan, J., and Ratcliff, D. S. NIMH Diagnostic Interview Schedule (DIS), *Arch. Gen. Psychiatry* 38:381, 1981.
24. Robins, L. N., and Smith, E. Longitudinal studies of alcohol and drug problems: Sex differences. In O. J. Kalant (ed.), *Alcohol and Drug Problems in Women.* New York: Plenum Press, 1980.
25. Ryan, C., and Butters, N. Learning and memory impairments in young and old alcoholics: Evidence for premature-aging hypothesis. *Alcoholism: Clin. Exp. Res.* 4:288, 1980.
26. Schau, E., and O'Leary, M. Adaptive abilities of hospitalized alcoholics and matched controls. *J. Stud. Alcohol* 38:403, 1977.

27. Schuckit, M. A. Alcoholism and sociopathy—diagnostic confusion. *Q. J. Stud. Alcohol* 34:157, 1973.

28. Tarter, R. E. Minimal brain dysfunction as an etiological predisposition to alcoholism. In Meyer, R. E., and Babor, T. F. (eds.), *Evaluation of the Alcoholic* (NIAAA Research Monograph No. 5). Washington, D.C.: U.S. Government Printing Office, 1981.

29. Tarter, R. E., McBride, H., Buonpane, N., and Schneider, D. Differentiation of alcoholics according to childhood history of minimal brain dysfunction, family history, and drinking pattern. *Arch. Gen. Psychiatry* 34:761, 1977.

30. Weissman, M., Myers, J., and Harding P. Prevalence and psychiatric heterogeneity of alcoholism in a United States urban community. *J. Stud. Alcohol* 41:672, 1980.

31. Wender, P. *Minimal Brain Dysfunction in Children.* New York: Wiley, 1971.

32. Williams, R., Goldman, M., and Williams, E. Expectancy and pharmacological effects of alcohol on human cognitive performance: The compensation for alcohol effect. *J. Abnorm. Psychol* 90:267, 1981.

33. Zucker, R. A., and Devoe, C. I. Life history characteristics associated with problem drinking and antisocial behavior in adolescent girls: A comparison with male findings. In: Wirt, R. D. Winokur, G. and Roff, M. (eds.), *Life History Research in Psychopathology.* Minneapolis: The University of Minnesota Press, 1975.

Donovan — Jesson — Jesson